One Canada

Creating the Greatest
Country on Earth

One Canada

Creating the Greatest Country on Earth

Cecil Young

Published by Trafford Publishing, 2004
British Columbia, Canada

© Copyright 2004 Cecil Young.
All rights reserved. No part of this publication may be reproduced, stored in a retrieval system, or transmitted, in any form or by any means, electronic, mechanical, photocopying, recording, or otherwise, without the written prior permission of the author.

Every effort has been made to identify and ackowledge quotations used in this book. If there were omissions or misidentification, the author would be grateful to be so informed.

Note for Librarians: a cataloguing record for this book that includes Dewey Decimal Classification and US Library of Congress numbers is available from the Library and Archives of Canada. The complete cataloguing record can be obtained from their online database at:
www.collectionscanada.ca/amicus/index-e.html
ISBN 1-4120-2235-5
Printed in Victoria, BC, Canada

TRAFFORD

Offices in Canada, USA, Ireland, UK and Spain
This book was published *on-demand* in cooperation with Trafford Publishing. On-demand publishing is a unique process and service of making a book available for retail sale to the public taking advantage of on-demand manufacturing and Internet marketing. On-demand publishing includes promotions, retail sales, manufacturing, order fulfilment, accounting and collecting royalties on behalf of the author.

Book sales for North America and international:
Trafford Publishing, 6E–2333 Government St.,
Victoria, BC v8t 4p4 CANADA
phone 250 383 6864 (toll-free 1 888 232 4444)
fax 250 383 6804; email to orders@trafford.com

Book sales in Europe:
Trafford Publishing (UK) Ltd., Enterprise House, Wistaston Road Business Centre, Wistaston Road, Crewe, Cheshire CW2 7RP UNITED KINGDOM
phone 01270 251 396 (local rate 0845 230 9601)
facsimile 01270 254 983; orders.uk@trafford.com

Order online at:
www.trafford.com/robots/04-0063.html

10 9 8 7 6 5 4 3

Table of Contents

Dedication .... *xiii*

Acknowledgements .... *xv*

Why I chose Canada .... *xvi*

Why I wrote this book? .... *xviii*

Canada Now 1

Introduction 2

    Proud to Be Canadian 5

    National Anthem of Canada 9

    Hymne national du Canada 9

    The meaning of "O Canada" 10

Towards Confederation 13

    Canada before the Europeans 13

    Arrival of the Europeans 13

    The Birth of Confederation 14

Why do we Need Government? 18

    Governing 18

    Politics 18

    The Political Party 19

    Political Patronage – A Reward System 20

    Government - Theory 23

    Government - Reality 24

State of Canadian Federalism 28

    Bureaucracy 34

National Unity *36*

Canada's Deficits *39*

Canada-USA Relationship 42

Adopting the "American Way of Life" *53*

Canada and the World 57

Canadian Geography 61

Canada 62

Canadian Governance *64*

Provinces and Territories 70

Planning a Great Country 103

Fundamental Rights *105*

Creating One Canada - Ten Principles *106*

One Canada 107

Who is Canadian? 108

The Role of Government 114

Two Levels of Government *115*

Administrative Regions *116*

The National Government 117

The Power of Parliament *118*

Head of State – Governor General *119*

The Governing Council (The Executive Branch) 123

Head of Government - Prime Minister *123*

The Senate (The Legislative Branch) 127

The People's Representatives - Senators *127*

The Supreme Court of Canada (The Judicial Branch) 130

Local Government 133

    Mayor and Councilors *133*

    Mayors' Executive Board *137*

Financing Governments 138

    Financing the National Government *143*

    Government Services Fee – The Amount *143*

    Financing Local Government *145*

    Local Government Services Fee – Property Value *146*

    Local Government Services Fee – Automobile *147*

The Economy 148

    What is the economy? *149*

The Election Processes 153

    One Vote, Two Parts *154*

    The Party's Candidate *156*

    The Election Process, Part One - Private *157*

    The Election Process, Part II - Public *158*

    Simple Majority *159*

    Recalling Politicians *160*

    The Election Campaign *162*

    What is Proportional Representation? *163*

    The Undecided Voter *166*

    Preferential Balloting *168*

    Election Spending Limits *170*

Government Political Financing *171*
For Governor General *173*
Political Contribution *173*

The Departments 175

Department of Agriculture and Food 181

Department of Arts & Culture 181

The Canadian Handbook *182*
National Holidays *185*
Focus on the Family *189*
Marriage *190*
Homosexual Relationships *192*
Prostitution *195*

Department of the Attorney General 197

Department of Canadian Heritage 197

Department of Communication 197

Broadcast Television *198*
CBC LeisureWorld *199*
CBC SportsWorld *200*
CBC Education *200*
CBC NewsWorld *201*
Cable and Satellite Systems *201*
Canadian Film and Television Productions Fund *203*
National Telephone System *203*
Post Mail *205*
Unsolicited Mail *205*

National Voice and Data Distribution Conduit	*206*
Fiber Optic Cable	*206*
Department of Consumer Relations	209
Consumer Credit Reports	*212*
Department of Education	221
Educational Development	*225*
What should we be teaching our Children?	*229*
Age of Majority	*240*
Department of Energy	242
Department of Environment	245
Department of Finance	249
Taxation	*249*
The Birth of Canadian Income Tax	*250*
Government Service Fee – The Amount	*261*
Government Service Fee - Collection	*262*
Financial Reporting	*263*
Department of Health	263
National Drug, Dental and Health Plans	*263*
National Dental Care Plan	*264*
National Drug Plan	*265*
Marijuana – Drug or Medicine?	*265*
Department of Housing	268
Department of Human Services	270
Guaranteed Annual Income (GAIN)	*270*
National Pension Plan (NPP)	*271*

National Child Care Plan *274*
National School Breakfast and Lunch Program *275*
Department of Immigration 278
What is Canadian Experience? *280*
Immigrants *282*
Department of Industry 286
Made In Canada *288*
Department of Intergovernmental Relations 290
Department of International Relations 291
International Intelligence Gathering *293*
Department of Internal Security 294
Guns and Gangs *296*
Department of International Commerce 299
Department of Justice 300
Paying a debt to Society *300*
Criminal Record *300*
The Child Offender *302*
The Youth Offender *302*
The Adult Offender *304*
Death Penalty *304*
Department of Labour 306
Mandatory Retirement *307*
Department of National Defense 309
Strong Armed Forces *311*

x

  United Nations Rapid Deployment Force *314*

Department of Natural Resources 315

Department of Prisons and Corrections 315

Department of Public Information 316

Department of Public Safety and Emergency Management 318

Department of Revenue 318

Department of Science 319

Department of the Solicitor General 319

Department of Sports and Recreation 320

  Recreational, Amateur and Professional Sports *322*

  Amateur Sports *322*

  Recreational Sports *323*

  Professional Sports *324*

  International Sporting Events *325*

Department of Supply and Services 326

Department of Technology 326

Department of Travel and Tourism 329

  Promoting and Traveling Canada *329*

  Promoting Canada to Canadians *329*

  Promoting Canada to the World *331*

  Paradise in the Sun – The Caribbean Islands *331*

  Paradise in the Sun - Jamaica *333*

  Paradise in the Sun - Barbados *334*

Department of Transportation 335

 Roads and Highways construction................................ *337*
 Railway construction... *337*
 Public Transit... *338*
 Department of Veterans Affairs 340

Building One Canada **341**
 Taking Back Government 343
 Who will build One Canada?.............................351
 One Canada – The First Phase 356
 One Canada – The Second Phase 358
 Priorities in One Canada 358
 One Canada is Simplicity....................................359
 It is not enough...361
 If you believe 362

Canada Facts and Figures.....................................**363**
 Map of Canada...364

Bibliography..**374**

About the Author **375**

Dedication

I dedicate this book to my mother Jocelyn (Ellen) Young, my father Henry Young and my wife Jacqueline, my sons Stefan and Terence. Mother taught me perseverance and the value of hard work; Father, self-sufficiency and self-confidence; my wife, diplomacy and self-control and my children, to see the simplicity of life.

Acknowledgements

As one traverses the course of life, contact with people and participation in events help to develop character. The influences of others determine our perceptions and actions. The person I am today is a direct result of influences by countless people and events. I have learned something from every person I met. People from all lifestyles contributed to making me the person I am.

I would like to acknowledge three who made the most life-changing impact on my life. I thank my eldest brother Raphael for bringing me to Canada in 1972, at the tender age of seventeen. That act of generosity convinced me Canada is where I wanted to live the rest of my life. Thanks to my elder brother, Karlus, for offering his help and guidance after I returned to Canada in 1976. The greatest thanks I extend to my wife Jacqueline, who made the greatest impact on my life, molding me into the person I am today.

Cecil Young

Why I chose Canada

My parents had friends who lived in, and traveled to, England, the United States of America, and Canada. I had a brother living in England. We heard many good things from people who visited these countries and learned about England from my brother's letters. My exposure to the many peoples of the world came from living near, attending high school and working in Montego Bay, Jamaica, a leading tourist destination in the 1960's and 1970's. I mingled with Americans, Canadians, and English tourists at my father's workplace, and in the streets of Montego Bay. Learning about these countries intrigued me and I began to wonder, "What is over there?"

In the late 1960's, two events helped me to become more interested in Canada. Firstly, in 1967, Jamaican Prime Minister Donald Sangster became very ill, admitted to, and later died in a Montréal hospital. Local radio stations kept Jamaicans abreast of the Prime Minister's health and provided insights into Canada. Secondly, as I began high school, my brother Raphael moved from England to Canada. News of a popular politician named, Pierre Trudeau, the favourite to become prime minister of Canada filled the Jamaican media. In my last year in primary school, I noticed bags of bulgur, flour, and powdered milk, marked "Product of Canada" as the school canteen. Jamaican primary school children are very familiar with these food staples provided by the people of Canada. I learned from our teacher this was part of Canada's "food aid" program to poorer countries.

In high school, North American geography classes were studies of Canada and the United States of America. I could draw a map of Canada, layout all provinces, plot all major cities, knew the major produce and industries in each region. I wanted to live in Canada; it was a fascinating place. After our mother died in 1969, Raphael promised his three younger siblings a life in Canada, a thought that excited us. I arrived in August 1972 and was in awe. It was beautiful, Niagara Falls, Canadian National Exhibition, Ontario Place, picnicking in many parks, driving along roads and changing highways without stopping, ice and snow on the ground, Canada-Russia hockey games; a magnificent place I thought.

In 1972, I chose Canada, with Raphael's help, because it fascinated me from my early teenage years. In 1976, Canada chose me as part of its immigration policy. We are both the better for it. I am living a better life and touching many lives with my community service. Today, after more than a quarter of a century of living in Canada, I continue to choose Canada because it offers us freedom, prosperity and the opportunity to learn and use the best parts of other cultures. I love this country and you will not find a more patriotic Canadian than I am. I continue to choose Canada as it grows into greatest country on earth, built with the best parts of cultures from around the world into a near-utopian place.

Cecil Young

Why I wrote this book?

My early recollections of government and politics occurred between 1962 and 1972. In the general election campaign leading up to the 1962 Independence from Great Britain, Jamaica's conservative politicians sold the idea of an island government, independent from Great Britain. The social democratic politicians preached the dangers of an independent island government. My parents were followers of the conservative clan and my aunt and uncle were disciples of the social democrats.

"Vote buying" was commonplace during election campaigns. I recall the election campaign leading the 1967 general elections; people in my village were excited to receive a one-pound weight paper bag of flour, courtesy of the local conservative political candidate. Inside every bag were a British Half Crown piece, valued at two schillings and six pence, commonly referred to as a "two and six piece." The British Pound was the official Jamaican currency at the time. The villagers, including my parents, were excited to receive the flour and cash gift. At the time, my father earned about one British Pound and ten Schillings for a six-day workweek, so this "gift" was almost one half-day's pay. The money was a reminder to vote for the politician who provided the flour and money. That was vote buying and my first experience of it. **This was my first lesson in politics.** I later heard the flour was a gift to the Jamaican people from the people of Canada. These nefarious politicians used Canada's gift of food, intended for the Jamaican people, to bribe the very same people for which the gift was intended. **That was my second lesson in politics.** That was 1967; the year Canada celebrated its Centennial of independence from Britain.

As I grew older, I became more active in my village and politics. In

1972, I campaigned in my first general election and saw social democrats form the government. During my last three years in Jamaica, 1973 to 1976, I became one quarter of a group that created a Boys Club, was a volunteer Adult Literacy teacher, and, between 18 and 20 years, became a leader in my village, earning the respect of people as aged as my parents. During my late teenage years, I learned the true colours of politicians, the machinations of politics and ways of politicking. I recall adults referring to politics as "politricks," a word I could not find in the dictionary and later learned its meaning to be "politicians filled with trickery." Apathy and distrust of politicians and politics were commonplace, much as it is in Canada today. I observed politicians, backed by the rich and powerful, taking great pleasures in deceiving the multitude.

While people around the world are fighting and dying for the very freedoms we take for granted, our own freedoms are eroding daily in the name of safety and security and the fight against terrorism. I cannot understand Canadians' willingness to ignore government actions when **"From the bedroom to the board room, government affects everything we do."**

I am disheartened by the constant bickering between the governments in the Canadian Federation; by the selfish provincial politicians who are building their own kingdoms and monuments instead of working for the betterment of their population; by the business leaders who use and abuse their workers as fodder in the wealth accumulation machinery.

I am disgusted by career politicians whose sole purpose for being, are longevity in politics and the "pot of gold" at the end of their political careers.

I am disheartened by the large number of Canadians who have convinced themselves politicians are all the same.

I am troubled by the democratic road we are traveling as Canadians surrender control of the country to career politicians and corporate executives and the wealthiest amongst us.

I am discouraged by the majority of Canadians refusing to volunteer in their community, depriving the community and country of skills necessary to build Canada into the Greatest Country on Earth.

I chose to write this book to offer ideas on building Canada to be the Greatest Place on Earth to live in. It is my hope that this book will open the eyes of our politicians, business leaders and every Canadian so that we may create a place to live that is the Greatest Country on Earth. I hope this book serves as a catalyst for many Canadians to take back our country for our people.

Cecil Young

Canada Now

Over five hundred years, Canada evolved into a nation of First Peoples, English, French, and the many cultures of the world. During our evolution, people from all our regions made significant contribution to our world locally, nationally and internationally. In this section, Canada Now, you will learn about the birth of Confederation, our provinces, and territories and their contribution to Canada. You will also learn about the State of Canadian Federalism, Canada-USA relationship, Canada and the World, and the reasons we need government.

Introduction

One Canada is a vision of creating a strong and united Canada, out of the dysfunctional federation of ten provinces and three territories, leading to the Greatest Country on Earth. Canada was created to be a strong country, nurtured by the existing regions, eventually becoming greater than its parts. As Canada grew from infancy, the provinces, the Aunts and Uncles of Confederation, also grew and aspired to become independent countries on their own. Since the Centennial in 1967, the young Canada grew, exerting the rights given to it by the Constitution, the British North America Act. The provinces, having designs of nationhood, began resenting the young Canada, forcing it to gradually cede control of the nation, rendering the National Canadian government a nearly impotent custodian of Canadian citizenship, and almost equal to the provinces in stature. The Canadian Federation has devolved into a State of Feudalism, where "passing the buck" is the common denominator between the federal and provincial governments. Municipal governments blame the provincial governments for their ills; the provinces then blame the federal government with the "buck" passing in a vicious circle. Inside the vicious circle are the people of Canada bound in red tape while being taxed to death to pay for the ineffectiveness and inefficiencies of governments. With each provincial government determined to create its own kingdom within Canada, One Canada will never be a reality, unless a new paradigm of governance is developed for all of Canada.

The new paradigm is governance and service delivery at the local municipal level, supervised by the National government. The Fathers' of Confederation clearly defined the powers and responsibilities of the federal Parliament and the provincial legislatures. Had the clear divisions of power been followed, the Canada of today would be greater than the sum of its regions. For the first one hundred years of Confederation, the provincial governments, like caring aunts and uncles, helped nurture Canada through its adolescent years and into nationhood. Since Canada's centennial, the increasing provincial demands for greater powers and powers and control of their affairs forced the federal government to sign federal/provincial agreements, forcing the devolution of federal powers, thus weakening the federal government. One Jamaican Proverb, **"Two bull caan reign in a di same pen"***, sums up the relationship between the ten provincial and one federal governments, one of constantly locking horns together. The territorial governments, not elevated to provincial status and powers, are hardly in a position to lock horns with the federal government.

> * **Two bull caan reign in a di same pen** - *Jamaican patois;*
> **Two Bulls cannot reign in a herd** – *English translation;*
> **There can only be one leader** - *The Meaning.*

Now the time has come for the provinces to remove their blinders, let Canada grow into maturity, bringing greater prosperity to its people.

In 1867, The Fathers of Confederation created what they believed would be a great country, a great nation. In 1949, Newfoundland Premier Joey Smallwood convinced his people Newfoundland would benefit from joining the Canadian federation. In the second of two referenda, Newfoundlanders voted to complete Canada from "sea to shining sea." Premier Smallwood became one of the Fathers of Confederation. The creation of the Territory of Nunavut in 1999, gave recognition to many of our First Peoples.

While the physical boundaries of what is now Canada remain the same, Canada is a "smaller" country today. At Confederation, news traveling across Canada took several weeks, mainly by foot, horses, and carriages. The same were true for a person desiring travel from Nova Scotia to British Columbia. As Canada grew, those obstacles gradually wore down, to the point where news can travel the length of Canada in nanoseconds and travel is down to hours. With the advent of airplanes, electronics, the microprocessor and now the Internet, Canada is like a virtual community. Today, we have the best place on Earth to live. Some day we will have the greatest place on Earth to live, with the greatest standard of living, the greatest minds, and the greatest leaders, the friendliest and most caring people.

In our present governance form, it will be impossible to achieve the greatness that awaits Canada and the Canadian people in the 21st and 22nd centuries. The greatness is there for the taking; we must act now or another nation rise up to become the Greatest Country on Earth to live in.

Proud to Be Canadian

I have always been amazed at the lack of confidence many Canadians have in Canada and its achievements. In many areas of life, we have been at the forefront of many technological and scientific discoveries.

We are a proud people, just not a boastful people. We are a hardworking and industrious people, toiling away in anonymity, with the occasional accolade.

Many of us are not aware of the contributions Canadians have made to the world, primarily because of the media and advertising juggernaut to the south. This southern juggernaut inundates the Canadian psyche, media and educational system with their American achievements and contributions to the world, burying Canada's contributions.

"[Canadians are] the people who learned to live without the bold accents of the natural ego trippers of other lands."
Marshall McLuhan (1967)

I am proud to be Canadian. Here are some of the reasons why:

1. Up to the 15th Century, First Peoples develop a strong confederation of nations amongst themselves;
2. 1867, Fathers of Confederation created Canada;
3. 1879 - Sir Sandford Fleming suggested dividing the world into twenty-four equal time zones, with a standard time in each zone. In 1884, twenty-five countries adopted the idea;
4. 1842 - Kerosene developed in New Brunswick, Canada. Kerosene is a staple fuel for many developing countries;
5. 1852 - First submarine communication cable in North America, laid between Cape Tormentine, New Brunswick and Carlton Head, Prince Edward Island;
6. 1854 - First oil company in North America established;

7. 1856, first commercial oil well in North America went in to production at Enniskillen, Ontario;

8. 1858 - Trans-Atlantic communications cable laid between Trinity Bay, Newfoundland and Valentia, Republic of Ireland facilitating the first telegraphic message between Europe and North America;

9. 1874 - Alexander Graham Bell, of Brantford, Ontario invented the telephone.

10. 1874 - Henry Woodward, of Toronto, patented the first incandescent lamp with an electric light bulb, (later selling his share of the patent to Thomas Edison, an American credited with inventing the light bulb, after improvements he made in 1879);

11. 1877 - An American company, using a Canadian patent, set up a telephone in Canada.

12. 1906 – The first publicly-owned electrical utility in the world, The Hydro-Electric Commission of Ontario created (later called Ontario Hydro);

13. 1914-1919 – Canada's contribution to World War I;

14. 1920's - Pablum, a well-known and popular baby food, invented at Toronto's Sick Children's Hospital, by Dr. T. G. H Drake, Dr. Allan Brown, and Dr. Frederick F. Tisdale;

15. 1922 - Dr. Frederick Banting and Dr. Charles Best discovered insulin, daily shots of which help to control diabetes for millions in the world today;

16. 1927 – Nellie McClung, Irene Parlby, Henrietta Muir Edwards, Emily Murphy and Louise McKinney, the "Famous Five" women, submitted a petition for an interpretation of the word "Person" in section 24 of the British North America Act, 1867;

17. 1929 - The decision on the petition of the "Famous Five" found that "Person" includes female persons, thereby making women eligible for appointment to the Senate of Canada;

18. 1939-1945 - Canada's contribution to the Allied war effort in World War II;

19. 1956 - Lester B. Pearson proposed the United Nations Emergency Force to stabilize the Suez Canal crisis; a concept that emerged into United Nations Peacekeeping;

20. 1958 - Avro Arrow, a technical masterpiece at the forefront of aviation engineering during its time;

21. 1967 - 100th anniversary of Canadian Confederation; Expo 67 in Montreal celebrated a century of nation building and hosted the world in a showcase of technology and culture;

22. 1971 - Greenpeace was formed specifically to protest violations of the environment;

23. 1972 - Canada launched the world's first domestic communication geo-stationary satellite;

24. 1972 - The Canada-USSR hockey "Summit" Series;

25. 1976 - The world's tallest freestanding structure, the CN Tower, opened in Toronto;

26. 1980 - Victory of the "Yes" side in the Quebec referendum;

27. 1981 - The technologically advanced Canadarm unveiled in space aboard the U. S. space shuttle Columbia;

28. 1988 – Sprinter Ben Johnson won Olympic Gold medal for the 100m sprint in a world record time of 9.79 seconds;

29. 1996 - Sprinter Donovan Bailey (100m sprint) and Men's 4x100M relay won an Olympic Gold medals;

30. 1997 – The 12.9km Confederation Bridge, linking New

Brunswick and Prince Edward Island, opened to traffic;

31. 2000 - National Men's Soccer team's victory in the Gold Cup;
32. 2002 - Canada's National Men's and Women's Olympic Gold Medal victory in (ice) hockey, both over the USA;
33. 2003 - National Women's Soccer team made it to the semi-final of the FIFA Women's World Cup of Football.

The list of achievements for Canada goes on and is the subject of published books.

Our history is filled with Canada's firsts and accomplishments; our knowledge is bereft of these accomplishments.

Other Reasons for being Proud to Be Canadian

Canadian Weather – Winter, Spring, Summer and Fall, there is always something to do for everyone.

Canada was the world leader in creating the International Court of Justice.

Canadians invented the Ski-doo, Jet-ski, Velcro, Zipper, and the Zamboni. Canadians also invented the long distance, shortwave and battery-less radios.

Most of all, I am Proud to Be Canadian for the freedoms I enjoy.

Our freedoms afford us the opportunity to:
- Live where I please;
- Move around freely and safely;
- Pursue any lifestyle I desire;
- Express and defend my opinions;
- Practice my religious belief;
- Associate with whomsoever I choose.

National Anthem of Canada

O Canada!
Our home and native land!
True patriot love in all thy sons command.

With glowing hearts, we see thee rise,
The True North strong and free!

From far and wide,
O Canada, we stand on guard for thee.

God keep our land glorious and free!
O Canada, we stand on guard for thee.

O Canada, we stand on guard for thee.

Hymne national du Canada

O Canada! Terre de nos aïeux,
Ton front est ceint de fleurons glorieux!

Car ton bras sait porter l'épée,
Il sait porter la croix!

Ton histoire est une épopée
Des plus brillants exploits.

Et ta valeur, de foi trempée,
Protégera nos foyers et nos droits.

Protégera nos foyers et nos droits.

The meaning of "O Canada"

Our home and native land!

As immigrants, my wife and I have called Canada home for more than a quarter century. Canada is no less a home for us, and we are no less loyal, than any Canadian-born. We believe in, and support, Canada above all others. We are nevertheless proud of our Jamaican heritage and the valuable lessons learned from our parents, family, and friends whilst growing up in Jamaica. To our Canadian born sons, Canada is their homeland. For the four of us, Canada is "our home and native land," a home we are proud to help build into a better place.

True patriot love in all thy sons command.

Patriotism is the love for our country and is not the exclusive right of those born in that country. Patriotism is not only defending the land from invaders or fighting to protect the values we believe in, it is working hard everyday to produce and contribute to the building of our land. Canada commands patriotism from all its men and women who consider themselves Canadians. "True patriot love in all thy sons command" means we must all put Canada first. Only the person that puts Canada first is a Canadian.

With glowing hearts, we see the rise

My family is very proud to call Canada home, to be Canadians and even more proud when Canada is recognized around the world for its leadership, breakthroughs in medicine, science, technology, space and communications; its support for peacekeeping and peace making; victories in world class sporting events and its important roles in past wars. Every time the flag is raised in recognition of our accomplishments, our hearts glow with pride, proud to be Canadians, proud to see Canada rise.

The True North strong and free!

We believe that Canada will gain strength from its people, its technological advances, and its social conscience to become strong, with a people that are free to pursue their hearts' desire. With our huge land area, harsh winters, diverse population and cultures, Canadians must be strong and free to live a full and rewarding life.

From far and wide, O Canada, We stand on guard for thee.

With its huge landmass, and its people spread far and wide, all Canadians must be vigilant in protecting the interest of Canada as a country and Canadians as a people. Protection is repulsion of all external forces intent on harming Canadians and destroying Canada. We must protect our people and country from people wanting to conquer us with their culture and belief system. We must even protect ourselves from Canadians who seek to build protectionist walls around our borders. In our midst are people who promote hatred, bigotry, incite violence and the division of society into rich and poor, haves and have-nots. We must protect Canada from people who feed off the devilish side of our species. Clear across Canada, we must stand on guard against those who would want to destroy Canada in favour of short-term material gain. Over the centuries, we came across the Earth, "from far and wide," to create Canada, to be Canadians and must continually "stand on guard" to defend our land, our brothers and our sisters.

God keep our land, glorious and free!

It is the right of every Canadian to have their own belief system, whether that is in a God, Allah, and Buddha, another deity or none at all. Whether devoutly religious, agnostic, or atheist, our leaders are guided by their belief system, which will be paramount in their minds when deliberating and debating a decision. Those beliefs will influence their decisions and they must be considerate of the other of beliefs out in the land. Leaders cannot separate their belief system from the affairs of state. Hence, separation of state and religion is impossible. In my Catholic Christian belief system, all things live by the grace, and under the influence of God or the Devil. Our belief in, and guidance from God, will help us to keep our land "glorious and free."

The belief that our Constitution guarantees a separation of church and state are misguided. An idea imported from the USA, it is an example of our indoctrination and adoption of the "American Way" of life." Those believing in the separation of church and state are doomed to fail at leadership. Our failing leadership, whether in government, or in our own lives, is a testament to the failure to be guided by the teachings of the church. Religious teachings must be brought back into our lives or we will continue to wander life filled with moral bankruptcy and plagued by violence, dishonesty and other immoral behaviours.

"When the religion of a people is destroyed, doubt gets hold of the higher powers of the intellect and half paralyzes all the others. Such a condition cannot but enervate the soul, relax the springs of the will, and prepare a people for servitude. When there is no longer any principle of authority in religion any more than in politics, men are speedily frightened at the aspect of this unbounded independence. Despotism may govern without faith, but liberty cannot. Religion is much more necessary in democratic republics than in any others.

How is it possible that society should escape destruction if the moral tie is not strengthened in proportion as the political tie is relaxed?" *Alexis de Tocqueville*

Towards Confederation

Canada before the Europeans

For millennia, First Peoples inhabited the areas we now call Canada and the United States of America. Historical records indicate vibrant and orderly First People societies existed, in tribal or band form, right across North America. The First Peoples created their own cultures instead of building upon a culture transplanted from elsewhere. An entire confederation of First Peoples existed for centuries before the Federation of European people came into existence as the Dominion of Canada in 1867. The highly structured First Peoples confederation governed themselves with laws and decisions, passed down through the ages by word of mouth. First Peoples have richly contributed to the present Canadian cultures. The kayak, snowshoes, toboggan, soapstone and woodcarvings, exceptional paintings and artworks, lacrosse and a rich and vibrant culture of music and art are among the contributions First Nations peoples made to the Canada of today. The most significant contribution First Peoples made would ultimately cause them pain and suffering.

Arrival of the Europeans

After the European discovery of North America in the early 1500's and their subsequent influx thereafter, the conquest and disenfranchisement of the First Peoples began. Much of the "discoveries" of Champlain, Cartier, and other famous European "discoverers" were with the help of First Peoples. The white European's conquests of the land from Atlantic to Pacific to Arctic were aided by First Peoples' ingenuity and knowledge of the terrain, rivers, lakes, and natural resources. As European settlers and their settlements expanded westward, First Peoples were killed and enslaved, their land captured by settlers or forced and deceived into selling their land while under duress. Five hundred years later, First Peoples live in apartheid-style "reservations," under the watchful eye of governments, never being able to fully control their own destiny and promote their native culture and way of life they enjoyed before the Europeans arrived.

The Birth of Confederation

The Canadian federation began its evolution from the days First Nations Peoples walked across the ice bridge of the Bering Strait. The British North America Act of 1867, (BNA), an act of the British government, created the Dominion of Canada from the colonies of Canada, Nova Scotia, and New Brunswick. The provinces of Nova Scotia and New Brunswick retained their previously established boundaries, with Canada divided into the provinces of Ontario and Quebec. Despite granting general powers to the federal government, and describing provincial powers, the Dominion of Canada did not enjoy independence from Great Britain. Important powers, such as dealings with other states, immigration, command of the armed forces and especially the power to change the BNA itself, stayed in the hands of the British parliament. Canadians proposed the "Kingdom of Canada" as name of the new nation. In fear of offending the Americans, the British changed the name to "Dominion of Canada". It is believed "Canada" comes from the Iroquois word "Kanata" meaning "village" or "community." Canada came into being by means of land acquisitions and divisions. Here are some important timelines in the creation of Canada.

- 1867- The Dominion of Canada created from the colonies of Canada, Nova Scotia, and New Brunswick.
- 1870 - Canada acquired Rupert's Land and the Northwest Territory to create the Northwest Territories.
- 1870 - The province of Manitoba created and in 1877 became larger with the adoption new boundaries.
- 1871 - British Columbia joins the federation as a province with the boundaries it acquired prior to 1866.

1873 - Prince Edward Island joined Confederation as the seventh province.

1876 - The District of Keewatin created out of a large part of the Northwest Territories.

1882 - The Federal government created four new districts, Assiniboia, Saskatchewan, Athabaska, and Alberta.

1905 – The eight and ninth provinces of Canada, Alberta and Saskatchewan, were created;

1925 - Canada officially claimed a sector of the Arctic laying between 60th west longitude and 141st west longitude.

1949 - After a narrow victory in the second of two referendums, Newfoundland joined Canada as the tenth province.

1999 – The territory of Nunavut, carved entirely out of the Northwest Territories, became Canada's third territory, fulfilling the Inuit people's dream of native self-government.

The three territories, Northwest, Yukon, and Nunavut all have the same status and powers as each other, but do not have the powers accorded to the provinces by the Constitution. At the end of the twentieth century, the Canadian federation consisted of ten provinces and three territories. With Nunavut becoming a territory in 1999, we came full circle; Canada became a federation with the inclusion of a large portion of our First Nations peoples, now beginning a new journey to the self-government, lost nearly half a millennium ago.

The implementation of the British North America Act (BNA), in 1867 sowed the seeds of Confederation, creating a federation of "countries" in a larger country. The four jurisdictions from which Canada was created had effective governance structures. Provinces and the new provincial governments were created to maintain this governance structure and to nurture Canada into a nation and country. At the end of the twentieth century, the "federation of countries" consisted of ten provinces, three territories and one internationally recognized country, Canada. The smaller countries are the ten provinces, and to a lesser extent, the three territories. The BNA grants the provinces exclusive powers over major areas such as taxation, education, and health. Additionally, the BNA grants the federal government exclusive powers over major areas such as the military, banking, currency, immigration, citizenship, marriage and divorce, and prisons. The Canadian federal government is responsible for The Northwest, Nunavut, and Yukon Territories.

The Constitution Act of 1982 gave us the single most important section of our constitution, The Canadian Charter of Rights and Freedoms. For decades prior to 1982, Prime Ministers and Premiers attempted to create a new constitutional framework for Canada, but fell short as the Premiers of the existing "countries" could not agree on the greater good of the one country, Canada. The Federation of Regions envisioned by the Fathers of Confederation has devolved into a Canada of fourteen geographical regions, representing fourteen countries, in a federal, and now feudal, system of government in the twenty-first millennium. The feudalism is a product of the acquisition of lands and cultures in the first half century of Canada's creation.

Here are the names of the ten provinces, three territories and the year they became part of the Canadian Federation.

Table I

Province or Territory	Joined Confederation
New Brunswick	1867
Nova Scotia	1867
Ontario	1867
Quebec	1867
Manitoba	1870
Northwest Territories	1870
British Columbia	1871
Prince Edward Island	1873
Yukon	1898
Alberta	1905
Saskatchewan	1905
Newfoundland	1949
Nunavut	1999

Why do we Need Government?

Governing

Various authoritative bodies govern Canadians. From the top we have a Monarch whose position is hereditary and one of privilege. The Monarchy extends into the House of Commons, a chamber of elected people's representative and a Senate, a chamber of appointed members. In our personal sphere, employers govern our daily lives. Even events around us govern our lives. Governing is exercising continuous sovereign authority over individuals, peoples or other bodies such as a country or corporation. The ability to control, direct, or strongly influence actions, and ultimately prevail over individuals and organizations is the art of governing. The ultimate goal of governing is to exercise restraining or directing influence and to have power over those being governed.

Politics

Politics is the art and science of winning and holding control over a government, of guiding or influencing governmental policy. Politics is competition between interested groups or individuals for power and leadership resulting in political activities characterized by artful and often dishonest practices. We see politics in all aspects of our lives. In the community, groups develop strategies to influence its membership, supporters, and decision makers, inside and outside each group. At work, employees play coworkers against each other to gain an advantage with the boss. On sports teams, players, and parents seek favour with team official to gain advantage over other players and parents. Our every move in life is influenced by politics and by those who practice politics. In every organization, from a simple married couple to the larger society of millions, the art and science of politics is practiced to exert control over one or more persons. When we say "I don't like politics", "I don't like politicians" or "Politicians are crooks", we are forgetting we are all politicians, to one degree or another, practicing politics to meet our own personal objectives. The practices of politics generate reverence, love, hate, and loathing, depending on the constituency affected. The highest forms of politics we know, and are generally loathed by the population, are political parties and government. Political organizations include political parties, trade unions, professional associations, and special interest groups.

The Political Party

A political party is an organization whose sole purpose is to gain political power in order to implement the policies, programs, and ideas of its members. Our registered political parties have differing rules for membership and processes for electing a leader and the party's nominee in general elections. The credentials for membership in a Canadian political party vary according to their respective constitutions. From the young age of fourteen years, you may belong to a political party. A permanent resident may be eligible for membership in one party but not another, which requires Canadian citizenship. Being a member of more than one party is permissible in one political party whilst exclusive membership is required in others. Another party may allow affiliated membership to groups and organizations. Regardless of our individual positions, there is a party waiting for us to become a member of and participate in the democratic process. Political parties use differing methods of electing their leaders. A popular method is the delegate selection. Each constituency elects delegates from amongst it local membership. These delegates then attend the party's national convention where, in addition to voting on the parties' resolutions and amending bylaws, a leadership vote might be required. Some parties have a one member-one vote system wherein each member directly votes for the leader, using in-person, Internet, and mail-in ballots. Each method has their merits; each is susceptible to manipulation and each usually does not effectively reflect the wishes of the membership.

The political party is the cleverest institution in the land. Imagine a group of people deciding to create an organization with little or no money or other material assets. Imagine its operations financed by direct individual contributions and indirectly by the taxes of the people. A political party has very little assets in relation to the power it wields. All the expenses and financial risks are borne by the people while the political party and all the elected members reap all the rewards. Is it any wonder it is call a "party?" A person seeking a new job opportunity must pay the entire job search expense out of his pocket. Not so, for the person seeking a spot in our elected chambers most of their job search costs are paid for by others. A friend of mine seeking to be a member of parliament brought that point home to me. I enquired about the amount of his personal monies he will be contributing to his political campaign. I was stunned to learn he did not intend to contribute any of his own money and expected the people to pay for his entire job search, while he alone reaped the benefits of his new job. Either way, we the people are on the hook, whether he won or lost.

Political Patronage – A Reward System

If you have never heard of political patronage, you must have been very isolated from the world. Political Patronage is present in every political party and government throughout our world. What is 'patronage," in the political sense, and why does it happen? Political patronage is the power to distribute or appoint people to governmental or political positions. Political Patronage is a reward system used by grateful politicians to reward loyal supporters. Long before the public sees an aspiring politician, loyal and hardworking supporters are in the background, "pounding the pavement" to drum up support. Supporters are volunteers giving time and effort, all for the love of politics, the candidate, or future rewards. Supporters sell party memberships, make countless telephone calls, organize fundraising functions, and stand by the aspiring politician through thick and thin. As political careers flourish, usually the same people make themselves available to work and support the politicians. Support manifests itself in the form of time, effort, money, goods and services to the political campaign. Long-serving volunteers expect rewards in the form of government contracts, appointments to one of the many government boards and agencies, and a host of other special considerations. Lots of money is required to conduct an effective party internal nomination and the later public general election campaign. There are always a few individuals and corporate supporters ready to write a cheque, and give time and effort, whenever requested to do so. They also must to be rewarded for their loyalty.

Political Patronage also stem from long-serving politicians who never made it into government cabinet, remaining a back-bencher for a political career spanning one, two or three decades, along the way being loyal party supporters by continually winning their seats for the party and staunchly supporting the party in the "house". These members of the legislatures are usually rewarded with higher profile appointments to crown corporations, international diplomatic postings and many other "plum" positions. Patronage is also pumping government money into constituencies to ensure the governing party member wins in the next election.

> **"(Jean) Chrétien said to me about six months ago," Mills recalls, mimicking the ex-prime minister's accent, 'Denis, you're my most expensive MP.' Since his first election victory in 1988, Mills says Ottawa has pumped more than $1.2 billion into the riding for a wide variety of projects."**
> *(Excerpted from the Toronto Star, January 24, 2004, interview with Toronto area MP Dennis Mills.)*

Whether it is putting a government office in a constituency, paying for a cultural festival, or creating agencies to dole out government contracts, patronage will always be with us. Whether it is an appointment to the Senate, a national committee or as one of Canada's representative to another country or international body, patronage is a reward after a career in politics as either an elected member or a "backroom boy" or a "spin doctor." A government makes tens of thousands of appointments throughout its life. These appoints run the gamut from the experienced and qualified for the job to the political patronage. Do political patronage appointments hurt anyone or the country? It most certainly does, but not as much as the political opposition would want us to believe. Opposition to patronage appointments is mainly to gain political points, as opposition parties, when they become government, continue the practice of patronage appointments.

The greatest disservice of political patronage appointments is the possibility of denying a qualified Canadian a job, in favour of a lesser-qualified person with the right political "connections." The beneficiaries of political patronage appointments are not all dummies or incompetents, as opposition parties and citizens organizations want us to believe. Many are qualified and experienced Canadians who once had flourishing careers before entering politics and who have gained a wealth of experiences whilst serving in one of our legislatures or working closely with the leaders of political parties, with the added bonus of having political connections and loyalty to a political party.

Corporations also benefit from political patronage, a reward for their political contributions or the service provided by their executives. Many senior members of Canadian corporations are also senior members of political parties, overtly or covertly. These executives and senior managers sign members to political parties and work for, and make financial contributions to, their candidate of choice during the nomination process and general election. Every good corporate executive uses every avenue to grow his business and knows good political "connections" produces additional political contacts and new corporate contacts that may result in a lucrative contract for his company.

Patronage will never go away; just practiced in a different form by every political party after gaining power of government.

Government - Theory

Government is the act or process of governing by giving authoritative direction or exercising continuous control over the performance of functions for a political unit. Government is an organization, machinery, or agency through which a political unit exercises authority and performs functions. We know government as a complex set of political institutions, laws, and customs for the management of the population. In comparison to the population, government represents a small group of people holding simultaneously the principal political executive offices of a nation or other political unit and being responsible for the direction and supervision of public affairs such as groups in a parliamentary system constituted by the cabinet or by the ministry. The small groups forming our federal government are the Members of Parliament, Senators, and public servants necessary for governing as well as similar positions in the provincial governments.

Headquartered in the capital city, governments are either a unicameral or a bicameral entity. Canada's federal government is bicameral parliament, with a House of Commons and a Senate, while our provincial governments are unicameral, having only a house of elected representatives.

Government - Reality

We cannot work, play, eat or drink; sell or own anything; we cannot go to a soccer, football, or hockey game without feeling the effects of government. We cannot watch television, go to a movie or live theater without the feeling the presence of government. We cannot have sex, marry, raise, and educate children without the hand of government touching us. We cannot be sick, born, die and be buried without government directing our course of action. Even after death, when our Last Will and Testament is read, the effects of government are evident. Through the legal infrastructure government manages, or mismanages, the growth of industry, wealth of individuals and corporations, quality of social programs, the environment, and the general quality of life of its citizens.

Government is like an octopus, with tentacles reaching into every facet of society. Government is a monolithic and all encompassing entity that moves at snail's pace, believing it will exist forever.

"From the bedroom to the boardroom, politics affect everything we do." *Cecil Young, Ward 8 Candidate, Mississauga City Council, 1991.*

We know of God and governments and we think both are irrelevant in our lives. Government is made up of men and women, with all their faults. Government behaves as though it is an institution of, with divine powers vested from, God. We may choose to ignore the actions of government as we go about our daily lives; in the end, we will reckon with the government as the government sees fit. Judge for yourself the actions of government and compare with this passage from the Bible.

> **Luke 20 Verses 21-26 (New King James Version)**
> *21 And they asked him, saying, Master, we know that thou sayest and teaches rightly, neither accepts thou the person of any, but teaches the way of God truly:*
>
> *22* **Is it lawful for us to give tribute unto Caesar, or no?**
>
> *23 But he perceived their craftiness, and said unto them, Why tempt ye me?*
> *24* **Shaw me a penny. Whose image and superscription hath it?** *They answered and said, Caesar's.*
> *25 And he said unto them,* **Render therefore unto Caesar the things which be Caesar's, and unto God the things which be God's.**
> *26 And they could not take hold of his words before the people: and they marveled at his answer, and held their peace.*

Government is a business operated by the political party whose candidates are elected in the most constituencies in the legislative assembly. Government represents the views, and implements the policies of its master, the political party. While the government is the party, the party is not the government. Political parties do not have the authority to make decisions over the population. Political parties have great influence and control over its members that are elected to the federal House of Commons, provincial legislatures, and local councils and appointed to the Senate. Contrary to popular belief, government is not the composition of the total number of Members of Parliament elected by the majority party. Neither is government the same as the total composition of our Parliaments or the Senate. A majority government in our present system marginalizes Opposition Members of Parliament, reducing them to "whiners" and "complainers," rather than the voice of the people for which they were elected. Even within the government, the majority of its Members of Parliament, the "backbenchers," are nearly irrelevant. Control of members in our legislatures rests in the hands of the Prime Minister and his cabinet and the Premier and his cabinet. There is cadre of senior aids who further control the actions of cabinet.

While several members from government and opposition parties belong to various committees, governments regularly ignore the findings and recommendations of these committees, rendering the committee members and parliamentarians irrelevant. In our parliamentary process, most Members of Parliament behave like sheep being led to slaughter and must obey the commands of the party Whip, the Member of Parliament, for each political party, who is appointed by the party to enforce party discipline. A failure to "toe the party line" may result in suspension or expulsion from the party, forcing a duly elected Member of Parliament to sit as an independent. If a government Member of Parliament has greater political ambitions, such as moving from the backbenches into cabinet, or even to someday lead his party, then he had better "toe the party line." Even an Opposition Member of Parliament must toe the party line, for he may be denied the position of "departmental critic" in the opposition's shadow cabinet or a cabinet position when his party forms the government. A member suspended or expelled from his party have little chance of being the party's nominee in the next general election.

Government is a business with the Prime Minister being the Chief Executive Officer, the Ministers being Departmental Vice-Presidents, with the remaining government and opposition members forming the "Board of Directors of Canada." Members of Parliaments are like corporate directors, required to "rubber-stamp" Cabinet decisions, with little or no debate. Government produces many goods and services, much like a private business. We are not taxpayers, as politicians and taxpayers organizations would have us believe. We are citizens and residents of Canada and consumers of goods and services produced and delivered by the government and its agents. The assets of the government are not the assets of the people, neither are the liabilities.

Canadians may not make any claim on the governments'; assets; neither may the Canadian people be sued for the liabilities of their governments. If the people owned government, why then are contracts between the government and another entity not made public. If the government belonged to the people, then we have a right to see those contracts. If the government belonged to the people, then why do we need a Freedom of Information Act to have access to government documents?

In bad economic times and faced with decreasing revenues, governments and businesses have two options; reduce production and delivery of services and reduce staff. Government has one other option not generally available to private business, the authority to print more money. Like the private sector, governments borrow money on the open market by issuing government bonds. In a time of slower economic activity, government would not increase taxes for fear of triggering an economic slide into a recession. As revenues decrease, governments favour borrowing to pay for, and maintain, the normal level of service to the people. Any significant reduction in services, or tax increases, would certainly bring an outcry from Canadians, and quite possibly electoral defeat for the governing party. Facing increased demand for services, government has raised its service fees through increased taxation, inevitably followed by an outcry from individuals, business leaders and the opposition members of the "house." Whenever revenues increase, government either spend to improve the quality of services it provides; reduce its service fees by implementing a tax reduction; or by making cash refund directly to the people. Over the past two decades, we have simultaneously experienced massive tax cuts and decreases in services as irresponsible politicians play political games with the people. People are always glad to get a "tax cut" without expecting a corresponding decrease in government services.

Compare government actions to businesses such as banks, insurance, cable television, telephone and investment companies who raise fees whenever revenues fall and increase dividends to their shareholders when profits exceed expectations. We will never see the day when a business reduces it fees or prices, for prolonged periods, and maintain its level or service and profitability.

If we demand a tax reduction, we are demanding a reduction in the level and quality of government services.

If we demand lower prices, we are demanding lower wages.

State of Canadian Federalism

Confederation brought about hope to create a federation of regions that would compliment each other and lead to a greater country. National political parties were formed and for the first one hundred years enjoyed plurality right across the country and could legitimately claim to be a national party having representation in every province. Simultaneously as we became a "Me First" society, support for political parties splintered along linguistic, regional, and social lines. The federal political party wishing to become the federal government must now depend on regional voter support. Winning the provinces of Ontario and Quebec is crucial to forming a federal government and with a little help in the Atlantic and western regions, a party could claim itself as a national government. The lack of national support for any one political party is a direct result of discontent within the federation. In the last thirty years of the twentieth century, Quebecers elected separatist members to their provincial and federal legislatures in order to gain parliamentary legitimacy for their cause, separation from Canada. Western Canadians supported new political parties as a means of forcefully getting the attention of the federal government. Western Canadians also supported the social democratic parties to ensure the availability and universality of social programs and the cooperative nature of social democracy. Ontarians supported established parties having a tradition of supporting a strong central government and protection of Canadian unity. The bickering between governments is not new, having gone on for decades. It is now at a feverish pitch specifically because of the splintering of the national representation into regional blocks. As the national voice was becoming a whisper, the provincial voices became louder and louder and is all that is heard by the people. The federal system of governance has become the feudal system of government.

After coming to Canada, I quickly became involved in the community, particularly in politics and sports, learning the sheer size of government bureaucracy is killing innovation, desire, and generally creating despair among hard working people. Today a sense of frustration permeates the citizenry. Ignored by their governments, Canadians feel robbed by the very institutions established to protect their interests. Canadians harbour strong feelings of resentment to politicians, businesses and the wealthy that have hijacked government for their own self-interest.

The many levels of government create an environment where it is easy to "pass the buck" to another level, whether higher or lower seems irrelevant. The endless bickering and jurisdictional squabbles between levels of government is forcing Canada to stumble like a drunkard to the greatness that awaits it. In my corner of Canada, the constant bickering between school boards, municipal, regional, and provincial governments over money and jurisdiction delayed hospital construction, road expansion, program cuts or elimination, increased user fees and reduction in the quality of education. The bickering continues today and like many family quarrels, money and power are the root causes. Many of the concerns at the various levels of government are legitimate and are recognized as impediments to building a stronger and more vibrant Canadian society. Provinces have always, and will continue, to demand greater transfer of federal powers, and more money from, the federal government. Separatists' governments, classifying Quebec as a "distinct society" wants political sovereignty from, and economic association with, Canada; the ultimate goal is complete separation of the province from

Canada. Quebec separatist, when they form the next government, will wait for "the winning conditions" before deciding on a referendum on sovereignty, probably with another muddled question.

> **"Canada is divisible because it's not a real country."** *Lucien Bouchard, M.P., Leader of the Bloc Quebecois (BQ), 1995 Quebec Independence (Referendum) campaign.*

Premier Lucien Bouchard clearly understood the Canadian federation is not working and cannot work under its present structure. He was wrong in his belief that Canada is not a real country. He was equally wrong in believing Canada is divisible. Canadians watched as another province promoted economic sovereignty from, and political association with, Canada. Other provinces resisted and resented official bilingualism. One provincial premier and a national party leader suggested the federal government should just hand over all the money to the provinces with no strings attached. Both the premier and national party leader called Canada "a community of communities," with the premier later pronouncing the federal government an agent of the provinces and should be following the wishes of the provincial governments. Were it not for the strength and vision of Statesman and Prime Minister, the late Right Honourable Pierre Elliot Trudeau and an eminent team, Canada would have disintegrated to a "balkanized" state, and probably would not have existed today as a country.

Alberta and British Columbia are fed up with being ignored by the federal government and is demanding a greater voice for the western provinces. So they should, and rightly so! They are equal partners in the federation. Manitoba, Saskatchewan, the Atlantic provinces and Newfoundland and Labrador, while voicing their opinions on the problems of, and the need to rework the federation, goes along for the ride because they do not have the population or economic clout to make a difference. Ontario and Quebec are the big provincial players in the federation; they have the population, economic power, and constitutional influence to control the federation, and usually do. The frustrations provinces have with the federal government are real and reflective in recent comments by Albertans suggesting putting up a "firewall" around Alberta's money and political authority to keep Ottawa out. In their zeal to become autonomous countries, provinces have enacted laws that are restricting the equality of all Canadians, regardless of where they are from. Provinces have a residency requirement for its residents to receive social assistance and to purchase land. A professional certified in one province might require re-certification in any one, and all other provinces.

Political parties courted the ultra-right and catered to the "mean-spirited" side of humanity as a means of being elected. Once elected these politicians appease the gullible electorate by stirring up hatred and mistrust for one another, pitting one level of government against another, and one group of Canadians against another. It is common to see the provinces take contrary positions on everything the federal government does, except gladly taking money from the federal government, balking in unison at any suggestions of accountability. Over the decades, provincial governments achieve unanimity in telling the federal government to "just give us the money," and stay out of our business. Our politicians are a no longer respected people, often loathed by the population. The "Honourable" men and women in our legislatures have denigrated one another for their beliefs, opinions, and actions, splintering the legislatures into 'cliques". In its zeal to satisfy proponent of a free market economy, governments have abandoned the principle of universality of government services, leaving the underprivileged to fend for themselves and at the mercy of peddlers of deceit. Government actions, and in some cases inaction, sowed the seeds of discontent.

Provincial governments are parochial in nature, serving its own self-interest, and unable to envision a border further than their own. Having control over their municipalities, provincial masters have handcuffed municipal governments who must depend on "handouts" from the provincial treasury. Municipalities, having very little authority to raise funds, must struggle to meet the needs of its people. With the constitutional division of powers of federal and provincial government and the control province exercise over municipalities, we have a recipe for bickering and "do nothing" governments. The federal government is unable to offer direct help to municipalities, as the provinces will balk in unison at federal government interference in provincial matters. However, the provinces will gladly accept any federal cash earmarked for helping the municipalities, keeping most of it in provincial coffers. The present constitutional framework prevents the federal government from implementing national programs and must tread carefully lest it is accused of stepping into areas of provincial jurisdiction. We have an abundance of bickering at all levels of government caused by the self-serving actions of generations of politicians. With federal, provincial, municipal, regional, quasi-governmental bodies and school boards fighting over jurisdiction, we have created bureaucracy on top of bureaucracy, operated by "do-nothing" politicians who are only interested in getting re-elected.

The federal government, having miserably failed at protecting the national interest, has helped in creating a fragmented Canada. The provinces, having contempt for the federal government, are now behaving in a manner that is alienating their cities, beginning the internal fragmentation of the provinces. Our city governments, sensing the national fragmentation, are now appealing to the federal government for financial assistance, despite cities being provincial jurisdiction. The outcry from city mayors for funding from the federal government will result in jurisdictional squabbles between the provincial and federal governments. The provinces will perceive any direct transfer of money to the cities as an encroachment on provincial jurisdiction. No doubt, Quebec will be the most vociferous opponent of any direct contact between the federal and city governments. To show their frustration over jurisdictional squabbles and the lack of action from their provincial masters, some mayors have mused about their cities become autonomous from the provinces. In One Canada, cities will be semi-autonomous and be able to better control their destinies. Only after we have One Canada will cities be able to meet their funding requirements.

The federal government has continued the destructive path of devolution of its powers through the backdoor, by using federal-provincial agreements instead of constitutional amendments, without meaningful accountability by the provinces. This devolution of powers have exacerbated the fragmentation of Canada, creating many classes and types of Canadians, none of whom are equal to the other, belonging to another province, another country and rarely to Canada. Granting a province jurisdiction over immigration and allowing a province to opt out of national programs with full compensation, are but two examples of the failure of the national government to protect Canada first.

Demanding Provinces

At every First Ministers' conference, Premiers demand more powers and monies from the Prime Minister and federal government. The Premiers believe the Canadian government is too powerful and too centralized, collecting too much money from the provinces and not sending back an equal amount to them. Sir John A. MacDonald, during the debates leading to confederation, had foreseen the state federalism when he said:

> **"Here we have adopted a different system. We have strengthened the General Government. We have given the General Legislature all the great subjects of legislation. We have conferred on them, not only specifically and in detail, all the powers which are incident to sovereignty, but we**

> have expressly declared that all subjects of general interest not distinctly and exclusively conferred upon the local governments and local legislatures, shall be conferred upon the General Government and Legislature.
>
> We have thus avoided that great source of weakness, which has been the cause of the disruption of the United States. We have avoided all conflict of jurisdiction and authority, and if this Constitution is carried out,. . . we will have in fact, as I said before, all the advantages of a legislative union under one administration, with, at the same time, the guarantees for local institutions and for local laws, which are insisted upon by so many in the provinces now, I hope, to be united. . . . "

Sadly, successive federal and provincial governments have ignored, and continue to ignore, the constitution in pursuing their own self-interest of "Kingdom Building," creating Canadian Feudalism of the 21st century.

Bureaucracy

In every organization, there is a governing structure and hierarchy required to orderly conduct business. The policies, procedures, and management structure of an organization are best referred to as "corporate bureaucracy." The larger the organization, the bigger the bureaucracy and the more difficult it is to manage and effect change. Government is the largest and most important organization in the land and is therefore the largest bureaucracy in every country. The increasing sizes of our collective bureaucracies breed inefficiencies and incompetence. Canada's four levels of government, federal, provincial, regional and municipal, and quasi-government bodies, such as school boards, exists in a bureaucratic structure that under serves us. The bureaucracy governing our lives is overwhelming in its ineffectiveness, with the amount of money needed to feed the bureaucracy being almost incomprehensible. It seems that every time something must be done, there must be endless consultations, reports, and rebuttals between, and from all levels of government and "stake holders." This is bureaucracy on top of bureaucracy, better known a "Red Tape." Red Tape ensures the people are not served, money is wasted, and progress is denied or reduced. The increasing complexity of our bureaucracies, both in public and corporate governance, stem from both our personal inability to take responsibility for our actions and the increased litigious nature of our present society. Since we have moved away from assigning blame to a mentality of "no fault," we have created bureaucracies to shift and share blame and suffering to everyone else.

"Bureaucracy consumes money but produces very little in return" *Cecil Young, All Candidates Debate, Mississauga Ward 8 City Council election campaign, 1991.*

The federal and provincial governments are all pulling in different directions and are destroying the fabric of a nation Canadians built over centuries. With four levels of government in some areas, solving the problems facing Canadians is taking decades instead of a few years, despite the multitude of solutions available for each problem. We, the Canadian people have been "hung out to dry" by our governments and its co-conspirators, the large business and wealthiest of Canadians, and have become the "football" in the political football game. Canadians are justified in their anger about feeding the bureaucracy with their hard-earned wages.

After World War II, Canada began developing and implementing universal access to government services in a move to ensure all Canadians had access to service, regardless of their means. We implemented national health, Canada Pension Plan, and employment insurance plans and many other programs, dubbed the "social safety net." As the number of social services programs grew to protect the less privileged in our society, we were offering generous corporate tax breaks to encourage the growth of industry and the creation of jobs. We began to create a society where everyone could prosper with hard work and perseverance. The financial costs for the social services and corporate tax incentives became too expensive and prohibitive. In the period 1970 to 1995, governments found they were struggling with recurring yearly deficits leading to massive cumulative financial debts.

By the beginning of the 1980's, the dark and mean-spirited side of humanity began to rear its ugly head with the advent of the "Me First" society of greed and selfishness. Larger businesses and wealthier Canadians demanded the governments rein in social service benefits. These co-conspirators were not satisfied with reducing benefits; they wanted complete elimination of the social safety net and threw their support behind politicians who were very willing to destroy the programs designed to help less privileged people. The unprecedented display of greed and selfishness touched all facets of our lives. Common sense and compassion went out the door in the pursuit and accumulation of wealth at the expense of others. Faced with financial deficits and massive debts and securing the support of large corporations and wealthier Canadians, the federal and provincial governments began the gradual and systematic destruction of education, healthcare and social services; selling their actions to the people as "cost cutting" measures. Government cost-cutting measures and the hijacking of government by large businesses and the wealthy are only now are bearing fruits in the form of illiteracy, adult and child poverty, homelessness, corporate financial scandals, increased crime and violence and deteriorating infrastructure in our cities.

National Unity

Since the proclamation of confederation, national unity has been on the national agenda, sometimes as a burning desire and at other times a lukewarm idea. For one hundred and ten years, national unity was about the peoples and cultures of English and French Canadians, the two "founding" peoples and cultures representing the European colonizers. Our preoccupation with the two founding peoples ignored the vibrant cultures and people of our native sons and daughters. The vibrancy of First Peoples nation was created thousands of years before the English and French arrived in North America. Styled "Two Solitudes" and "One Country, Two Histories" the debate about Canadian culture pitted English Canada against the predominantly French-speaking people in Quebec, and to a lesser extent French-speaking Canadians in other provinces. At various times since confederation, federal/provincial conferences have attempted to bring equality to both solitudes and recognize Quebec, its language and culture as a "distinct society," deserving a special place in the federation. Even as we entered the twenty-fist century, the debate about Canadian culture is between English and French, completely ignoring the other cultures that have gained prominence since the centennial of confederation. As Quebecers gained confidence about their place in confederation, frustration and resentment of the status quo, the dominance of the English, grew feverishly to rhetorical pitch. The **Front de Libération du Québec**, better known as the **FLQ,** was a Quebec separatist group with a determination to separate Quebec from Canada. The mostly illegal tactics of the FLQ culminated in the October Crisis of 1970 and a new era in national politics began. In 1968, three years prior to the October Crisis, Rene Lévesque, a former Liberal, led a movement that culminated in the creation the Parti Quebecois, PQ. The PQ is a political party that advocates social democracy and the separation of the province of Quebec from Canada, creating an independent country. The rise of the PQ to government in 1976 sent shivers down the spine of the power brokers of English Canada. In panic, corporations moved out of Quebec, further fueling the separatist cause and increasing mistrust of

English Canada. The two solitudes were now at loggerheads, setting the stage for 1980 and 1995 Quebec referenda on separation. The muddled 1980 question, when deciphered, was about political sovereignty from, and economic association with, Canada, followed by a referendum on any political changes negotiated between Canada and Quebec. In a firm 60/40 split, Quebecers rejected the question. The 1995 referendum was explicit in its intent to negotiate a new economic and political partnership with Canada. However, the Quebec National Assembly bill supporting the question explicitly stated, **"If the negotiations prove to be fruitless, the National Assembly will be empowered to declare the sovereignty of Quebec without further delay."** Quebecers narrowly voted NON, with a 50.6% to 49.4% split, choosing to stay in Canada, deferring the question of separation to another day even as the English and French continue their historical quarrel over equality and their respective cultures.

Canada did not stagnate during the decades long English and French debates on equality and cultures. First Peoples began to assert themselves in the federation; western Canadians gained new economic powers and immigrants began to influence the political landscape. National unity is no longer an English/French issue; it is now wrapped in First Peoples rights and freedoms, western Canadian equality and the cultural and linguistic realities of a multicultural Canada. This blend of cultures and peoples afford Canada a unique opportunity to develop into the Greatest Country on Earth and to lead the world to peace, freedom, and prosperity.

First Peoples

Since the arrival of the Europeans, First Peoples have been struggling to regain their rights and lands and to have provisions of treaties with the Europeans honoured as written and to remedy land claims. The centuries old struggles to resolve the issues are very large black marks on

Canada and its love and support of human rights. We were in the forefront of the long and hard fight to bring down apartheid regimes in Afrikaners' South Africa and Rhodesia. We were able to defeat apartheid in less than a century but unable to solve our First Peoples problems over centuries. The issues are complex but in the interest of directing our efforts and resources to building One Canada, the national government must resolve all outstanding First Peoples claims within a period not exceeding one decade.

One Canada offers a solution to the new reality. The new regions of Canada will recognize the four building blocks of Canada; First Peoples, English, French, and adding the Multiculturalism builders.

Canada's Deficits

> *Deficit* – a deficiency or impairment in mental or physical functioning; inadequacy or insufficiency; the amount by which a sum of money falls short of the required or expected amount; a shortage

The dysfunctional state of Canadian federalism is traceable to Canada's deficits; **intellectual, social, democratic, patriotic, and financial.** Our intellectual deficit leaves us vulnerable to manipulation by politicians, governments, corporations, and wealthy Canadians. Our social deficit created the greedy and heartless "me" generation whose mantra, "the survival of the fittest," resulted in increased poverty, homelessness, hopelessness, gang and gun violence, and disrespect for people and property. Our democratic deficits forces us to be governed by our inferiors; politicians who are constantly manipulated by their self-serving advisors and political partisans. Our Patriotic deficit diminishes the value of Canadian citizenship, surrendering control of our affairs to foreigners who brainwash us into believing if something originated outside Canada then it must be of better value than similar Canadian-made products. Our financial deficits continue to pile up monetary debt that drains significant financial resources away from programs required to better the Quality of Life for Canadians.

Intellectual Deficit

The intellectual deficit stems from our fear to be heard and be held accountable. We teach children mediocrity is acceptable; competition is bad; playing to win is undesirable and to stand out is unwanted. We stifle creativity, hamper excellence, lay blame elsewhere, and encourage conformity. We shy away from tough decisions, preferring to keep our opinions to ourselves and to adapt ourselves to our surroundings. In essence, we are programmed not to "rock the boat," or else we will be labeled "shit disturbers." Our intellectual deficit stifles debate, which is necessary in a healthy and vibrant democracy.

Social Deficit

Our social deficit is a measure of our humanity. With increased discrimination against the elderly, ever-increasing number of homeless persons, violence, and gang warfare plaguing society, bullying in schools, family breakdown, hooliganism, and illegal drug usage, our social deficit is on the rise. Splintering our population into special interest groups, decay in our moral values and the absence of basic human values such as respect, caring and loving one another, will make elimination of our social deficit a difficult task in the generations ahead. The greater our individuality and the stronger our selfish desires, the more profound our social deficit become.

Democratic Deficit

Gradually, we are loosing our freedoms ever so subtly it is hardly missed. We refuse to participate in politics, giving up our voices and control of our lives to our inferiors. Our leaders create "control centres" around themselves, ensuring isolation from other elected representatives and the population. Power in our legislatures is confined in a select few, rendering the majority of parliamentarians impotent. Our many legislatures and council chambers are filled with long serving and docile career politicians under the control of manipulative political "bag men" and "spin doctors." The solution to our democratic deficit is rejuvenation of our legislatures with newer members from time to time through fixed terms of service for politicians.

Patriotic Deficit

Canadians have a most superior inferiority complex, grown over time, and nurtured by foreign ownership of our resources and businesses, cultural domination by foreigners and our belief that if it is "Made Elsewhere" it is better than "Made in Canada." We believe that if we are very smart and very good we should be working and living in the USA or Europe. We continually compare ourselves to Americans. We lack the confidence to believe in our achievements and ourselves. We are afraid to blow our own horn lest we are branded as pompous. We are afraid to defend Canada and all Canadians, apologizing at every opportunity to hide our lack of patriotism. Patriotism is firmly standing up for the values we cherish, the land we love and is the responsibility of good citizenship.

Financial Deficit

Financial deficits are synonymous with governments. We are now accustomed to governments spending more that they take in and borrowing to finance debt. Governments spend like water going over Niagara Falls without regard for the sources of its money, the people. If government needs more money, it takes more from the people, reduces services, and prints more money. Deficits are a part of the political process, not part of governing, and are a means of buying votes with grandiose government schemes to curry favour with the voters, the wealthy and corporations. Governments are not the only ones operating with deficits. Individual Canadians are burdened with debt to the point where many are borrowing money to pay back the money they borrowed earlier. It is astonishing to know that many Canadians are one pay cheque away from bankruptcy, as reported in the media. Financial deficits of the past generation resulted in a national debt of almost than $700B and a combined provincial and territorial debt exceeding $250B in 2002. That is a staggering $29,000 for ever man, woman, and child in Canada in 2002. Will we ever pay of this nearly one trillion dollar debt? Should we even bother to pay it off? The answer is a resounding YES. The yearly-accumulated interest could well pay for many social programs that will improve the quality of life for all Canadians.

Canada-USA Relationship

> **"Americans should never underestimate the constant pressure on Canada, which the mere presence of the United States has produced. We are different people from you and we are different people because of you. Living next to you is in some ways like sleeping with an elephant. No matter how friendly and even-tempered is the beast, if I can call it that, one is effected by every twitch and grunt. It should not therefore be expected that this kind of nation, this Canada, should project itself as a mirror image of the United States."** *Prime Minister, The Rt. Hon. Pierre Elliott Trudeau.*

With their often-repeated credo of "Life, Liberty, and the Pursuit of Happiness," the United States of America (USA) represents the best and worst in humanity. The USA produced some of the greatest minds, and best technologies; more millionaires and billionaires than any other country; most devastating military machines, and deadliest weapons of mass destruction, of the past five hundred years. Many around the world have tried to emulate the American "way of life," and to some degree have, including all the good, the bad and the ugly facets of American life. With the USA's almost unbridled freedoms come crime, broken inner cities, and massive disparity in financial well-being. The American bombast and financial influence are well known around the world. Many countries have studied the American society, selecting those values that will enhance their societies, being careful not to import the worst of America.

Canada shares the world's longest undefended land border with the United States of America and, until recently, Canadians and residents pass freely across the border. Geographically Canada in envied for such a close relationship with the USA. Paradoxically, that closeness means Canada is consistently taken for granted by all US Administrations and treated as the 51st state. Nevertheless, we are friends and friends are often taken for granted and sometimes even ignored. Throughout our histories, Americans have taken Canadians for granted, remembering us only when our help is required, and abandoned when convenient. Canadians continually look to Americans for approvals and recognition for any action or deed Canadians performed. It is as though "daddy" must give us his blessings or else we are inadequate, inferior, and not belonging. These days, Americans do not give much thought to Canadians and Canada's interests, except when it is in America's interest. When we rescued their hostages in Iran, Americans were grateful. When we accepted America-bound aircrafts and thousands of passengers, in the wake of the September 11, 2001 bombings in New York, Washington and Pennsylvania, Canada and Canadians did not merit attention in their President's speech. The outcry from many Canadian quarters, who felt slighted by the Presidents ignorance of Canada, was unbelievable. Once more, we needed some approval or blessings from Americans for helping them out. Would America help us out if those bombings were on our soil? We most certainly would not merit the incessant attention Canadian media gave to the tragedies of New York, Washington and Pennsylvania.

America paid much attention to pre-confederation Canada. In the early part of the nineteenth century, the Americans publicly stated their intentions, and made overtures, to annex the northwestern parts of Canada. In 1866, the US House of Representative adopted the "Annexation Bill" to acquire all of **"Nova Scotia, New Brunswick, Canada East, and Canada West, and for the organization of the Territories of Selkirk, Saskatchewan, and Columbia,"** essentially all of what is now Canada. That Annexation Bill drove fear in the hearts of British North Americans, playing an important role in the 1867 Confederation into the Dominion of Canada. The Americans also coveted Alaska, claimed by the Russians. In 1867, Russia sold Alaska to the Americans, and almost immediately, a boundary dispute developed with Canada. The Russians had claimed more land than an 1825 treaty, between the Russians and the British, gave them and the USA came along to claim these same quantities lands. In 1903, the government of the United States of America used its influence with Canada's colonial master, the British Monarch, to gerrymander the Alaska-Canada boundary, denying the Yukon a Pacific Ocean port and denying British Columbia full access to the Pacific Ocean. The American's goal was to link Alaska to the contiguous United States of America at Washington State which would have completely cutoff British Columbia from the Pacific Ocean. The Americans claimed Canada had no entitlement the Alaska panhandle since Canada did not exert its political and military influence over the panhandle. Despite doubts about the validity of the Alaska-Yukon border, no Canadian government has ever attempted to revisit the settlement mechanism used to determine the Alaska-Yukon-British Columbia boundaries. Even though a century has passed since the gerrymandered border was decided, Canada must seek to reopen the debate with a view of getting a settlement that will give the Yukon a Pacific Ocean access and full and complete access to the Pacific Ocean and Straits for all of British Columbia.

The long running softwood lumber dispute pits Canadian lumber producers against their American counterparts, who are using protectionist measures to force provincial governments to charge higher American prices to Canadian lumber companies. This economic blackmail violates fair trade practices, but to the Americans, fair trade is for their benefit only. Canada is a party to the World Trade Organization (WTO) and we signed the Free Trade Agreement with the Americans, and the North American Free Trade Agreement (NAFTA), which added Mexico, yet our manufacturers do not have free trade with the USA consumers. Our manufacturers are constantly harassed by subsequent American administrations, costing Canadian jobs.

Whether you share the sentiment, **"Damn Americans…., I hate those bastards,"** or you believe their President is a "moron," it is imperative to clearly understand and effectively partner with the Americans and not be beholden to them, as some Canadians amongst have espoused. Canada-USA relationship must be well managed by Canada, confidently knowing Americans are *our* best friends always, and we are but one of *their* friends of conveniences. We must quite clearly understand that in the American psyche, the USA is the only important country in the world, believing they have the god-given right to impose their will on the rest of the world. To this end, America culturally and militarily invaded other countries, converting those citizens and governments into American surrogates and puppets. The American invasion of Canada is through our laws, economy, culture, and to a lesser extent, our military, and security services. In their one military foray into Canada, the War of 182, the Americans were beaten back, though Canada lost land in the Maritimes.

The political demands of the provinces are routed in American "stateism," learned from educating many of young adults, our corporate and political leaders, and professionals, by the colleges and universities of the United States of America. Sir John A. MacDonald said it best in the late 1860's:

"Ever since the union was formed the difficulty of what is called "State Rights" has existed, and this had much to do in bringing on the present unhappy war in the United States. They commenced, in fact, at the wrong end. They declared by their Constitution that each state was sovereignty in itself, and that all the powers incident to a sovereignty belonged to each state, except those powers which, by the Constitution, were conferred upon the General Government and Congress."

The American stranglehold on the Canadian economy is reflected in the large percentage of Canadian businesses controlled and owned by American companies. American ownership and control of companies in strategic sectors of the Canadian economy, enable the American government to cripple Canada, if Canadians refused to "play ball" with them. With more than eighty-five percent of Canada's exports shipped to the USA, closing the border for one week would seriously hurt the Canadian economy. Therefore, we are forced to "know-tow" to the directives of the Americans, out of fear of economic retaliation; a fact none of our politicians will openly admit it. Any retaliation will also hurt the USA economy that also depends on this the largest bilateral trade relationship in the world, approaching one trillion dollars. The USA's "America First" policy shut the border on all Canadian beef with the reported case of a single cow with the Bovine spongiform encephalopathy (BSE) or "Mad Cow Disease." The American action devastated the Canadian beef industry with farmers loosing of millions of dollars everyday the border is closed. When the Americans found a single case of Mad Cow disease in their cattle, many countries banned the importation of all US beef; Canada banned only those beef products and live cattle likely to carry mad cow disease. The Americans claimed their beef industry never had BSE on its own and their single case of BSE was traced back to an infected animal born on a Canadian farm in Alberta.

While Severe Acute Respiratory Syndrome (SARS) were devastating the Canadian tourist industry, the USA never reported a definitive case, classifying all their cases as "suspected" of SARS. Any admission of SARS in the USA would devastate their tourism industry, as it did Canada's. There is widespread speculation that SARS existed in the USA at the same time it was ravaging Canada's health care system. We will never know the truth about SARS in the USA. There is a perception that in the USA the truth is a casualty on the road to profits. That is probably true for countries adopting the "American Way of Life."

American law provides for sanctions against foreign companies utilizing the assets of American citizens and companies seized by Cuba's communist government. The long arm of this law crosses into Canadian jurisdiction, overriding our laws, threatening to declare Canadian corporate executives, with business operations in Cuba, as "persona no grata" (not welcomed) in the USA. An American company with operations in Canada had to remove Cuban-made pajamas from its Canadian stores, to comply with US laws. Somehow, our Canadian government felt it had to exert pressure on this American company to restock the Cuban-made products on its store shelves and begin an investigation to see if the retailer had violated Canada's Foreign Extraterritorial Measures Act. Canada maintained diplomatic relations with Cuba despite American pressure to sever it. As the pajamas were not banned in Canada, why was an investigation required? This American company should have been ordered to immediately place the pajamas back on its shelves or face the maximum $1.5 million fine provided for in the Foreign Extraterritorial Measures Act. The USA reserves the right to apply its laws to any country of the world even as it rejects any country applying their laws on Americans. The USA wants to carry out any act, legal or illegal, anywhere in the world without being subjected to the rule of international law. That is the main reason the US administration have refused to ratify the treaty creating the International

Court of Justice, proving the USA is the only importing country in the world, with the god-given right to impose its will on the rest of the world.

> **"When the Prime Minister of Canada went to Washington he was treated with about the same consideration by the president as his two dogs were except that he was not lifted by his ears."** *John Diefenbaker - March 21, 1967, House of Commons*

This sentiment, expressed when Prime Minister Lester Pearson visited Washington, could have been made after visits by former Prime Ministers Pierre Trudeau and Jean Chrétien. The Canadian establishments have always chided these two prime ministers for maintaining a strong sense of independence from American administrations. Prime Minister John Diefenbaker cancelled the Avro Arrow fighter plane program, the best technical fighter plane of its time, in 1959. Since that time, there has been speculation the American president of the day ordered Prime Minister Diefenbaker to cancel to Avro Arrow program, although the official line is it was too expensive to build and deploy such and technologically superior fighter aircraft. America elected John F. Kennedy as their president in 1960 while John Diefenbaker was still prime minister of Canada. The ultra-nationalist Canadian Prime Minister did not get along very well with President Kennedy with America's trade embargo on Cuba and the Cuban missile crisis being the "straws that broke the camel's back." The Prime Minister refused to put the Canadian armed forces on advanced readiness, at America's request. The Canadian armed forces defied the Prime Minister and put themselves on advanced readiness, demonstrating it would follow American presidents instead of the Canadian Prime Minister. According to Prime Minister Diefenbaker, Kennedy told him bluntly that, **"When I tell Canada to do something, I expect her to do it!"** I suspect that covertly, the USA pressures

Canada to act in the best interest of the USA and we gladly agree. I believe in the coming years and decades the directives controlling the Canadian government will be overtly made, as they were in the Diefenbaker years. The Diefenbaker government was toppled after a series of damaging press conferences, press releases, and smear campaign orchestrated by foreign agents and Canadian collaborators. Richard Sanders, in A People's History of the CIA, quotes then RCAF Public Relations Director Commander Bill Lee as saying, **"It was a flat-out campaign. We identified key journalists, big labour, key Tory hitters and. . . Liberals. We wanted people with influence on members of cabinet. In the end, the pressure paid off. "**

"President Kennedy spent one million dollars and 400 operators to defeat me in 1963." *John Diefenbaker - MacLean's Magazine, January 1973.*

With the defeat of the Diefenbaker government, **Canada had it first bloodless "coup d'etat."**

US Immigration and Customs Agents operate on Canadian soil to pre-screen persons seeking entry into the USA and to inspect cargo containers before they are shipped to US destinations. Allowing foreign Immigration and Customs Agents to enforce foreign laws on Canadian soil is a gross and blatant violation of Canadian territorial sovereignty. These agents must be sent back to their home soil to enforce their home laws. Canadian Immigration and Customs agents operating on foreign soil must be brought back to Canadian sovereign territory, protecting the territorial sovereignty of other countries.

The cultural invasion of Canada permeates our radio, television and film industries, and our education system. Very little explanation is required here, as the lives of every Canadian are touched by this invasion. As part of the North Atlantic Treaty Organization (NATO), Canada need not worry about military invasion by the United States of America. Any invasion of Canada would trigger a mutual defense pact in the NATO agreement. Even though the USA reserves the right to act in its own self-interest if a military invasion of Canada was necessary, I suspect it would think long and hard before doing so. Canada could expect military help from Germany and France, and strong condemnation from other NATO member countries. Sadly, our colonial master would be silent on any military invasion of Canada by the USA. We have set up ourselves for quick conquering, by almost any other nation, having destroyed our once proud, strong, and effective military. An American military invasion of Canada would last about a long as it takes the Prime Minister of Canada to drive from his official resident at 24 Sussex Drive, in Ottawa, to the National Parliament buildings about three kilometers away.

National and provincial laws are revised and new laws drafted to reflect American jurisprudence. Many Canadians speculate our security and intelligence services are under the control of the US security and intelligence services because of recent revelations. We will never know, because our government will never admit it, continually hiding behind the "national security' blanket. With our "Superior Inferiority Complex" to Americans, many Canadians have welcomed the cultural, economic, and legal invasions from the United States of America by adopting the "American Way of Life." Many more will welcome a military invasion when it comes early in the 22nd century.

Canadians must recognize the disconnection of the American people from their federal government, a chasm created over generations of people's apathy and indifference to politicians and the political process. A closer look at Canadians' relationship to their governments will reveal a crack that is widening, soon becoming a chasm. This chasm is under construction as our provinces adopt the "state rights" of the American Union of the states and provincial premiers belief they now have the same powers as the prime ministers and their provinces should be equal in stature to the country. The chasm in America and the one under rapid construction in Canada will result in curtailed freedoms and the eventual death of democracy from undernourishment. The American government controls its population by fear, continually telling them they are under attack from fanatics, hell bent on destroying Americans; that their country is continually in danger and that peace loving Americans want to surrender America to the control of the rest of the world. The luck of the national American governments is that many Americans do not think about the consequences of government actions, blindly going about their lives as they try to make mortgage and loan payments, pay huge healthcare premiums, and prescription drug costs.

> **"Beware the leader who bangs the drums of war in order to whip the citizenry into a patriotic fervor, for patriotism is indeed a double-edged sword. It both emboldens the blood, just as it narrows the mind. And when the drums of war have reached a fever pitch, the blood boils with hate, and the mind has closed, the leader will have no need in seizing the rights of the citizenry. Rather, the citizenry, infused with fear and blinded by patriotism, will offer up all of their rights unto the leader and gladly so. How do I know? For this is what I have done. And I am Caesar."**
> *Attributed to Julius Caesar (without certainty)*

American administrations continually refer to threats to their society and "way of life" in order to rally the support of its people. Continually crying "wolf" and one day, no one will show up to help the Americans when they will be really in need. In the 1950's, Americans were told there is a communist under every stone. In the 1960's, nuclear war was inevitable while in the 1970's it was the economic power of the Far East that would destroy the American economy. The American leadership of the 1980's pronounced big government and its regulations as killers of innovation and prosperity. The scapegoats of the 1990's were the welfare state, high taxation, and unions who would burden the American taxpayer. The bogeyman of the twenty-first century is terror from Islamic Religious fundamentalist.

Nevertheless, America is our friend and brother. America began its road to a federal system almost a century before Canadians created their federation. America became a sovereign nation almost two hundred years before Canada shook off the shackles of colonialism, becoming a fully sovereign Canada after repatriating its constitution from its colonial and imperial master. From the days of American black slaves, marooned in Nova Scotia instead of being transported back to Africa, to the Loyalists fleeing the war of independence and settling in Upper Canada, to the underground railroad that brought slaves into Canada, the bonds of family and friends on both sides of the border have been strong. It is near impossible to speak with a Canadian citizen or resident whom do not have a family or friendship connection to someone living in the United States of America. Many Canadian citizens and residents have mothers, fathers, brothers, sisters, other relatives, and friends in the United States of America. That makes Canada and the USA part of one big family. Family members and friends often take one another for granted; even ignoring one another for periods, and often expecting an "understanding" from the other on whatever action the one or the other might take. America, the older and wiser brother will want to impose its will on the little brother, Canada. As in a family, the little brother, for a time will yield to the older brother. Eventually, the little brother will grow up and want to do things his own way, creating friction within the family and particularly with the older brother. That is independence and it happens in families and relationships. In many instances, Canada has yielded to America's wishes and in as many instances, Canada has stood up to American pressures. Both countries are the better for standing up to one another and when necessary yielding to the other.

In Jamaica, an idiom says, **"The family tree bends but it never breaks."** The bonds in the Canadian and American "family tree" will bend with the many disagreements between Canada and the United States of America, from time to time staining the relationship. Each country will protect their own self-interest, within their borders, and in the framework of the entire world. Each country will protect the other when both interests' are served. Canada must chart and support an independent policy of law, order, and good governance, bringing freedom and prosperity to the peoples of the world and enhancing Canada's worldwide stature. Canada's brand of quiet diplomacy and its proximity to the USA provides a unique sphere of influence for Canadians to dampen America's bombastic foreign and domestic "America First" policies. Canada-USA relationship will never break; it will bend from Prime Minister to Prime Minister and President to President and, with the tremendous effort expended in cultivating and maintaining that relationship, will always swing back to the strong relationship it has been for more than two centuries.

Adopting the "American Way of Life"

The American cultural machinery is a behemoth churning out songs, plays, movies, and television programs that overwhelms Canada. American electromagnetic waves, from television, radio, and satellite stations, knowing no borders, are easily accessible to more than 90% of the Canadian population. With a population ten times ours, the American market makes it very cost effective to produce television programming that is very affordable to Canadian broadcasters. Therefore, instead of producing local programming, Canadian broadcasters purchase them from American producers and reap the rewards of huge advertising dollars.

The Industrial Revolution gave the USA the financial power to dominate the world for the past one hundred and fifty years. In so doing, it muscled itself into the economies and culture of every country of the world. The USA government imposes a tax on every country and citizen of the world, using its proxies, American owned companies. Every country in the world subsidizes the "American Way of Life." Every citizen of the world pays for the American military might. Many American political leaders and citizens consider the United States of America as the world's policeman with an obligation to defend democracy and capitalism and to enforce the "American Way of Life" in foreign countries. Many Americans believe their country is not the world's policeman and should be protecting the American homeland first, and to hell with the rest of the world. Those who believe America is the world's policeman are the ones that control the power of American government and the military. America has an obligation to be the world's policeman as it charges a fee to every country in the world through American proxies' transference of wealth into the American treasury.

As the years go by, an ever-increasing number of our children are completing their post secondary education in U. S colleges and universities, paid for by various American-financed scholarships. An American education creates an erosion of Canadian values, the proponent of the American culture and the adoption of the US style of government and politicking. Increasingly, politicians have taken to attacking their opponents using American-style innuendos, half-truths, and character assignations. Not too long ago, attacking a politician's personal life was taboo. However, as newer and less capable candidates seek elected office, their darker side rises to the top. Most politicians and aspiring politicians, unable to articulate their positions on almost any subject, resort to obnoxious comments and name-calling in an effort to divert attention away from their own capabilities and lack of intellectual assets. The American invasion has permeated the political parties at all levels, to the extent that American "spin doctors" and negative, demeaning political advertising are now part of our political landscape. Our political leaders believe that anything originating in Canada must be of inferior quality. Hence, the adoption of American toll roads, American Healthcare, American Justice, American negative political campaign advertising. Our right-wing politicians have adopted the American way of belittling the poor, the unfortunate and the helpless and adopted the American way of blaming all the ills of society on the unions, welfare recipients, and the young.

Many of our television-broadcasting operators contribute very little to promotion and protecting the main Canadian culture and the multicultural mosaic. Ever since their existence, cable and the broadcast television industries have wrapped themselves in the Canadian flag, go on bended knees, begging the Canadian Radio Television Commission (CRTC) to relax Canadian content regulations. Year after year, these organizations are very profitable, contribute a pittance to develop Canadian culture and talent, and help in the destruction of Canadian culture and institutions. The American film industry has a significant presence in Canada, thanks in large part to a favourable exchange rate and a generous tax credit program. While our tax dollars create local production and acting jobs, the lead actors are mostly Americans, promoting a storyline is set in America, and the landscape does not reflect Canada. Using the hard-earned dollars of the Canadian taxpayer, we pay the American film and television industry to employ American actors, promote American culture, American politics, and American jurisprudence, American glorification of gangs, crime, murder and violence and the American obsession with guns and war machinery. While we give generous tax credits to foreign producers to glorify their way of life, we starve our own film industry of the funding required to create films depicting Canada and Canadian culture. Our homegrown actors barely eke out a living from their acting careers in Canada, with many moving to the "good 'ole USA" to become big stars, making big money. The mostly American made films shown in Canada depict actions against our laws and our belief system. Our audio and video broadcasting system, having the greatest influence on our lives, are sources of education, entertainment, indoctrination, and intellectual reprogramming. It is imperative that these medium be free of any broadcasts that break our laws or council their audiences to break our laws.

As federalism disintegrates, Canadian politicians look to the USA as saviour for the ailments of Canada. Our political and business leaders blindly copy American political platforms and business practices, respectively, with a lag time of about five years, even though these political platforms and business practices are failures in the USA. Trade between Canadian provinces and American States is much easier to accomplish than trade between provinces because of restrictive trade practices of individual provinces. There are more meetings between provincial premiers and state governors then there are between provincial premiers themselves or with the prime minister of Canada. Communication in the federation is healthier in the north-south direction than the east-west direction. As our political and business leaders facilitate the deeper economic and political integration of country into the USA, their dominance over us will eventually colonize Canada. In less than one quarter of a millennium, Canada would have gone from being a colony of the British to be a colony of the United States of America.

On the world stage, America is the governing administration and American multi-national corporations, while Americans are its people. In most parts of the world, the American Administration, represented by it President and his administration, is either loved or hated. Conversely, Americans are mostly well liked by the people of the world. Attacks on Americans in the hotspots of the world are attacks on the President and his administration since the attackers are unable to attack the upper echelons of government and the multinational corporations. Was the attack on the World Trade Centre in New York City an attack on Americans, the American Administration or the American financial sector?

Canada and the World

The United Nations has consistently rated Canada as the best place on Earth in which to live. That is a tall order for such a large country with a small population, the smallest population in the Group of Eight countries, USA, Russia, France Britain, Italy Japan, Canada, and Germany. In a 1997 report, the United Nations (UN) cited child poverty as a major problem for Canada's future. Our children are our future. If they live in poverty, our future is doomed. Studies have shown that children attending school on hungry stomachs do not learn as well as those with filled stomachs. Poverty leads to low self-esteem, which leads to lack of confidence, further leading to depression and illness, possibly resulting in crime and violence. Despite the glowing report card from the U.N., we are a nation divided. A small group of Canadians caters to, and feeds off, the worst in human nature. Canadians are world-renowned for compassion, equality, and fair mindedness and for its peacekeeping and peace making efforts. Those qualities are in danger of disappearing as the ultra rightwing rear its ugly head. Selfishness, intolerance, and inequality are on the rise. Racism and violence are on the rise, partly because there are those among our leadership who are greedy, selfish, and uncaring. In our present society, a few are taking much from the many, leaving many poor and destitute. While we are the best place on Earth to live, we have several social problems, which have denied many Canadians the right to live a free and full life. Many Canadians have become un-equals in our society. Adult poverty is a major problem that will explode in our collective faces in the form of increased demand on our health care, security and housing services.

Many employed adults are victims of adult poverty because they do not earn enough money to purchase the necessities of life, housing, clothing and food, never mind saving for retirement or education for their children.

The fundamental spirit of the human race is self-preservation and survival of the human race. We, therefore, will instinctively take action to ensure we are housed, clothed, and fed. If society continues to deteriorate, hunger and homelessness will increase; poverty will be commonplace, with the poor and destitute will rise up in violence against their oppressors. A leader will arise from our midst, who will mobilize the underprivileged and unfortunates in societal anarchy. The resultant tyranny will spread fear amongst law-abiding people who will flee to other more secure countries.

> **"How far you go in life depends on your being tender with the young, compassionate with the aged, sympathetic with the striving and tolerant of those who are weaker than you - because someday, you will be one of these."** *George Washington Carver, . (1864-1943), born an American slave, becoming a well-respected scientist and educator*

Canada is renowned for compassion, fairness and as the voice of reason. Canada is always expected to seek a peaceful solution for the world' conflicts and is usually called upon to lead any peacekeeping and peace making efforts. We have admirably met these expectations, despite stretching our military to extraordinary lengths. We must continue these roles and live up to the world's expectations. As the world evolve into a new military and economic order of the two extremes of strength and weakness, rich and poor, the middle grounds of compassion, respect and cooperation will all but disappear to be replaced by animosity, dominance and ignorance. Canada must lead an effort to re-invigorate the United Nations (U.N.) General Assembly and United Nations

Security Council. After more than one half century, the United Nations is in danger of sliding into irrelevance as the mighty and their surrogates seek to impose their will on the world. The democratic nations of the U.N. must use diplomatic, economic, and military means to root out the despotic leaders and governments of the world, from their country and the U.N. The U.N must no longer hide behind the dual shield of "sovereign nation" and "internal domestic affairs" as tyrannical national or tribal leaders massacre their people.

Canada must work to have a permanent seat on an expanded U.N Security Council that includes regional and middle power representation. The present U.N Security Council represents the colonialists, imperialists, and superpowers of an era long gone. An expanded U.N. Security Council must include additional permanent members from Africa, South America, and Canada.

Given a choice of living is a homeland or foreign country free of both terror and poverty with hope for a brighter future, refugees and immigrants will always chose their home country. Canada must work with the U.N members to create economic and political conditions around the world that will stem the flood of refugees and immigrants to the burdened nations that are free and stable. The new model of Canada proposed in this book will create a new economic and political order for Canada. Canada must work with the nations of the world to create a new economic and political order through financial and military means. The multinational corporations of the world are more interested in fattening their bank accounts by exploiting poorer countries and their people, with the help of devious governments and their local surrogates. Canada may need to stand alone to ensure these multinational corporations invest in the people and countries they are currently exploiting, by removing any advantages gained from exploiting the poor of the world. The proposed financing model for One Canada will help to reduce the advantages gained from exploiting the poor and transferring jobs out of Canada.

Canada must use its quiet diplomacy to convince the richer countries to use their financial muscle to build and support infrastructures in developing countries. Two of the world's largest events, the Summer Olympics and the FIFA World Cup of Football rank among the largest infrastructure construction projects in the world. Financing by the G10 countries would afford developing countries in Africa, Asia, and the Caribbean jointly hosting these events, creating both short-term and permanent jobs, with an improvement in the quality of life in developing countries.

The breeding ground for terrorism is the fertile minds of people with idle hands, financed by the fanatical minds of people with money and a cause. The rich and powerful nations, businesses, and individuals of the world control the other nations of the world and are more interested in maintaining, and even increasing that power, than creating the conditions for all people to lift up their standard of living. Every nation of the world, no matter how small, poor, rich, or powerful is important to creating Canada as the Greatest Country on Earth. Canada must use the general forum of the United Nations and private diplomatic and leader-to-leader meetings to encourage all nations to embark upon a program to reduce poverty, famine, homelessness, landlessness, and war around the world. We will be financially richer and safer after significant reduction of these root causes of terrorism.

Canadian Geography

In this section, you will learn about Canada, the second largest country in the world, and its ten provinces and three territories. Canada has an economy greater that one would expect with its population. We are blessed with an abundance of natural resources and well-educated people, producing some of the best products in the world using the latest technologies. The synopsis of each province and territory shows the contribution each make, and their importance, to Canada.

Canada

Canada's geographical land area of 9,984,670 sq Km supports a population of 31,629,700. Canada's population continues to grow with the yearly addition of almost quarter of a million immigrants, from every country of the world. The major cities and populations centres are St. John's, Halifax, Charlottown, St. John, Quebec City, Montreal, Ottawa (Capital), Toronto, Windsor, Winnipeg, Regina, Calgary, Edmonton, Kelowna, Vancouver, Victoria; all connected by a national transportation system of air, water and land links. The Dominion of Canada was proclaimed a country after the confederation of regions in 1867. The word "Canada" is thought to originate from "kanata," a Huron-Iroquois word for "village" or "settlement." Jacques Cartier first used "Canada" to refer to the village of Stadacona and the entire area under Chief Donnacona. Maps in 1547 designated everything north of the St. Lawrence River as "Canada." In 1791, "Canada" was first used with the division of the Province of Quebec into the colonies of Upper and

Lower Canada. In 1841, Upper and Lower Canada re-united under the name "Province of Canada." At Confederation in 1867, "Canada" became the name of the new country. Spanning almost one-half of the North American continent, Canada has six time zones, Newfoundland, Atlantic, Eastern, Central, Mountain and Pacific.

The National Flag

The search for a truly Canadian flag began in 1925 with the formation of a committee of the Privy Council for the purpose. The committee did not complete its work. In 1946, a parliamentary committee with a similar mandate received over 2600 submissions, yet Parliament never voted on any of these submissions. With the 1967 Centennial of Confederation approaching, the government of Prime Minister Lester Pearson advised the House it wished to adopt a distinctive national flag. Once more, in 1964, committees of the Senate and House of Commons began calling for submissions for a new flag design. The official ceremony inaugurating the new Canadian flag was held on Parliament Hill in Ottawa on February 15, 1965, after the long arduous journey beginning in 1925. The following words, spoken on that momentous day by the Honourable Maurice Bourget, Speaker of the Senate, added further symbolic meaning to our flag, "The flag is the symbol of the nation's unity, for it, beyond any doubt, represents all the citizens of Canada without distinction of race, language, belief or opinion. "

The Maple tree is officially the national arboreal (tree) emblem of Canada. Forming part of our national flag, long after it first served as a Canadian symbol as early as 1700, the Maple Leaf is forever etched in our consciousness as the most-prominent Canadian symbol. Since the early 1700's, many organizations, from the military to newspapers, used the maple leaf as their emblem.

The Beaver - attained official status as an emblem of Canada when an "act to provide for the recognition of the beaver as a symbol of the sovereignty of Canada," received royal assent on March 24, 1975.

The Parliament Buildings - Few symbols are as evocative of Canada  as the Parliament Buildings, with the Centre Block and distinctive Peace Tower flanked by the East and West blocks. In 1841, Lower and Upper Canada joined to form the Province of Canada. In 1857, Queen Victoria chose Ottawa as its permanent capital because it lay a more secure distance from the American border. With Confederation in 1867, the buildings were immediately chosen as the seat of government for the new Dominion of Canada. The Centre, East, and West blocks of the Parliament Buildings were built between 1859 and 1866. The Peace Tower was built to commemorate the end of the First World War.

Canadian Governance

The British North America Act of 1867 (The BNA Act), created the Canadian federation, with Ontario, Quebec, New Brunswick and Nova Scotia as the four founding provinces. Two orders of government were established: the federal government, with its seat in Ottawa, Ontario, and the provincial governments, with their legislative institutions modeled on those of Britain. In 1867, Canada's sparse population and very large area made for weak links between regions. Strengthening links between these regions were a primary consideration for Canada's founding fathers. They gave the Canadian federal government powers over immigration, indirect taxation, criminal justice, penitentiaries, defense, and trade and commerce as a means of strengthening the links between the regions.

The provinces were given powers over education, health and social services, the administration of justice, prisons, and direct taxation. Some powers were shared between governments, necessitating the two levels of governments consulting each other about matters of mutual concern. One of the best practices of the Canadian federal government is the principle of "equalization payment." Enshrined in the Canadian Charter of Rights and Freedoms, the Parliament and the government of Canada is committed "to the principle of making equalization payments to ensure that provincial governments have sufficient revenues to provide reasonably comparable levels of public services at reasonably comparable levels of taxation." This commitment solidified a distribution arrangement, which had been formally introduced through federal legislation in 1957.

Canada is a geographical region made up of fourteen (14) countries, in a federal system of government. The ten provinces have near-autonomous government while the three Territories, under the control of the federal government, enjoy a reasonable measure of autonomy. When confederation was proclaimed 1867, regional leaders at the time wanted to nurture the federation of regions into one nation. By the 1999 proclamation of the territory of Nunavut, Canada evolved in to a federation of ten provinces and three territories. The provinces, having control of taxation, health care, education, transportation (except railway), municipalities, and all the other powers granted in the Constitution are countries on their own. Were it not for the exclusive powers granted to the national legislature over immigration, international relations, and the military, provinces would enjoy full national status as any member country of the United Nations. The federal government encourages the provinces to behave as nation states. L'Franchophonie is an international organization of French-speaking nations. The nation state that is Canada is a member, so is the Canadian provinces of Quebec and New Brunswick. Are these provinces not then representing themselves as nation states? There are many instances of provincial governments maintaining trade missions and political representative in nation states of the world. At these trade missions and political offices, is it a province being promoted at Canada's expense? All diplomatic and trade representations abroad must promote Canada first and then the regions of Canada. The national government must not allow any province to promote itself as a nation state, but as a region of Canada

At 9.9 million square kilometers, Canada is the second largest country on Earth. There is no doubt that Ontario and Quebec, dubbed Central Canada, controls the levers of confederation with, arguably, Ontario controlling the economic levers and Quebec controlling the political levers. Alberta and British Columbia have jointly gained a hand on these two levers while attempting to develop a third, "Western Canadian" lever. The remaining provinces and territories are "just along for the ride" on the confederation rollercoaster. They do not have the political or economic power to create a fourth lever of less fortunate provinces and territories. In time, they will gain the economic, political, and cultural influence to create that fourth lever. A fifth, Cultural lever is in the making. The hands of English, French and multiculturalism, will control the cultural lever. The single most important lever controlling Canada is political; comprised of the levers of economics, language, and culture.

In the following pages, Table II shows land area; Table III lists population; Table IV is electoral districts of Canada, the provinces and territories and the percentage relationship to Canada.

Table II - Land Area

	Area (km²)	% total area
Canada	9,984,670	100.0
Nunavut	2,093,190	21.0
Quebec	1,542,056	15.4
Northwest Territories	1,346,106	13.5
Ontario	1,076,395	10.8
British Columbia	944,735	9.5
Alberta	661,848	6.6
Saskatchewan	651,036	6.5
Manitoba	647,797	6.5
Yukon	482,443	4.8
Newfoundland and Labrador	405,212	4.1
New Brunswick	72,908	0.7
Nova Scotia	55,284	0.6
Prince Edward Island	5,660	0.1
Source: Natural Resources Canada		

Table III – Population

As of July 1, 2003	Total	% Total
Canada	31,629,700	100.00
Ontario	12,238,300	38.69
Quebec	7,487,200	23.67
British Columbia	4,146,600	13.11
Alberta	3,153,700	9.97
Manitoba	1,162,805	3.68
Saskatchewan	994,800	3.15
Nova Scotia	936,000	2.96
New Brunswick	750,600	2.37
Newfoundland and Labrador	519,600	1.64
Prince Edward Island	137,800	0.44
Northwest Territories	41,900	0.13
Yukon	31,100	0.10
Nunavut	29,400	0.09
Source: Statistic Canada		

Table IV – Electoral Districts

As of April 1, 2004	Number	% total area
Canada	308	100.0
Ontario	106	34.4
Quebec	75	24.4
British Columbia	36	11.7
Alberta	28	9.1
Saskatchewan	14	4.5
Manitoba	14	4.5
Nova Scotia	10	3.6
New Brunswick	10	3.2
Newfoundland and Labrador	7	2.3
Prince Edward Island	4	1.2
Nunavut	1	0.3
Northwest Territories	1	0.3
Yukon	1	0.3
Source: Elections Canada		

Provinces and Territories

Alberta

Proclaimed a Province 1905, Alberta is named after Princess Louise Caroline Alberta, fourth daughter of Queen Victoria. Alberta is the province lying in the transition zone between the prairies and the Rocky Mountains. Alberta, resting in the Mountain Time Zone, occupies 661,848 sq Km or about 6.6% of Canada's total land area sustaining life for a population of 3,153,700, about 9.97% of the population of Canada. Alberta's two largest cities are Edmonton, Calgary, with many other smaller towns and villages; all connected by more that 168,014 km of roads, rail and air; links. In 2001, net immigration to Alberta was a positive 16,290 persons. When named, Alberta was one of four provisional districts of the North-West Territories, and included only part of the present province with the same name. Alberta offers spectacular beauty to residents and visitors alike. Stretching 1223 km from North to South and 660km East to West, Alberta includes Banff National Park, Canada's first and oldest, and Jasper National Park, Canada's largest mountain park. Wood Buffalo

National Park is the World's second largest and Canada's largest national park. Dinosaur Provincial Park contains one of the world's richest dinosaur finds. Drumheller is home to "Reptile World," Canada's largest public display of live reptiles and the World's largest Tyrannosaurus Rex.

Alberta is home to the World's largest indoor shopping and entertainment complex, West Edmonton Mall and the largest ski area in Canada - Lake Louise. Every summer, the Calgary Stampede attracts Canadians and tourists from around to experience the world of the Wild West. The world's largest oil sands development, the Suncor/Syncrude Oil Sand Plant, is in Fort McMurray. In 1947 a major oil discovery at Leduc, near Edmonton changed Alberta's destiny forever. Worldwide, Alberta is the ninth largest oil producer, second largest natural gas exporter, and third largest natural gas producer. Alberta exports 65% of its oil and 51% of its natural gas to the USA; sells 13% of its oil and 33% of its natural gas within Canada; produces 55% of Canada's conventional crude oil, 80% of its natural gas, 49% of its coal, and all of its oil sands. Alberta is heavily dependent on energy resources, and with oil sands reserves estimated at 1.6 trillion barrels of bitumen; the energy sector would be playing a very important role in Alberta's future for many years to come.

British Columbia

Queen Victoria proclaimed the province of British Columbia in 1871, with the "Columbia" referring to the Columbia River named by American Captain Robert Gray for his ship Columbia. British Columbia entered confederation on the condition that the province will always have a permanent connection to central Canada by railroad. The mainland is about 1250 km from north to south, and about 1050 km from east to west. Covering 9.5% of Canada, including Vancouver Island, the 944,735 sq Km, of British Columbia supports a population exceeding four million, representing 13.11% of Canada's population. More than 50,000 km of roads, 6800 km railroad and major air routes link British Columbia's major cities, Victoria, on Vancouver Island (Capital); Vancouver, Kelowna, Nanaimo, Prince George, with the smaller towns and villages. British Columbia's main land transportation route across the Rocky Mountains is through the Crowsnest, Kicking Horse, and Yellowhead Passes. The Alaska Highway is the route to the north. Immigration to British Columbia is mostly from the Far East, with some from other provinces. British Columbians operate on the Pacific Time zone, some four and one half hours behind Newfoundlanders. Forestry, mining, fishing, and agriculture are the mainstays of the British Columbia economy. Other important industries such as eco-tourism, agric-tourism, film, and high technology provide additional revenues. The Okanagan Valley is famous for its fertile lands and production of fruits and vegetables. British Columbia produces apples, cherries, plums, and raspberries, large amounts of hydro electricity, and natural gas. Film and television productions make British Columbia the third-largest production centre in North America. The natural beauty of British Columbia accounts for the more than 22 million yearly visitors to the west coast province. The spectacular beauty of the Rocky Mountains is majestic. Whistler-Blackcomb area, north of Vancouver, is an excellent ski resort and a year-round recreational center. Vancouver-Whistler will be hosting the 2010 Winter Olympics. Clayoquot Sound, on the west coast of Vancouver Island, is one of the largest and richest rainforest known on the planet. Clayoquot Sound is home to ancient Sitka Spruce, Douglas Fir, Western Red Cedar, and Western Hemlock; trees that are up to 1700 years old and are about 100 meters (300 feet) tall. Clayoquot Sound is a United Nations Educational, Scientific, and Cultural Organisation (UNESCO) declared Biosphere Reserve.

Manitoba

The name for the province of Manitoba, which became a part of the federation in 1870, probably comes from either the Ojibwa word "manito-bah" or the Cree "manito-wapow," meaning "strait of the spirit" in reference to The Narrows of Lake Manitoba. 3.68% of Canadians live in Manitoba's 647,797 sq Km. In that 6.5% of Canada's land area, we will find Manitoba's largest cities of Winnipeg (Capital), Brandon, Flin Flon, Saint Boniface. The transportation infrastructure consists of about 2870 kilometers of railroad, more than 18,000 kilometers of highways; an international airport in Winnipeg, with air links to other cities and towns. Immigration to Manitoba is almost negligible. Manitoba is in the Central Time Zone.

Canada's centre-most province, and most eastern of the Prairie Provinces, Manitoba measures 1225 km from north to south and along the southern border with the USA, the east to west distance is 447 km, although at its widest point Manitoba measures 793 km. Manitoba's economic engine is driven by manufacturing, agriculture, mining, and hydro-electricity. Manitoba enjoys a rich population mix of people from every continent in the world, providing a cultural diversity common in Canada. Scottish, English, and French Canadian settlers joined the Aboriginal people after confederation. Russians, Mennonites, Icelanders, Ukrainians, and Germans settlers migrated to Manitoba in subsequent years. After World War II, additional immigrations came from Europe, the Caribbean, South America, Africa, and Asia.

Manitoba gave birth to Louis Riel, a Métis, perhaps the most controversial figure in Canadian history who led his people in their resistance against the Canadian government in the Canadian Northwest. A promising student, born in the Red River Settlement (in what is now Manitoba) in 1844, he did not graduate from his priesthood training or his attempt at lawyer training. By 1868 Riel was back in the Red River area. Ambitious, well educated and bilingual, he quickly emerged as a leader among the Métis of the Red River. In 1869-1870, he headed a provisional government, which would eventually negotiate the Manitoba Act with the Canadian government. The Act established Manitoba as a province and provided some protection for French language rights. Riel was the undisputed spiritual and political head of the short-lived 1885 Rebellion. On May 15, 1885, Louis Riel surrendered to Canadian forces, taken to Regina where he stood trial for treason. On 1 August 1885, a jury of six English-speaking Protestants found Riel guilty but recommended mercy. Judge Hugh Richardson sentenced him to death. He was hanged in Regina on 16 November 1885. His execution was widely opposed in Quebec and had lasting political ramifications.

Winnipeg's most famous character is Winnie the Pooh. During the First World War, troops from Winnipeg were being transported to Europe, via eastern Canada. In White River, Ontario, a Lt. Harry Colebourn bought a small female black bear cub from a hunter who had killed its mother. He named her 'Winnipeg', after his hometown of Winnipeg, or 'Winnie' for short. Winnie became the mascot of the Brigade and went to Britain with the unit. Promoted in rank to Captain, Harry Colebourn loaned Winnie to the London zoo in December 1919, after his unit was posted to the battlefields of France. The bear lived until 1934 and was a major attraction for the zoo. Author A. A. Milne started to write a series of books about Winnie the Pooh, publishing a titled book in 1926. Milne published several other Pooh books and today, millions of Winnie the Pooh books have been sold around the world.

Canada's youngest Governor General the Right Hon. Edward Schreyer, is from Manitoba, where he was a dominant political figure for many decades, rising to become Premier.

New Brunswick

Named after the British Royal House of Brunswick, New Brunswick is one of Canada's Atlantic Provinces, occupying 73,908 sq Km, about 0.7% of Canada's land area. New Brunswick is one of the founding provinces of the Canadian Federation in 1867.

The population of 750,600, about 2.37% of Canada's population, lives in the major cities of Fredericton, (Capital) Saint John, Moncton, and Edmundston. From north to south New Brunswick measures a maximum of 370 km and from east to west a maximum of 400 km. New Brunswick is served by a transportation system of about 1000 km of railroad tracks, 21,000 km of highways and roads; an international airport in St. John and ferry services to Nova Scotia and fixed link bridge to Prince Edward Island.

New Brunswick is Canada's only officially bilingual province and the largest of three Maritime Provinces where about 33 per cent of its population is French speaking. For many years, there was a net migration of New Brunswickers to other provinces of Canada, mostly seeking a better life. New Brunswickers wake up to life in Canada on the Atlantic Time Zone, just ahead of Newfoundlanders.

Tourism, commercial fishing, and forestry are the major economic generators of the province. Tourists to New Brunswick enjoy meals of fresh seafood, experience the rich culture and heritage of the province, view the highest tides in the world, and swim in some of the warmest salt-water beaches north of the U.S. state of Virginia. Productive forest covers about 85 per cent of its land base. Commercial fishing is a major industry, with agriculture, minerals, and commodities contributing to the provinces wealth. New Brunswick is famous for potatoes – its seed potatoes are exported to over 30 countries around the world. The magnificent St. John River splits the province from north to south ending in the Bay of Fundy. In St. John, one may witness the reversing falls and the enormous tides of the Bay of Fundy, truly one of the world's great natural wonders. One hundred billion tonnes of water flows from the Atlantic Ocean into, and then out of, the Bay of Fundy, twice a day, creating rip-currents, up-swellings, swirling whirlpools and 16m tidal waves. It is a magnificent site to behold.

Newfoundland and Labrador

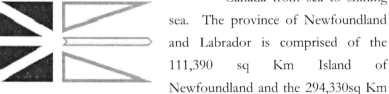

The Island of Newfoundland is located in the Gulf of St. Lawrence and the larger Labrador portion are on the eastern part of the Canadian mainland.

Canada's most easterly, and its newest province, Newfoundland and Labrador joined Confederation in 1949, after an affirmative vote in the last of two referendums, completing Canada from sea to shining sea. The province of Newfoundland and Labrador is comprised of the 111,390 sq Km Island of Newfoundland and the 294,330sq Km mainland Labrador region bordering on Quebec. The total area of Newfoundland and Labrador is 405,212 sq Km, representing 4.1% of Canada. Newfoundlanders make up 1.64% of Canada's population, at 519,600 persons, affectionately referred to as "Newfies." John Cabot first used the term "new found isle" in 1497. The name Labrador is from the Portuguese word "lavrador" or small landholder, and is probably attributable to João Fernades, a Portuguese explorer. St. John's (Capital), and Gander are Newfoundland's major cities. The mostly rural Newfoundland communities are connected to each other, Canada, and the world by about 8937Km of highways; 21 ferry routes and local and major air links. Every morning, Newfoundlanders are the first to wake up in Canada as they are located in Newfoundland Time Zone, the most easterly of Canada's time zones.

Crude and refined oil, fish products, newsprint, iron ore, and electricity account for most exported goods. Offshore oil is the highest valued commodity produced and is the leading contributor to export growth in recent years. On Valentine' Day in 1982, a terrible storm raged over the Grand Banks, off the coast of Newfoundland. The Ocean Ranger, the world's mightiest and "indestructible" oil drilling rig, pounded by waves of more than 20 meters high, capsized, perishing all 84 men on board; 56 of were Newfoundlanders. The sinking of the Ocean Range became Canada's worst maritime disaster since the Second World War.

For over 100 years, a ferry service between Port aux Basques, Newfoundland and Labrador and North Sydney, Nova Scotia provided a vital link to mainland Canada. Due to economic conditions, Newfoundland and Labrador suffers higher unemployment than is generally acceptable nationally. As unemployment rose, migration from the province increased, and for a long time, there were a large migration of Newfoundlanders to other provinces of Canada, mostly seeking a better life.

The 5428 Megawatts (MW) Churchill Falls is a joint project between Newfoundland and Labrador Hydro and Hydro Québec. Hydro Québec purchases almost all power from the Churchill Falls plant under a long-term fixed-price contract set in the late 1960's and expiring in 2041. The Newfoundland and Labrador government wishes to re-negotiate the rate paid by Hydro Quebec to reflect current market rates. Hydro Quebec essentially buys electricity from Churchill Falls at mid-1960's prices and resells it at current rates, reaping enormous profit, despite having about one-third ownership of Churchill Falls.

Nova Scotia

Nova Scotia is one of the founding provinces of confederation, agreeing to be part of the Dominion of Canada in 1867. Nova Scotia represents 0.6% of Canada's land area, covering an area of 55,284 sq. Km, supporting a population of 936,000, about 2.96% of Canada's total population. The major cities of Halifax, Dartmouth, and Lunenburg are connected to Nova Scotia's other cities, towns and villages by more than 2,600 Km of roads, 700 Km of rail, local and international air, and water transportation. Nova Scotia attracts a very small amount of immigrants, both from within Canada and other countries of the world. The first British settlers gave Nova Scotia its name, which is the Latin translation for "New Scotland."

Nova Scotia, located in the Atlantic Time Zone, consists of the mainland and Cape Breton Island, is almost surrounded by the famous Bay of Fundy, Atlantic Ocean and the Northumberland Strait. Long before Europeans arrived, the Mi'kmaq people (pronounced "Mig-maw") lived here for thousands of years; many still do. Nearly 100 years after the

British arrived, French settlers arrived on the western part of Nova Scotia and "renamed" it Acadia. Nova Scotia is home to largest fort ever built in North America, Fortress Louisbourg, now one of Canada's national historic sites. Nova Scotia is home to Canadian Navy, the Halifax Shipyards, and the Halifax Citadel, a British built fort on top of Halifax's highest hill. Halifax is home to the oldest paper in Canada, the Halifax Gazette, first published in 1752. Many black American slaves, freed before the U. S. Revolutionary war, started a new life in Nova Scotia, setting the stage for Nova Scotia becoming a part of the Underground Railroad, helping many American slaves escape to freedom in Canada, where slavery was against the law.

Nova Scotians have been fishing for more than 400 years, bringing in large catches of lobsters, scallops and other fish including haddock, halibut, flounder, and herring. Nova Scotia is the world's largest exporter of lobster. Trees mostly cover Nova Scotia, making forestry a big part of the economy, as does natural gas and high-grade gypsum. The Annapolis Valley is picturesque with its rolling hills and fertile valleys. The 298 km Cabot Trail loops around the northern tip of the Cape Breton Highlands. This breathtaking trail offers spectacular views of ocean, exciting drives up on down the steep roads and a view of ferries to and from Island of Newfoundland. Camping in Cape Breton Highlands National Park and swimming in its crystal-clear waters is a memorable experience of my vacation in the Atlantic Provinces. Nova Scotia blessed Canada, and the world, with musicians like Anne Murray, Rita MacNeil, Hank Snow, the Rankin Family, Natalie MacMaster, Sarah McLachlan, and Holly Cole; artists like Alex Colville and Maude Lewis; writers Robert MacNeil and Alastair McLeod and actor Donald Sutherland. Sir Robert Borden (1911-1920), Sir John Thompson (1892-1894), and Sir Charles Tupper (1896) are three Prime Ministers of Canada produced by Nova Scotia.

Halifax cemeteries bear the remains of hundreds of victims of the World's largest peacetime maritime disaster, the sinking of the luxury ocean liner, the Titanic, on its maiden voyage, in April 1912. The Maritime Museum of the Atlantic has the world's finest collection of Titanic memorabilia. The Halifax Explosion of December 6, 1917 distinguished Halifax as the only North American city that suffered huge damage in the First World War. On that fateful day, two ships, the Imo and the explosive-laden Mont Blanc, collided in Halifax Harbour. The resulting explosion of the Mont Blanc generated, at the time, the largest "man-made" explosion in history, destroying the entire north end of the city of Halifax. The massive explosion engulfed most of Halifax injuring and killing more than 8000 and leveling hundreds of buildings.

During World War II, the port of Halifax was the point of departure for trans-Atlantic supply ships for Britain's war effort. Convoys carrying food, fuel, ammunition, supplies and the men of the Canadian Navy, braved Nazi submarines as they traveled across the Atlantic Ocean to England.

Ontario

The formerly Upper Canada is one of the four founding provinces of the new Dominion of Canada in 1867. Ontario is the second largest province covering 10.8% of Canada. Within its land-area of 1,076,395 sq Km resides a population exceeding twelve million, about 36.89% of Canada's population. More than 80% of Ontarians live in urban centres along the Great Lakes. The major urban centres are Toronto (Capital), Hamilton, Kingston, Kitchener Mississauga, Niagara Falls, Ottawa, Sudbury, Thunder Bay, and Windsor. Ontario's most popular vacation spots include Niagara Falls, Thousand Islands, and Georgian Bay

As the most populous province, Ontario's transportation system is an intricate network of air, water, and land systems. The land system comprises 16,000 Km of highways, including Canada's busiest, the 800Km long Highway 401 and the 1800 Km long Highway 11 (Yonge Street). The Great Lakes-St Lawrence Seaway system brings ocean-going ships into the heart of Canada. The national VIA Rail and Ontario's GO Train commuter service provides rail transportation to many Ontarians. There are extensive passenger and commercial rail network connecting with the other provinces of Canada. The air transportation system operates at hundreds of smaller airports and airstrips, with major airports in Ottawa, Windsor, North Bay, Sudbury, and Thunder Bay, with Canada's largest and busiest airport, Lester B. Pearson International in Toronto. The busiest international crossings between Canada and the USA are located in Ontario at Windsor and Fort Erie, where tens of thousands of truck transport trailers cross both ways. The Greater Toronto area, with about four million residents, suffers the worst transportation gridlock in all of Canada, is getting worse everyday, without any short- or long-term solutions in sight.

Ontario continues to attract the largest percent of immigrants to Canada, particularly to the Greater Toronto Area. The large multicultural community makes it easier for new immigrants to settle in Canada, as help and comfort is readily available from large and effective cultural groups. Ontario operates on the Eastern Time Zone, one and one half hours behind Newfoundland and three hours ahead of British Columbians. The name "Ontario" is derived from an Iroquois word meaning "beautiful lake or beautiful water" and was first used for Lake Ontario, one of the five Great Lakes.

Ontario is the second largest province, with the longest east-west distance being 1,690km and the longest north-south distance being 1,730km. Even people living in Ontario are amazed at its massive size, bounded on the south by the Great Lakes-St. Lawrence Seaway system. This shipping transportation route stretches from Thunder Bay on the western end of Lake Superior through Lake Huron; down the St. Clair River into Lake Erie; through the Welland Canal, bypassing the Niagara River and Niagara Falls, into Lake Ontario; and continuing along the St. Lawrence River to the Atlantic Ocean. This major waterway brings many products of the Prairie Provinces to Ontario, Quebec and World markets. Within a one hundred kilometer radius of Toronto's CN Tower reside more than ten percent of Canada's population, representing more than one hundred cultures of the world.

Ontario played a very important part in the freedom sought by many American Negro (black) slaves, fleeing from the American south. The Underground Railroad was not a railroad built and operated underground, like a subway system. The Underground Railroad was a loose network of escape routes, beginning in the Southern United States and winding its way into Canada. Slaves escaping from America, when caught would be beaten, tortured and may face death as a lesson to those contemplating freedom. Historians believed the action of Ontario's Lieutenant Governor Colonel John Graves Simcoe, who in 1793 introduced a bill to prevent the introduction of further slavery into Upper Canada, contributed to slaves coming to Ontario as free people. During the American civil war, more and more British Loyalists and their slaves escaped to Canada and particularly Ontario. Many Loyalists and former slaves returned to America after the civil war were over, leaving their marks in many parts of Ontario. Harriet Beecher Stowe, more than one hundred and fifty years ago wrote the book, Uncle Tom's Cabin, about the Reverend Josiah Henson's contribution to the Underground Railroad. Ontario's St. Clair Parks Commission operates Uncle Tom's Cabin Historic Site, commemorating Reverend Josiah Henson's life experiences of helping fleeing slaves.

One in three Canadians resides in the province of Ontario, the economic engine that powers the Canadian economy. Natural resources, agriculture, industrialization, finance, tourism, services, and culture drive today's Ontario economy, contributing 41% to Canada's Gross Domestic Product (GDP) and almost 60 per cent of all manufactured exports from Canada. Ontario have the highest distribution of businesses in Canada, controlling 41 per cent of all Canadian assets, and exporting 93% of its produce to the USA. Toronto is the economic centre of Canada having the headquarters for many national banks, insurance companies. While other stock exchanges operate in Montreal and Vancouver, the premier stock exchange in Canada, the Toronto Stock Exchange, is located in that city.

The many cultures from around the world thrive, and are celebrated, in Ontario with festivals such as Manitoulin Island's Wikwimekong (Native), Caribana (West Indian) and Taste of the Danforth (Greek) in Toronto, and Kitchener's Oktoberfest (German). Many other festivals celebrate the many cultures and agricultural heritage of Ontario. The world's largest freshwater island, Manitoulin Island, in Georgian Bay is a part of Ontario. Niagara's Horseshoe Falls, the CN Tower, and Ottawa's Capital region all attract tourist from around the world. Niagara Falls is world-famous as the "Honeymoon Capital" of the World, attracting 18 million visitors a year. In 1954, Canada's first subway system opened in Toronto. The Thousand Islands, in the Kingston area, is breathtaking as is the Ten Thousand Islands in Georgian Bay. Canada's first Prime Minister, Sir John A. McDonald was first elected in the Kingston area and went on to represent other parts of Ontario. Since confederation, Ontario has played a leadership role in Canada on economic and constitutional matters.

Despite Ontario's refusal to become officially bilingual, Ontario is the voice of moderation in the federation, soothing the ruffled feathers of Atlantic economic depravation, Quebec nationalist and Western alienation.

Prince Edward Island

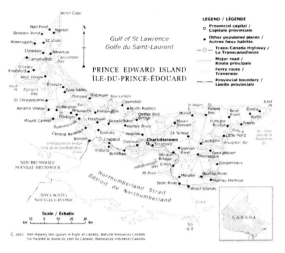

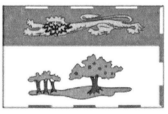

Prince Edward Island, Canada's smallest province, hosted the initial conference where the concept of a federation was discussed prior to July 1, 1867. Although a party to the discussions, Prince Edward Island (PEI) did not join confederation until 1873, six years after the creation of the Dominion of Canada. Prince Edward Island is a mere 5,660 sq. Km, 0.1% of Canada's total land area. Representing 0.44% of Canada's population, the 137,800 persons calling PEI home are concentrated in its two major cities, Charlottetown (Capital), Summerside, and the many smaller towns. Moving around P.E.I is by 5,440 km of roadway, ferry service to Nova Scotia, the 12.9Km Confederation Bridge and local air transportation links. Over the years, many Islanders immigrated to other parts of Canada seeking better life. Prince Edward Island is in the Atlantic Time Zone. The present name, Prince Edward Island, was adopted in 1799, in honour of Prince Edward, Duke of Kent, father of Queen Victoria, the British Monarch whose reign under which the Dominion of Canada was created. Prior to 1799, the island was called Epekwitk, meaning, "resting on the waves," by the Mi'kmaq First Peoples nation. Europeans later changed the pronunciation of the name to Abegweit. The British called it

St. John's Island. Prince Edward Island, fondly known as P.E.I, is Canada's smallest, yet most populous province. Located in the Gulf of St. Lawrence on Canada's east coast, P.E.I is separated from mainland Canada, New Brunswick, and Nova Scotia, by the Northumberland Strait. The 13-kilometre Confederation Bridge connects Prince Edward Island to New Brunswick, replacing the ferry service and maintaining a "transportation link" guarantee P.E.I obtained as a condition of joining the Canadian federation. Charlottetown, the capital P.E.I is of historical significance to Canadians as the "birthplace of confederation." Here, in 1864, the future fathers of the Canadian federation met to discuss the very concept of Canada. Province House National Historic Site is a blend of the past and present. The meticulously restored Confederation Chamber, in the west wing, preserves a part of Canada's history while the business of today's P.E.I is conducted in the Provincial Legislature, located in east wing. The main industries in P.E.I. are agriculture, tourism, fisheries, light manufacturing, with P.E.I. most famous for its potatoes, fish, and lobster. Prince Edward Island's 1.2 million annual visitors enjoy the pastoral scenery, relaxing white sandy beaches, and relaxing pace. One of Canada's most famous authors, Lucy Maud Montgomery, creator of Anne of Green Gables, was born in P.E.I. Tourists flock to Cavendish to visit Anne's historic home, Green Gables House, one of PEI's most popular attractions. Our 1995 visit to P.E.I. took us to PEI's red sand beaches and parks. My heart pounded with pride as I walked the Confederation Chamber, imagining the great debates that must have taken place there.

Quebec

Once called Lower Canada by the British, Quebec is a founding province of the Dominion of Canada. Canada's largest province is 1,542,056 sq. Km in area, about 15.4% of Canada's total land area, supporting a population of nearly eight million people, representing 23.67% of Canada's population.

Quebec's major Cities are Quebec City (capital); Montreal, and Trois Riviere. The numerous towns and villages are connected by rail, road, and air, with Trudeau and Mirabel International airports being the largest airports. Under agreement with the Federal government, Quebec is the only province that selects its own immigrants, mostly French speaking, as it tries to preserve the French language and culture within the Canadian federation of mostly English speaking provinces and a powerful English speaking southern neighbour. Proclaimed a Province in 1867 Quebec is part of "Central Canada" that is located in the Eastern Time Zone. The word "Quebec" comes from the Algonquin word meaning "narrow passage or strait."

North American by virtue of its geographic location, Québec is French in origin with the French civil code the backbone of its justice system, even as it operates with the British parliamentary governance system. Increasingly cosmopolitan from recent waves of immigration, Québec is a pluralist, modern, and dynamic society. Québec is a province with a distinct French-Canadian or Quebecois culture and strong sense of history. Quebec City, home of the famous Winter Carnival, has historic old world charm with its walled city and cobbled stone streets. The historic battles between the French and the British were fought on The Plains of Abraham. The picturesque Laurentian Mountains are renowned as an excellent winter destination. The roots for separatist sentiments were planted on the Plains of Abraham in 1759 when the English armies under General Wolfe defeated the French troops under General Montcalm, during the war between the colonial powers. The Quebec economy is sustained by manufacturing, agriculture, electricity production, mining, meat processing, and petroleum refining sectors. Quebec exports electricity to Canadian provinces and even larger amounts to bordering American states, trade goods such as forestry and agricultural products, iron and steel.

Quebec's Quiet Revolution

The Quiet revolution was a period of intense social change, of modernization of Quebec and of a profound redefinition of the role of Quebec and French Canadians within Confederation. In the early 1960's, Quebecers believed French Canadians should not play a second-class role in socio-politico-economic matters within Quebec. The government of Jean Lesage became the symbol and tool of a whole people on the road to self-assertion as it created provincial hospitalization scheme, departments of education, Cultural Affairs, and Federal-Provincial relations. The government created many agencies and corporations to assert Quebec's desire to control its destiny. The major creations are Hydro-Quebec, formed by nationalizing private hydroelectric facilities; Quebec Pension Plan; the Caisse de Dépot et de Placement, a Credit Union, and electoral and social reforms. Financing these bold measures at asserting its role in Canada, Quebec created a large provincial bureaucracy, substantially increased all forms of taxation, resorted to heavy borrowing, and continuously raided the federal treasury by demanding an ever-increasing share of the taxes collected in the province. Relations between the governments of Canada and Quebec were strained during the Quiet Revolution as Quebec demanded more autonomy, refused federal initiatives in provincial matters and implemented its own programs and reforms, necessitating the transfer of fiscal powers from the federal to the provincial government, and demanding French Canadians be recognized as equals in Confederation. Even as they welcomed the Quebec reforms in redefining Quebec's place in Confederation, the other provinces and the federal government resisted Quebec's stance. The Quiet Revolution brought about a new way for Quebecers thinking of themselves; increasingly French and a French nation within Canada. Quebec, through its actions, sought special status within the Canadian Federation by demanding greater control of economic, social, political, and administrative matters, even if those matters were explicitly federal. In 1965, Quebec withdrew from more than thirty joint federal-provincial programs with full fiscal compensation from the Federal government, with Prime Minister Lester B. Pearson suggesting Canada "would develop along the lines of an equal partnership between the two founding people." Quebec's increasing demand for more money and special status resulted in the rest of Canada becoming angry and tiresome, demanding the federal government "put Quebec in its place" and standing firm against the demands for more money and a special status. The Quiet Revolution succeeded in gaining greater powers for Quebecers, greater share of federal money and an entrenchment of the French language in the government of Canada. Despite not signing the Constitution Act of 1982, Quebec enjoys a place of prominence within Canada and subsequent Quebec governments, of all stripes, have used the power of the constitution and federal money to further a separatist or more autonomous agenda, with a distinct society flavour.

The nationalism fever created during the Quiet Revolution and Canada's brand of democracy resulted in the formation of a political party, the Parti Quebecois, dedicated to Quebec's political independence but with and economic association to Canada. In the 1980 referendum, 50.9% of Quebecers rejected the question on negotiating sovereignty-association with Canada. The 1995 referendum asked Quebecers to vote on a shorter question to which was attached a "Bill." The question did not ask for outright separation from Canada, instead proposed negotiating a different political relationship between Quebec and the rest of Canada, and if that new relationship cannot be negotiated, Quebec would unilaterally declare itself an independent country. One percent of Quebecers rejected the question, bringing Canadians very close to entering an unknown political arena. Quebec's demands, actions, and successes during the Quiet Revolution embolden other provinces to make similar demands on the federal government. The weakness of the federal government in its acquiescence to increasing provincial demands created the dysfunctional state of Canadian Federalism.

Saskatchewan

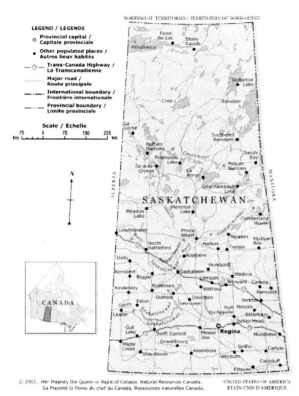

"Saskatchewan" is a derivative of "Kisiskatchewani Sipi," a native Cree nation word meaning swiftly flowing river. Saskatchewan became part of Canada in 1905, enlarging Canada with the addition of 651,036 sq. km or 6.5% of Canada's total area. The 994,900 residents of Saskatchewan contribute 3.15% of Canada's total population. A transportation system of about 3700 km railroad track; 2,500 km highways, urban and rural roads and major airports in Regina and Saskatoon connect the people of Saskatchewan to each other, Canada and the rest of the world. Saskatchewan's major cities are Regina (Capital), Saskatoon, Prince Albert and Moose Jaw. From both airports, airlines operate services to the northern communities. Saskatchewan, located in the Central Time Zone, is the only province that does not change to Daylight Saving Time in the summer, remaining on Central Standard

Time all year round. Saskatchewan is a long, narrow swath of territory stretching 1225 km north to south and with widths of 632 km along the USA boundary and to 446 km along the northern boundary. Saskatchewan shares Lake Athabaska with Alberta. The economy is powered by agriculture, technology, natural resources, manufacturing, and finance. Saskatchewan, producing 54% of wheat grown in Canada, was once known as 'The World's Bread Basket'. A well-developed mining industry, along with oil, natural gas, uranium, gold, potash, and high agriculture production brought Saskatchewan's economic stability. Saskatchewan is the world's largest producer of uranium and potash, commanding more than one quarter of world's production for each product. Uranium is most famous for its uses in nuclear power plants, while potash is used primarily in fertilizers. Saskatchewan is the second largest oil, and third largest gas, producer in Canada. Saskatchewan accounts for about twenty percent of all cooperative associations in Canada, encompassing every segment of its retailing and distributing trades. With a significant percentage of its population belonging to cooperative associations, is it any wonder Saskatchewan became the birthplace of publicly funded Medicare in North America. Tourists are attracted to the breathtaking sunsets stretching across endless horizons, Northern lights that twinkle and dance in the night air.

The most famous Canadian from Saskatchewan, a giant in Canadian politics, is Tommy Clement Douglas. Born in Falkirk, Scotland, Tommy Douglas served as Premier of Saskatchewan (1944-1961); the first federal leader of the New Democratic Party (1961-1971); served three periods as Member of Parliament (1935-1944 for the CCF), and (1962-1968, 1968-1979 for the NDP). His best-known accomplishment is being the father of Medicare while Premier of Saskatchewan.

Northwest Territories

Once a part of a vast area of the northwestern portion of North America, referred to as the "Northwest Territory," this is Canada's first administrative region, not accorded full provincial status. The Northwest Territories stretches northerly from its border with Saskatchewan Alberta and British Columbia to the North Pole. The Beaufort Sea, rich in hydrocarbon resources, is on the western side of the Northwest Territories. The mainland stretches just beyond the Arctic Circle while the remainder is made of islands such as Banks, Melville Victoria and Prince Patrick. The Northwest Territories represent 13.5% of Canada's land area, covering 1,346,106 sq. km, yet having a population of 41,900, about 0.13% of Canada's population. The major city of the Northwest Territories is Yellowknife, its capital. The Mackenzie River drains most of the Northwest Territories into the Mackenzie Bay/Beaufort Sea area. In the MacKenzie delta are two other centres "southerners" might hear about, Tuktoyuktuk and Inuvik. The single most important land transportation route is the Dempster Highway. Transportation is mainly by water in the warm weather and ice roads in the winter. Proclaimed the Northwest Territories 1870, variations of the name Northwest Territories have been used to describe lands in the west and north of what is now Canada. Originally, the term was applied to all lands north and west of Lake Superior. The Northwest Territories is in the Mountain Time Zone.

From 1870 to 1905, the name "North-West Territory" was used for the region formed from the union of Rupert's Land and the North-Western Territory. Since then, large parts of the area have been removed to form Manitoba, Saskatchewan, Alberta, the Yukon, and Nunavut. The Northwest Territories include several of Canada's greatest rivers, biggest lakes, and most important National Parks. This is the land where the world's best northern lights dance during the dark winter months and where the sun never sets during the summer. Two of Canada's most famous parks are the Nahanni National Park Reserve, and Wood Buffalo National Park. The Nahanni protects a portion of the Mackenzie Mountains Natural Region. In 1922, Canada's largest national park, and one of the largest in the world, Wood Buffalo National Park, was established to protect the free-roaming bison herds of the area. In 1978, Nahanni National Park Reserve became the first site in the world to be granted World Heritage Site status by United Nations Educational, Scientific and Cultural Organization, UNESCO. Mining, government, and tourism are the cornerstones of the Northwest Territories economy. Over half of the population is located throughout 33 communities, with the remainder located in the only city of Yellowknife, the capital. No political parties are represented in the Legislature of the Northwest Territories. The government of the Northwest Territory operates under the consensus system that allows Members of the Legislative Assembly (MLA) to be elected as independents in their local constituencies. The legislators then elect ministers and a premier and together they manage the affairs of the territory for the betterment of their people.

Nunavut

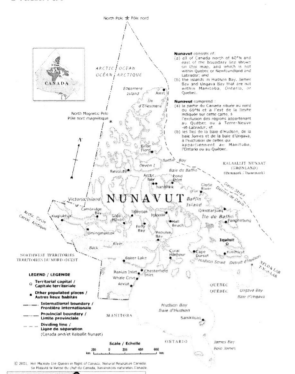

Canada's newest territory came into being in 1999. Its name, Nunavut, means "our land" in the Inuktitut language. A large portion of Nunavut is on the Canadian mainland, while the reminder is on many islands, most notably Ellesmere and Baffin. Victoria Island is shared by Nunavut and the Northwest Territories. Nunavut, with its 2,093,190 sq km is the largest administrative area in Canada. Nunavut represents 21% of Canada's land area. However, its population of 29,400 residents is only 0.09% of Canada's population. This sparsely populated territory is accessible by few unpaved roads, air and water transportation. Nunavut's government is headquartered in Iqaluit, on Baffin Island, with Bathurst as its other major city. Other community settlements of note are Resolute and Alert on the northern tip of Ellesmere Island. The vast geographic area that is Nunavut is in the Mountain Time Zone and consists of 26 communities, physically isolated by great distances. Access to most communities is by water and, the most important, air links, while unpaved roads connect a few communities to each other.

The economy of Nunavut is largely dependent on the harvesting traditions of the Inuit majority. Tourism, mineral exploration, and extraction are growth industries that promise to transform the Nunavut economy. The territory's Inuit people are famous for their soap stone carvings, and prints. In the mid 1990's a soap stone carving played an important role as defensive weapon when Prime Minister Jean Chrétien, it is said, confronted an intruder who had entered the prime minister's residence. The people of Nunavut rely on trucked water and sewage as there are very few, and inadequate, facilities to process water. Unlike the provinces, every drop of oil is imported from the rest of Canada, brought in by ships and air, and must be stored in tanks over the winter when the ocean freezes and shipping is impossible. Unlike provincial governments, the Nunavut government is non-partisan. In this consensus style government, the people elect members of the legislature in a democratic parliamentary government. Members of the Legislative Assembly (MLA) then elect ministers and a premier. The MLA's, Ministers and the Premier establish government priorities, based upon issues identified in the election, and together they manage the affairs of their people, mostly free of adversarial politicking of provincial governments and political parties.

Yukon

The Yukon Territory became part of Canada in 1898. The name "Yukon" is derived from a Native name "Yu-kun-ah," for the great Yukon River that drains most of the Yukon Territory. Covering an area of 483,450 or 4.8% of Canada's land area, the Yukon Territory is the smallest of the three Territories. Whitehorse and Dawson City are the major population centres accounting for most of the Yukon's 31,000 people. This small population is a mere 0.1% of Canada's population. The transportation needs of Yukoners are served by more than 4800 Km of roads and by air and rail links. The Yukon Territory is in the Pacific Time Zone.

The mineral industry forms the base of the Yukon's economy. Tourism, government services, retail trade, construction, and fur production also support the territory's economy. Archaeologists theorize that the first people of the Yukon crossed a land bridge from Asia to northern Canada more than 10,000 years ago. Yukon First Nations people hunted caribou, moose, and mountain sheep in spring and fall, and spent summers fishing for salmon, having close ties to traditional lands; a connectedness that is at the heart of current land claims negotiations.

The Yukon has eight different language groups, seven are Athapaskan, and one is Tlingit.

In the 1870s, gold prospectors drifted into the Yukon from gold fields and in 1896, made the big gold strike on Bonanza Creek. After news of Klondike gold reached southern Canada and United States, thousands of hopeful gold seekers headed north. By 1898-99, Dawson City, at the junction of the Klondike and Yukon rivers, was home to 40,000 people, becoming the largest city west of Winnipeg. For many years, the Alaska-Canada boundary remained unsettled. Attempts to settle the issue with the Russians before 1867, then the Americans after Canadian confederation were fruitless. The Klondike gold discoveries made the settlement of the Alaska-Canada boundary dispute an urgent issue. A joint Anglo-American High Commission was established in 1889 to decide if any of the Pacific panhandle fell within Canada. After five years of discussion, the British commissioner sided with the three American delegates and outvoted the two Canadians. In 1903, the panhandle was given to Alaska, and the Yukon was cut off from the Pacific Ocean. The Yukon was denied free access to the Pacific Ocean by our friends, the Americans, and colonial master, the British Monarch, each protecting their respective interests. Coal deposits, silver and lead were mined in the Yukon from the early 1900's. Many Yukon people continue to hunt and trap through the 1920s and 1930s.

Planning a Great Country

Greatness awaits Canada in this the third millennium. We must want and plan to build the Greatest County on Earth. In this section is presented the reasons for remodeling Canada on a system of governance that reduces bureaucracy, allowing governance to be as close to the people as possible. One Canada is created by restructuring the administrative regions into multiple local governments and one national government. The present election process within a political party and during an election campaign will be a revelation for many Canadians.

Planning a Great Country

We must begin by planning to build a greater country and people by developing strategic plans encompassing terms of 5, 25, 50, 100, and 250-year terms. Where do we want our Canada to be, and what should the accomplishments of Canadians be at the end of each period? Why would we even want to plan as far as two hundred and fifty years? We know not all of us alive today will be around in two hundred and fifty years. Canada will be around and our descendants will continue to build on our legacy. Certainly, the Canada of today will be very different from the Canada two hundred and fifty years hence, as it was different two hundred and fifty years ago. Our descendants will want a safe and vibrant country in which to live, and as custodians of Canada, we have an obligation and owe them the courtesy of preserving the natural resources, improving the human resources and developing new products and services to enhance their lives. Politicians begin campaigning for the next general election on the morning after the last general election. Every decision taken by government politicians are predicated on the population's perception and response to a specific government action. Political expediency is at the heart of all government decisions. The importance of public perception and imagery over good governance are the reasons governing political parties hire "spin-doctors," "backroom boys," media and image consultants, and marketing professional. The opposition parties are not immune from hiring "spin-doctors," "backroom boys," media and image consultants, and marketing professional, as they hope to be the governing party. These unelected "spin-doctors," "backroom boys," media and image consultants, and marketing professionals massage government information into palatable radio and television sound bites, glossy marketing brochures and propagandist print media advertising; all using public funds to promote the governing political party. Political parties are using public money since political contributions are tax deductible from the donors' gross income. The corporate executives are worried about the next fiscal quarter and the short-term share prices rather than the long-term sustainability and valuation of the corporation. Rarely do our elected representatives' plan beyond the next general election and rarely do corporations plan beyond the next fiscal quarter.

Fundamental Rights

Sir John A. MacDonald and the Fathers of Confederation knew their lives had a finite period and that one day they will all pass on to another life. Yet, they came together and created a country that would outlast them. Their vision culminated in the Constitution that clearly enumerated the levels of government and their responsibilities. Their vision and leadership are very valid even after more than thirteen decades years. The fathers of confederation were Statesmen.

In creating a family, any organization, or a country, there are fundamental rights that must be protected for good governance and the enjoyment of life. Freedom, personal privacy, and human rights must be protected at all costs. The fundamental rights of freedom and choice must never be surrendered in the name of security. The more rights we give up to protect our freedoms, the less secure we will be. Our civil liberties define and protect us from those who would want to control our every action. As fear grips the world, giving up freedom little by little are sold to us as being in the best interest our personal and national security. The majority must never surrender one iota of civil liberties in the name of catching perpetrators. In surrendering our civil liberties to government, corporations, security and law enforcement agencies, when and where will it end? It will end whenever we have surrendered all our liberties, culminating in a fascist or totalitarian governance regime.

Creating One Canada - Ten Principles

In creating One Canada to become the greatest country on Earth, our leaders must remember that all Canadians:

1. Are equal one to another;

Have a right to

2. their own belief system;
3. live a life free from all forms of discrimination
4. live in a safe and secure environment;
5. be free to pursue their hearts desire;
6. receive an education;
7. a legal infrastructure to protect all;
8. live anywhere in Canada they desire;
9. own property anywhere in Canada;
10. Know that everything cost someone something.

One Canada

Building the greatest country on earth requires the political will of the elected representatives, people, and businesses. We require a new geographical and political structure to build one Canada. With hundreds of federal and provincial parliamentary seats, thousands of seats in municipal councils and school boards and many thousands of appointed positions to quasi-judicial boards and agencies, along with their attendant civil servants, **we are over governed**.

Creating one Canada is drafting a constitution, using the best parts of our present constitution, preserving the Charter of Rights and Freedoms, presenting it to the people in a binding referendum, and then implementing its provisions. The Federal government must take the initiative to lead the country over the objections of the provinces. This may require several challenges to the Supreme Court of Canada and invoking the "notwithstanding" clause in the current constitution. The House of Commons and the Legislatures cannot be solely trusted to create and adopt a new constitution. One only need look back at the results of the Victoria Accord (1970), the Meech Lake Accord (1990) and the Charlottetown Accord (1992) to see why the Legislatures and the House of Commons cannot be solely trusted to create a constitution. The Federal Government Clarity Act sets out the conditions for which a province may pose a clear question of secession to its population. Regardless of the Federal government's position, and any action it might take to determine the clarity of the question and the legitimacy of any vote in favour of said question, Canada is indivisible unless a 67% majority of voting age Canadian population says so, in a national referendum.

Who is Canadian?

"It is hereby recognized and declared that in Canada there have existed and shall continue to exist without discrimination by reason of race, national origin, colour, religion or sex, the following human rights and fundamental freedoms, namely,

(a) The right of the individual to life, liberty, security of the person and enjoyment of property, and the right not to be deprived thereof except by due process of law;

(b) The right of the individual to equality before the law and the protection of the law;

(c) Freedom of religion;

(d) Freedom of speech;

(e) Freedom of assembly and association; and

(f) Freedom of the press.

"I am Canadian, a free Canadian, free to speak without fear, free to worship God in my own way, free to stand for what I think right, free to oppose what I believe wrong, free to choose those who shall govern my country. The heritage of freedom I pledge to uphold for myself and all mankind."

From the Canadian Bill of Rights, July 1, 1960

This powerful definition of a Canadian, and the rights he is expected to enjoy, are long forgotten by our current crop of politicians, many of whom have also forgotten the Bill of Rights, 1960 and the Charter of Rights and Freedoms, 1982. It is not only the politicians that have forgotten the Bill of Rights, 1960 and the Charter of Rights and Freedoms, 1982. Many Canadians do not have a thorough understanding of the two powerful documents, having not been thoroughly educated on their meanings. Who is Canadian is also defined by colour, race, "look," and linguistic accent. An English or French speaking Caucasian (white) immigrant person readily blends into the fabric of Canadian society. Caucasian immigrants from other linguistic groups blend into our society after longer periods, often as long as it takes to loose their accents. Other shades of immigrants have a harder time blending into the Canadian society and even after centuries, never really blend into the "white" Canadian society.

Children of Caucasian immigrants, regardless of their parents' heritage, are readily accepted as "Canadians." Not so for children of "darker skinned" immigrants. Their born-in-Canada children are considered immigrants, even after generations of being in Canada. In my early days of employment in Canada, I was constantly asked, "Where are you from?" Whenever I replied "Mississauga" the follow up question would inevitably be "Where are you really from?" as though I could not be from Mississauga because I was not white. I fell into that trap of asking people where they were from, until I met a black co-worker of whom I asked the question, "Where are you from?" Her reply of "Nova Scotia" elicited the inevitable follow up question. I learned she was born and raised in Nova Scotia, a descendant of American black slaves marooned in Nova Scotia almost two centuries ago, instead of being taken back to Africa. My co-worker had never left Canada, not even for a vacation. I was surprised she was not an immigrant. I made the assumption that being black meant she was not from Canada; the same assumptions made by many white Canadians. As a dark-skinned immigrant, I was embarrassed after learning she was as true a Canadian as one can get. From that day onwards, I no longer ask anyone where they are from and whenever I am asked that question, I politely reply "Mississauga," if inside Canada and "Canada" if outside Canada. I am proud of my

Jamaican heritage and even more proud of being Canadian.

If you live here, you are Canadian and must put Canada first.

There are those in our society who constantly remind us that if you are white, you are Canadian and if you have darker skin then you are not Canadian and certain illegal activities and crimes are your domain. Herein lay the beginnings of Racial Profiling, the despicable act of conditioning ones expectation of the behaviour of a group of people based on their skin colour, race, or place of origin. In every society on earth, we coalesced into groups, whether voluntary or through government programs. We form linguistic, national, religious, colour and race groups in order to give ourselves comfortable surroundings. In so doing, we convince ourselves it helps us to adjust to the greater society. Unfortunately, over time, we get very comfortable within our cocoon of familiarity, never learning the intricacies of the greater society. By segregating ourselves to be among our "own kind," we loose the opportunity to participate in and influence the greater society. We also loose the opportunity to learn our new surroundings and we fail to teach the larger society our culture.

Listening to the ultra-rightwing movement, one could easily believe that the loss of Canadian identity is the result of immigration and the adoption of "foreign cultures" into the "white, Anglo-Saxon," and "French" cultures. Nothing could be further from the truth. We are loosing the Canadian identity because of regional, linguistic, and political animosity towards one another and against regions. As we bicker over these differences, self-serving politician and business leaders become disinterested in Canadian heritage and culture and heartily embrace everything foreign, mostly American and East Asian. Put a foreign name on a product and immediately we accept it is of better quality than Canadian made products. Our leaders find it easier to accept foreign domination than to make concessions and compromises to their Canadian counterparts in building a greater Canada. The regions of Canada are as diverse as the cultures within these regions. Canada is greater than the sum of its parts, a fact long forgotten by our kingdom building, self-aggrandizing politicians.

The animosity at the federal and provincial political levels has generated lack of cooperation and a general mistrust of our governments and of one another. We have lost our identity as Canadians, first as successive governments openly encourage, and fund the celebration of our differences by segregation. For more than a decade, a good friend of mine aspiring to be a member of one of our legislatures courted the various ethnic communities within the constituency. To gain their support this politician-to-be developed a political platform that suited each ethnic group. It was masterful politicking as each group did not communicate with each other and was mostly unaware of a customized political platform for each group. Here, we had the makings of a true politician, telling the people whatever they wanted to hear and not what is in their best interest, for the level of government he wished to represent. This was "balkanized" politics at its best. This kind of politicking is one reason we have lost our identity as Canadians. This celebration of diversity by segregation is a means of dividing the cultures and communities, preventing them from learning the machinations of the power structure and eventually becoming a part of the power structure. The controllers of the power structure encourage us to "tolerate" instead of accepting one another regardless of our differences. **That is why we consider ours a tolerant rather than an accepting society.** If we "tolerate" other cultures, rather than learn and accept, we will never build the Greatest Country on Earth. Instead we will fragment into regions struggling to find an identity and teetering on the brink of financial bankruptcy, and ripe for conquering.

The inequality of Canadians has created many obstacles to the enjoyment of life and liberty throughout the land. Some provinces have a residency requirement before a Canadian may purchase land; others require signs having French words significantly larger than English; still others have a residency requirement for a Canadian to collect social services benefits. There are many more instances of inequality and injustices. Everyday one province creates obstacles for residents of other provinces to meet before services are rendered. The obstacles are so great we do not have completely free and unfettered trade in goods and services from Newfoundland and Labrador to British Columbia, yet we have one stretching through the USA to Mexico. We may have free trade to Central and South America before we have one across Canada. A professional such as dentist, doctor, nurse, and auto mechanic, certified and license in one province, require a license and certification to ply his trade in another province. Environmental laws vary from province to province to federal government.

- Does the human body, realizing it had crossed into another political jurisdiction, morphs itself to conform to the laws of the new jurisdiction?

- Does the car built in Oakville, Ontario, become a technically different car if driven in British Columbia?

- Does the Chinook, blowing over British Columbia, and across Alberta and Saskatchewan, change the amount of pollutants it picks up or deposits on each jurisdiction, based on the environmental laws of said jurisdiction?

- When a Canadian becomes ill in one province, does she care that the health service required is available in her home province and de-listed in the province she is seeking care?

- Does selling a computer in Newfoundland and Labrador make

the computer functionally different from when sold in Manitoba?

Why then do we need separate provincial licensing and certification bodies for the many trades' and professional people? This treatment of Canadians by our governments is done purely for political and self-serving economic reasons, without any merit, and shows contempt for us. The myriad of licensing bodies, multi-jurisdictional regulatory agencies, self-regulatory agencies and multi-level governance is inefficient and causes massive government bureaucratic waste of goods, services and money while legitimate programs for the population is under funded or completely discontinued, in the name of saving money.

"What is a Canadian? A Canadian is a fellow wearing English tweeds, a Hong Kong shirt and Spanish shoes, who sips Brazilian coffee sweetened with Philippine sugar from a Bavarian cup while nibbling Swiss cheese, sitting at a Danish desk over a Persian rug, after coming home in a German car from an Italian movie. . . and then writes his Member of Parliament with a Japanese ballpoint pen on French paper, demanding that he do something about foreigners taking away our Canadian jobs." *Anonymous*

It is sad that someone would belittle a Canadian for enjoying the best the world has to offer. It is also true that by buying more foreign made products, we will eventually destroy our standard of living. As a trading nation, we must ensure while nibbling Swiss cheese as we sip Colombian coffee, trade is fair and free.

There is only one Canadian, the person that puts Canada first.

The Role of Government

> "We are going to be governed whether we like it or not; it is up to us to see to it that we are governed no worse than is absolutely unavoidable. We must therefore concern ourselves with politics, as Pascal said, to mitigate as far as possible the damage done by the madness of our rulers."
> *Pierre Elliot Trudeau, 1968*

In our pursuit of happiness, it is the responsibility of our government to create the necessary social and legislative infrastructure that allows us to start and grow businesses, rare and educate our children and plan for a retirement free from poverty and less dependent on government handouts. It is the role of government to encourage, educate and assist its citizens in the ways for creating individual prosperity, educate and encourage all of us to be "thy brothers' keeper" whilst reducing the intrusion of government regulation in our lives. The increase in prosperity, coupled with reduced government services fees will lead to a better quality of life, better social services and greater respect for government and its institutions. The government must lead by modernizing itself and keep abreast of the needs of its customers (the citizenry). The use of technology, reduction in the number of enforceable laws and better delivery of services will result in fewer expenses for the government.

Since World War II, our governments have gradually, and systematically, abdicated their responsibilities to lead the nation and its people. Instead, governments have adopted and implemented politically correct policies and programs, allowing the largest business and richest people to dictate government policy direction, for the benefit of a few and at the expense of the majority. A very small percentage of the population at the top of the financial chain continues to transfer wealth from the great majority, who provides the benefits to an increasing percentage of the population at the bottom of the financial chain. In the corporate world, larger businesses have the ear, and control, of governments, as their small and medium sized counterparts are taxed and harassed out of existence by our governments.

It is time to put the people and country first and lead the way to the greatness that awaits Canada.

Two Levels of Government

In one Canada, we must reduce the levels of government to two, a National, and a Local government. Government services would be delivered by the local government according to national standards created by both levels of government. This would ensure all Canadians receive the same level of services from coast to coast. Having a better and first-hand understanding of the people's needs, local governments are best able to meet the local needs of its residents and deliver services accordingly. The National government will manage defense, national and international affairs.

Today, municipal governments are starved for cash and must go begging to their respective provincial governments for funding. Irrespective of province, municipalities are restricted in their operations and are unable to meet the needs of its people. With two levels of government, a new funding formula will ensure municipalities have the required financial resources to meet the needs of its people, within a national framework. The elimination of provincial bureaucracies will free up money to finance municipal governments. As our municipalities grow and become more urban, people live in one and work in the other. The influx of people into one municipality during the daytime increases the demand for services such as roads, policing, parking, and snow clearing; creating a larger problem for infrastructure management.

Administrative Regions

One Canada would be divided into three hundred and fifty (350) semi-autonomous geographical and political regions, with a population not exceeding 750,000 persons, and varying in geographical size from urban to rural areas. This population base will ensure boundaries remain intact until the national population exceeds two hundred and sixty two million persons (262,000,000). The new administrative regions will allow for the dissolution of the apartheid-style Native Canadian reservation system, allowing for the creation of native self-government, with full constitutional power and control over their own affairs within the Canadian framework. Where a current First People's reservation exists, they will be guaranteed representation, education, and cultural protection by municipal councils for a fifty-year period. The new municipal governance necessitates the amalgamation of several villages, hamlets, townships, towns, and cities into one larger city, while very large cities would be reduced to manageable size. With twenty-four councilors in each municipal jurisdiction, villages, hamlets, and townships will have representation, and their voices would be heard on larger municipal council. The reduction in size of the very large cities would benefit the surrounding cities

All three hundred and fifty (350) local government regions would be officially bi-lingual English and French, with English and French mandatory from kindergarten to the graduation from high school. Each administrative region may also offer services in other languages, at their discretion, and as their residents demand. Given the multicultural and multilingual nature of Canada now, the new Canada will see many Canadians speaking many languages. The benefits of a multicultural and multilingual Canada would be enormous on the world stage and will lead the way to the greatness that awaits Canada. One Canada will be exotic, propelled by a vibrant multi-cultural, multi-national, and multi-lingual people supported by high technology, excellence in sports, and having the best transportation, health, and education systems in the world. We have all the ingredients to create an exotic country with class, pomp, and people of greater intellect. The new Canada would become the pre-eminent place on the planet: the chic and hip place to live.

We must stand up for Canada, stand up for ourselves, stand up for our fellow Canadians, and stand up for our beliefs. We must challenge ourselves by testing our physical and intellectual limits; we must test the laws of the land to ensure they work to protect all of us.

The National Government

It is time to decentralize the governance of our country by centralizing the management and delivery of services in local government jurisdictions and a national overseer government. The new legislature, the Senate, for a new national governance structure would have three hundred and fifty elected members. One Senator would represent each geographical jurisdiction. The geographical area would be varied in size and population, with the more populated urban areas being much smaller that the more sparsely populated rural areas.

Each Senatorial district would have support staff and offices to match its geographical size, allowing every citizen easy access to the Senator.

The governance of Canada will be vetted in the Governor General, the Legislative, Executive, and Judicial branches. The Senate would be the

Legislative Branch of the government. The Prime Minister, Deputy Prime Minister, and Cabinet Ministers would form the Executive branch and the Supreme Court of Canada would form the Judicial Branch. The Governor General will remain the Head of State and the Prime Minister would remain the Head of Government. In One Canada, the Monarchy would be abolished and the position of Governor General would be redefined to serve the people. The appointed Senate would be abolished and replaced with a unicameral parliament of elected Senators. All laws would require an affirmative vote of 67% of Senators, for enactment.

In one Canada, all governments will be amalgamated into a National and Local level with government services delivered by the level best suited to do so. The national government would consult local governments as it develops policies on all matters of governance such as financing, external relations, internal security, immigration, health, natural resources, employment, education and training, trade, natural resources, national defense, and the legal system. Local government would implement the policies according to its needs while conforming to national standards. As each region have its own characteristics, local government would be encouraged to meet its needs by customizing programs within the national framework. Municipal governments would not be allowed to opt out of any programs.

The Power of Parliament

Parliament is the most powerful institution in the land, capable of creating everything but life and destroying everything including life.

The new Senate would lead the way to national prosperity by creating the legal infrastructure in which its citizens operate. In so doing, the Senate will strive to be less intrusive in our daily lives, acting to protect the constitution and remedy any wrongs any citizen may cause upon another.

The Senate shall have one permanent committee per department with every member of the Senate being a member of a committee. Each Senate committee shall have not less than five and not more than eight members drawn from the Senate. Senators shall not receive any additional monies for being members of a committee. Many other committees of the Senate will be required to meet the administrative demands of government. The Senate must create any additional committees necessary to meet the needs of governance, with the tenure of these committees not exceeding the life of the Senate session. The Senate may create as many Ad Hoc committees, each presided over by a Senator, as it deems necessary to meet any additional demands of governance. Members of Ad Hoc committees shall be drawn from the public and shall be paid on a per diem basis. Regardless of tenure of a committee, every Senator must be a member of a committee.

Head of State – Governor General

With nearly a 400-year history in Canada, The Office of the Governor General is Canada's oldest continuing institution, representing the Monarchy as Head of State in the federation. The distinction must be made between the Head of Government and the Head of State. The Head of Government is the partisan Prime Minister, leader of the majority governing party while the Head of State is the reigning Monarch, represented by the Governor General, a non-partisan appointed by the Monarch on the advice of the Prime Minister. Our Head of State, the Monarch, is heredity, a position of privilege, and a resident of another country, representing that country when traveling abroad. Canada is never represented when its Head of State travels. The Head of State must be Canadian and represent Canada, and Canada alone, at all times.

An elected Governor General who shall become the singular Representative of the People, acting at all times in accordance with the wishes of the people and be above politics shall replace the Monarch as Head of State. The Governor General shall be the "Chief Canadian" as opposed to the Prime Minister being the "Chief Politician." These nicknames are not to be construed as derogatory but to be reflective of the apolitical and political positions they are, respectively. The Governor General shall be elected in years ending in three and on the last Thursday in April, for ten-year terms, and serving not more than two terms or part thereof. The Governor General shall appoint six full time advisors, each having at least 15 years experience in the fields of defense, economics, immigration, culture, law, and security. As the Governor General is the Peoples Representative, he must be knowledgeable, be aware of the current mood of the population, and act accordingly. His six advisors will provide opinions on the wishes of the people and the current direction of the government and advise the Governor General on any action he may take to ensure the people are protected against political decisions by the government.

In the event of resignation or death of the Governor General, the Senate shall affirm the appointment of one of the candidates, beginning with the first runner-up in the most recent election for Governor General. The appointee shall serve in office until the next duly constituted election date and may be a candidate for the Governor General position, in accordance with the laws for electing a Governor General. If all runners-up have been exhausted and the position remains empty, the President of the Senate shall be asked to fill the position for period not exceeding one hundred and twenty days. The Senate shall immediately call a general election to fill the position, with an election period not less than forty-five, and not more than eighty days. The Senate shall confirm, in the form of a motion and an affirmative vote, the results of the election for Governor General and the Chief Justice shall swear the Governor General into the position.

Qualifications for Governor General

The Governor General is expected to be a person with a wealth of life experiences, from family to employment and to community service. These experiences are truly necessary to hold the position of "Chief Canadian," therefore the qualifications to be the Governor General must be very high. The apolitical nature of the post demands the person seeking this office be removed from the political process several years before the election date. Persons seeking the office of Governor General must:

- have more that 30 years of work experience, since their first graduation from Canadian post secondary educational institution;

- Not have been a senior member or advisor to any national political party or campaign, in the two and one half years preceding the election date for Governor General.

- not be a serving member of Senate or local government council, except the President of the Senate, who may replace the Governor General upon his resignation or death;

- Not have been a member of the Senate for at two and one half years preceding of election for Governor General.

Role of the Governor General

The Governor General shall sign into law, legislation from the Senate and the National Executive Council; sign all national (state) documents; summons, opens and ends sessions of the Senate; officially declare election dates for the Senate and Head of Government; presides over the swearing-in of the Prime Minister, the Chief Justice of Canada, Ministers, and Senators. The Governor General shall regularly consult with his six advisors, and the National Executive Council, always acting on their advice. The Governor General may block or request amendments to any legislation, if, as the peoples Singular Representative, he feels the legislation does not serve the best interest of the people.

Prime Ministers and governments come and go at the behest of the people. They are political in nature and are expected to behave in a partisan manner suitable to their supporters, generally at the expense of the population. The continuity of government must be maintained while politicians are off campaigning and after changes in Prime Ministers or government. The Governor General shall be that continuity, representing the people within Canada and around the world, as the non-political Head of State, building bridges of friendship and understanding. The Governor General, on behalf of the People of Canada, will welcome World leaders, and national representatives to Canada. The Governor General is responsible for protecting his people from their political masters.

The Governor General shall have the responsibility of ensuring the governance of the people works as required by the law and according to Constitution, without himself carrying out the duties of the government. The Governor General is expected to question, and know the reason for, a government conclusion; and with the help of his advisors, draw attention to relevant considerations to ensure they are taken into account; must be mindful of influencing the outcome of discussions, being careful not to be an advocate of any partisan cause. In so doing the Governor General will have influenced politicians and government in a non-partisan manner, consistent with his duties of representing the overall interest of the people and nation.

Under normal circumstances, the Canadian Forces is under the command of the Senate. In times of armed conflict, the Senate must give its authority to declaring war on the aggressor with any deployment of personnel authorized by the Senate, yielding the technicalities of deployment to the Minister of Defense and the Governing Council. The deployment of Canadian forces in worldwide peacekeeping efforts shall be the prerogative of the Governing Council. However, if the territorial integrity of Canada is threatened, and the Senate fails to declare war immediately upon the aggressor breaching any point on the Canadian border, the Governor General shall have the authority to declare war and order the Governing Council to execute that order. Such authority shall be in effect for six months, during which time the Senate shall debate and authorize continuance or cessation of war. The Governor General shall not have the authority to dismiss the prime minister, senators, or ministers. However, the Governor General shall give his signature to the Senate's dismissal of the prime minister, another senator or the Prime Minster's dismissal of one of his ministers. With these exceptions, the Governor General shall exercise substantially the Constitutional powers presently invested in the current Head of State representative.

The position of Governor General conjures up images of being stately, stable, neutral, and apolitical. Having a uniquely Canadian as the Head of State does not mean we should abandon the dignity, stability, and stately aura of the position.

Remuneration for the Governor General

The Governor General shall be paid a salary equal to seventy five percent of the salary paid to the Prime Minister.

The Governing Council (The Executive Branch)

Head of Government - Prime Minister

The Head of Government shall be the Prime Minister. As a politician, the Prime Minister is the "Head Politician," most certainly behaving in a manner that will enhance the stature of his political party for the upcoming general elections. The Governing Council shall consist of the

One Canada

Prime Minister, Deputy Prime Minister, and forty (40) Departmental Ministers. Eligible voters in a Canada-wide national election shall directly elect the Prime Minister and Deputy Prime Minister. Candidates for Prime Minister and Deputy Prime Minister must be affiliated with a political party and must be the party's nominee for the positions and be selected according to respective party rules and the rules of Election Canada. Creating a political party is not a difficult process under present rules of Elections Canada; therefore, persons outside established political parties may create a new political party and run their own candidates in a national election for Prime Minister and Deputy Prime Minister.

Qualifications

Candidates for Prime Minister and Deputy Prime Minister must be a Canadian citizen; must have fifteen continuous years of Canadian work experiences, since the end of his/her first full time post secondary education or arrival in Canada. Those aspiring to be Prime Minister and Deputy prime Minister should ensure they gain as much community experience as possible.

Term of Office, Prime Minister and Deputy Prime Minister

The Prime Minister and Deputy Prime Minister would be elected for five-year terms, in years ending in zero and five, with the elections date being fixed for the fourth Thursday of May. No person shall serve more than three consecutive terms, or part thereof, in office. However, any person previously elected for three consecutive terms, my seek election providing one term have elapsed since the conclusion of his third five year period. Each pairing of candidates for Prime Minister and Deputy Prime Minister must be from the same political party.

Persons seeking the positions of Prime Minister and Deputy Prime Minister must deposit a sum equal to ten percent of the total spending limit as prescribed by Elections Canada. The deposit may be paid by the political party represented by the candidates or by the personal funds of the individual candidates. Upon each candidate receiving fifteen percent of the votes cast, Elections Canada shall refund the entire deposit, without interest payment.

Department Ministers

The Prime Minister shall appoint a Cabinet of Departmental Ministers consisting of thirty-five (35) Senators from his political party. The Prime Minister shall appoint five additional ministers, from the opposition parties, such appointment representing the percentage of elected senators for each opposition party, with the first 20%, or part thereof earning one Ministerial position and each full additional 10% earning one subsequent appointment. The ministerial positions occupied by opposition members of the Senate shall be at the discretion of the Prime Minister. The additional five ministers from opposition political parties shall always vote with the government Cabinet and not according to their individual political party positions. Departmental Ministers will serve at the pleasure of the prime minister.

Duties of the Governing Council

The Governing Council, consisting of the Prime Minister, Deputy Prime Minister, and the up to forty (40) Departmental ministers shall constitute the Governing Council. This council shall manage the day-to-day affairs of the country through the various governmental departments. However, the affairs of the country are under direct control of the Senate. The Senate may direct the governing council to a particular course of action, through a 67% affirmative vote.

Remuneration for the Governing Council members

The business of governing Canada is not unlike governing a very large Canadian corporation. Likening Canada to a corporation, the Prime

Minister is the Chief Executive Officer, the Ministers are the Departmental Vice-Presidents, and the Senators comprise the Board of Directors of the Corporation. Collectively they oversee a budget of many billions of dollars and manage the affairs of all Canada. The paltry compensation for the Government Canada's senior management team (Prime Minister, Ministers, and Parliamentarians) pales in comparison to the compensation of Canada's senior corporate executives. In 2003, the Prime Minister's salary was about five percent of the total compensation package of the lowest paid of Canada's Fifty Best Paid Executives. On base salary, the Prime Minister earned about one quarter of the lowest paid of Canada's Fifty Best Paid Executives. The most highly compensated of Canada's Fifty Best Paid Executives heads a company whose revenues are only seven percent of the revenues of the Government of Canada. If we were to compensate the Prime Minister in a manner similar to Canada's Fifty Best Paid Executives, the Prime Minister would earn a whopping $10billion per year. Is the job of Canada's Fifty Best Paid Executives more important to Canada than the job of Prime Minister? If we are to attract top business leaders into politics and the management of Canada, should we expect them to give up top executive pay for the privilege of being a parliamentarian? With the outcry accompanying any increase in parliamentarians' pay, do we have an expectation parliamentarians should be working for the lowest pay possible? Do we expect our Governing Council members to be paupers? If that is our expectation, we will certainly attract the kinds of people we most definitely do not want in politics. Is the low pay for members of parliament contributing to patronage, pork barreling, and the other unsavoury actions we have come to expect from politicians? We will never know the answer but we should mitigate the temptation by compensating the Government of Canada's senior management team in a manner similar to Canada's Fifty Best Paid Executives. I believe the Prime Minister is deserving of a base salary of one and one half million dollars ($1,500,000), the Deputy Prime Minister, seven hundred and fifty thousand dollars ($750,000) and Departmental Ministers, five hundred thousand dollars ($500,000) per year. The base salaries shall be adjusted annually at a rate equal to the average change in base salary for Canada's Fifty Best Paid Executives. The combined pay for the entire three hundred and fifty Senators and one Governor General, in their various positions, will be a very miniscule portion of the national budget.

Meetings of the Governing Council

While the Prime Minister, Deputy Prime Minister are elected by the people, and Departmental Minister are appointed, they shall not participate in Senate debates and votes or be members of any Senate committees. The Governing Council members present shall justify its actions to the full compliment of the Senate by presenting all pertinent facts and answer any questions Senators may have. The Governing Council members shall meet with the full compliment of Senators, in the legislative chamber, twice weekly to answer additional questions on government matters, policy, direction and any questions the Senators deem fit to be asked of the Governing Council. Final authority on any action by the Governing Council rests with the Senate and the Governing Council is accountable to the Senators.

The Senate (The Legislative Branch)

The People's Representatives - Senators

In our present governance model, as the scope of responsibility becomes larger, local issues and delivery of services gain less importance giving the perception some issues are not at all important. Today, Members of Parliament (MP's) are elected to serve in a national legislature, addressing issues of national concern. They are expected to bring to the national parliament the concerns of all constituents despite there probable irrelevance to other parts of the nation. The large scope of the national government forces categorization of all issues into national priorities, giving the impression local issues are of little concern. The Member of Parliament is perceived as ineffective by his constituents even though he might be hard at work on national issues. Depending on the province, elected representatives are referred to as Members of Provincial Parliaments (MPP's), Members of National Assembly (MNA's), or Members of the Legislative Assembly MLA's). They are elected to serve in provincial legislatures and are expected to bring attention to concerns of their constituents, in a similar manner as the federal Members of Parliament. Although the province is much smaller than the nation, prioritization of issues occurs in a manner similar to the national government and an MPP is similarly perceived as ineffective. Mayors and Councilors are elected to serve in Municipal Councils and directly deliver many services to the people. At this level, the local council is closest to the people and is best able to comprehend all the issues of concern to the people. There are hospitals, schools, roads and an airport in my city and I do not care to call many levels of government to get service. My only wish is to contact my municipal representative to address any issues I might have. A national government best handles issues of International Trade, National Defense, National Security, and International Relations, as they do not directly affect me.

Canadians elected to the Senate must ensure at least seventy-five percent of their assets are in Canadian financial intuitions or managed by Canadian financial managers, within sixty days of being sworn-in by the Governor General. It is impossible to expect our elected representative to be completely oblivious to the performances their assets, even when placed in a blind trust and managed at arms length. Do we want or expect these public servants to watch their assets dwindle away as they serve their country? We must ensure these positions of power and influence are not turned into positions privilege and profit-making by having the strictest of conflict of interest regulations, procedures to deal with conflicts of interest and guidelines to avoid conflicts of interest.

Senators shall be elected in representative constituencies. Regardless of geographical and population size, each semi-autonomous region shall have one Senator. Candidates for Senatorial positions must be Canadian citizens and having ten years work experience, since the end of his/her full time studies or arrival in Canada. Those aspiring to be Senators should ensure they gain as much community experience as possible. Candidates may have affiliation with established political parties and must obtain his party nomination in accordance with the party's constitution and the rules of Elections Canada. The Senate shall elect one of its own to the post of President of the Senate whom will be responsible for law and order in the Senate.

Remuneration for Senators

The geographical size of each jurisdiction would vary according to population density. Therefore, all Senators' salary would be equal and initially set at three hundred thousand dollars ($300,000). The base salaries of Senators shall be adjusted annually at a rate equal to the average change in base salary for Canada's Fifty Best Paid Executives. All Senators shall have one office, with three (3) full-time staff personnel, at the seat of the municipal government. In the larger, rural, and remote geographical ridings, Senators shall be allowed to have up to three (3) additional constituency offices, with up to three full-time staff personnel in each office.

Term of Office for Senators

Senators shall be elected for five (5) year terms, with elections being held in years ending with five and zero. The date of the election shall be fixed for fourth Thursday in May of the qualifying year. Senators would serve a maximum of three (3) consecutive terms or part thereof.

However, any person previously elected for three consecutive terms, my again seek election providing one term have elapsed since the conclusion of his third five year period. A Senator elected on a party banner must serve out his term under that party's banner. Any Senator so elected may change party affiliation at anytime but must first resign his position and seek re-election under his new party affiliation. Any Senator who no longer have the confidence of his political party, or who voluntarily leaves his political party, may sit as an independent Senator for the remainder of his term. This Senator need not resign from the Senate and seek re-election.

Persons seeking the position Senator must deposit a sum equal to ten percent of the total spending limit as prescribed by Elections Canada. The deposit must be paid out of the candidate's personal funds. Upon each candidate receiving fifteen percent of the votes cast, Elections Canada shall refund the entire deposit, without interest payment.

The Supreme Court of Canada (The Judicial Branch)

The Supreme Court of Canada, the final arbiter of our laws, would consist of nine (9) judges, recommended by the Prime Minister. One of these shall be appointed the Chief Justice of the Supreme Court of Canada. The Senate shall confirm the appointment of all judges to the Supreme Court of Canada, and at its sole discretion, may conduct such hearings as it sees fit in determining the suitability of the nominee for the position. The Supreme Court judges' appointment would be valid until each judge attains the age of seventy-five (75) years. Removing a judge from his position on the Supreme Court of Canada requires a sixty-seven percent (67%) affirmative vote from each of the Executive and Legislative branches of the government. No person shall be appointed to the Supreme Court of Canada unless he has had twenty years in the legal profession and five years as a Judge in a lower jurisdiction

These judges must be independent of the Legislative and Executive branches of government and be accountable to the constitution. While the Senate would be responsible for framing and adopting laws, the judges would be responsible for interpreting these laws to ensure they conform to the constitution of the land. While the Supreme Court of Canada interprets the constitutionality of parliamentary legislation, it must not have the authority to draft and enact laws. The Supreme Court of Canada, being composed of learned and experienced jurists, must council Senators in the application of the constitution. The responsibility to draft and enact legislation must be the exclusive jurisdiction of the Senate, as the democratic representative of the people. Senators must represent the wishes of their respective constituents and not their personal beliefs.

Supreme Court Decisions

The Senate frames and enacts legislations it believes conform to our Constitution and Charter of Rights and Freedoms. The learned and experienced jurists of the Supreme Court of Canada are the final interpreters of the laws of the land, issuing a definitive decision on the relationship of the legislation to the Constitution and Charter of Rights and Freedoms. From time to time, the Supreme Court has struck down laws for violating the Constitution, usually without regard for the intent of the legislation, thereby affecting the daily lives of the people. The sudden disruption of life caused by these decisions places the Supreme Court of Canada above the General Legislature of the peoples elected representatives. This is not a position the Supreme Court of Canada must occupy, therefore, any law struck down by the Supreme Court must remain in the status quo for a at least two years to allow a cooling off period for proponents on both sides of the issue. After the first anniversary of the Supreme Court's decision, the national government must signal its intention to rewrite the law to conform to the Supreme Court's decision. If the government chooses not to rewrite the legislation, said legislation dies on the second anniversary of the Supreme Court's decision. Should the government choose to rewrite the law, it will have a further three years from the date it signaled its intention to revise the affected legislation. Mandatory public consultation and Senate committee debates shall precede any new legislation.

Legislative Review Courts

The Senate creates legislations and makes laws required for the orderly governance of the country. Inevitably, governments will enact legislation in haste, trampling on the people's rights and freedom, as it tries to arrest perceived problems. Governments have hastily enacted legislation under the guise of "protecting the people" without first studying the effects on the population. Only after challenges in the courts did we realize these laws limited or removed our rights and freedoms. The Legislative Review Courts, consisting of nine judges appointed by the Senate, and reporting to the Supreme Court, shall review every piece of proposed legislation to ensure they conform to the Constitution, rendering a decision to the Chief Justice of the Supreme Court. The only function of the legislative Courts is to review proposed legislation and to scour current laws with a view to repeal, update or rewrite laws to meet or conform to society's evolution.

No doubt, we have created thousand of laws to govern ourselves. There must be countless antiquated laws that no longer meet our needs as we have evolved beyond their parameters. I recall an incident in my community where the landowner decided to clear-cut the forest many years before the land was needed for industrial buildings. I could not fathom the heartlessness of clear-cutting the trees. I later found out about a nineteenth century provincial law allowing the landowner to deforest the area and reap a property tax savings. This antiquated law, enacted when Canada's population was less than one-tenth its current size, was required to reward new homesteaders for creating farms out of forests. By removing trees form the land, this landowner effectively changed the property classification, reduced property tax assessment, thereby reducing the property tax payable to the municipal government. This is one law the Legislative Review Court would have ferreted out and repealed or modified to conform to the requirements of Canada in the twentieth century.

Local Government

Mayor and Councilors

A local government council, consisting of one (1) mayor and twenty-four (24) councilors, would administer each of the three hundred and fifty (350) geographical and political jurisdictions. Each jurisdiction will directly elect its mayor, with one councilor elected from each of twenty-four (24) separate constituencies. The Senators of the each jurisdiction shall be a member of the municipal council, having a voice, but no vote on council resolutions. The principal office of the mayor and councilors shall be located at the seat of the administration. In rural areas, councilors may maintain an office in their constituency, in addition to their principal office located at the seat of government, consisting of not more than three staff members. The local government would consist of twenty-four (24) departments, matching the naming and functions of the national government departments pertaining to local governance. These departments will serve local needs by delivering services designed to national criteria and customized for local consumption:

1. **Agriculture and Food** - Responsible for the protection of farmland, food production, and supervising the feeding of the

nation.

2. **Arts and Culture** – Promotion of film, music, theatre, and Art. Protection and promotion of our English and French cultures and our multicultural heritage;

3. **Attorney General** – chief law officer;

4. **Consumer Relations** - Responsible for the protection of consumer rights.

5. **Education** - Implement national curriculum from Kindergarten to University and Adult continuing education;

6. **Energy** - monitor energy consumption; develop energy conservation program;

7. **Environment** - monitor pollutants; enforce environmental laws; prosecute and revoke any local programs harming the environment;

8. **Finance** - Develop the municipal budget and monitor the expenses of all government departments; consult with the national Finance Department;

9. **Health** – Implement health and nutritional programs; ensure the health care is available to everyone; manage long term health care plan;

10. **Housing** – Develop and manage an affordable housing program;

11. **Human Resources** - Financial assistance, accommodation assistance; childcare services; pension and old age security; ensuring the availability of the basic necessities of life for those in need;

12. **Immigration** – Implement immigrant and refugee re-settlement programs; educate immigrants about Canada and the Canadian way of life;

13. **Intergovernmental Relations** - Liaison with the national

government to ensure services are being delivered as prescribed by the national standards;

14. **Internal Security** - Law enforcement by local police forces; liaison with the National police force and security agencies;

15. **Labour** - Implement a national apprenticeship program; act as a job placement agency and, in conjunction, with the Education and Training Department, act as retraining agency.

16. **Natural Resources** - Responsible for the management and protection of our naturally occurring resources such and forests, minerals and water;

17. **Prisons and Corrections** – Operate and manage prisons; rehabilitate felons before their return to society; monitor released inmates as they readjust to society;

18. **Public Information** - Responsible for the dissemination of government information; responsible for the public education on government services;

19. **Public Safety and Emergency Management** – Ensure the readiness and availability of emergency services to respond to large-scale man-made and natural threats and disasters.

20. **Sports and Recreation** - Manage sports and recreational program for educational institutions, community sports groups;

21. **Supply and Services** - Responsible for the procurement of goods and services on the government's behalf.

22. **Travel and Tourism** - Promote the municipality to Canadians;

23. **Transportation** – Within its boundaries, manage land, sea and air transportation; ensure these infrastructures are meeting the demands; in conjunction with the national government, manage

international transportation;

24. **Veterans Affairs** – Educate and promote the role of national and local Veterans' contribution to freedom and security in conflicts around the world.

Each of the twenty-four (24) departments shall have a permanent committee. Each committee shall have five members and be chaired by a councilor. The committee members shall be drawn from the public, with each member, except the councilor, being paid on a per diem basis. In developing the committee, the general council of the municipality shall ensure committee members from the public are experienced in matters the committee will handle or is an activist in community groups with a similar mandate of the committee. Councilors shall serve on one committee only, without additional remuneration.

Qualifications for Municipal Council

Persons seeking election to local government offices must be Canadian citizens, and have five years of work experiences after completion of their first post secondary education or arrival in Canada. At the local government level, candidates may not be a representative, implicitly or explicitly, of any political party and shall be an independent candidate whose sole interest must be dutiful representation of her constituents.

Remuneration of Council Members

While the national government may be likened to a large multi-national conglomerate corporation, municipal governments may be likened to large Canadian corporations. Not unlike these large corporations, municipal revenues and responsibilities will differ across Canada. We must compensate Council members in manner similar to compensation for executive in larger Canadian corporations. The mayor would be paid $300,000 per year while councilors would be paid $250,000 per year.

The suggested pay rates will account for $6,300,000 of each municipal budget. At each election, the national government shall set the yearly pay increase, for the term, for all elected representatives as a YES/NO question on the municipal ballot, empowering the people to financially reward the Mayor and councilors for their service of the past term of office.

Term of Office for Councilors

Local government representatives would be elected for five-year terms, in years ending in zero and five, with the elections date being fixed for the first Thursday in November of the qualifying year. No person shall serve more than three consecutive terms in office. However, any person previously elected for three consecutive terms, may seek election providing one term have elapsed since the conclusion of his third five year period.

Responsibilities

The Local government would be responsible for the administration and delivery of services within its boundaries. The national Government and the Mayor's Executive Board will set the parameters of government services, and with some customization for each jurisdiction, service levels will meet national standards. Local governments would not be allowed to enact any laws, regulations or implement any policies or procedures that contravene any national laws, regulations, or policies.

Mayors' Executive Board

The three hundred and fifty mayors from the administrative regions shall convene once each year at a National Mayors' Association meeting to elect the Mayors' Executive Board, consisting of thirty-five members. The National Mayors' Association will debate their individual and collective needs and develop action plans for presentation to the national government. This Mayors' Executive Board shall meet semi-annually to review the progress and accomplishments of the Mayors' action plans. The National Mayors' Associations shall establish twenty-four working committees to monitor the delivery of services to the people and liaison with the national department of the same name. The Mayors Executive Council shall meet with the National Governing Council at least annually.

With a National Governing Council, The Senate, The National Mayors' Association, The Mayors' Executive Board, and the Local Government councils working in concert, the wheels of government will turn more smoothly and efficiently, delivering levels of services Canadians have never seen.

Financing Governments

Throughout the world, the single most influential tool of government is taxation. Personal taxation may be as cruel as losing all your earnings in a communist system and equally cruel in a system of no taxation. The liberal medium is a system that invoices its customers for the services it provides them, without having the customers feeling cheated. Several years ago, I worked in an industrial factory where I saw this sign, "Stop Organized Crime, Abolish Revenue Canada." At the time this was the mantra of many a Canadian worker. Despite the name change at Revenue Canada, workers' perceptions are that the tax department's sole purpose is to squeeze out as much money as possible from every worker. This perception contributes to the population engaging in financial activities that reduces the amount of monies paid to the government in the many forms of taxation.

Worldwide, taxation is a means for government to collect a premium for the services it provides to the populace. Taxation carries the stigma of inequity and implies a heavy burden on the population. Indeed, it is a heavy burden for the middle seventy percent of the population. They pay the largest amount of income taxes, while those at both ends pay less for using government services. Government services include tangibles such as health care, education, roads, and intangibles such as the legislative functions of government. Since the 1980's, political parties and interest groups have been advocating the massive reduction of all forms of taxation. These groups usually hit on Medicare, Social Services, Employment Insurance, and regional support programs and the size of governments. However, none have advocated the reduction in the number of levels of government, an area where the biggest cost saving would occur. Governments need money to provide the required services of a just and orderly society while building a strong nation; the amount it needs depends on the size of government. Whether the tax is Goods and Services (GST), Provincial Retail Sales (PST), Fuel, Employment, Property, Income Taxes, or an Income Surtax, all are taken from the same pocket on each taxpayer. Media reports suggest the multitude of levied taxation consumes 52% of a person's income. This is an unacceptably high percentage, compared with other developed countries, and creates an unbearable burden for many Canadians. Money in the pockets of Canadians will be better spent than money in the government's pocket.

For corporations, income is monies left over after accounting for all expenses relating to the production of its goods and services. A corporation deducts from its revenues, the cost of all goods and services needed to produce its products. The automobile manufacturer is allowed to deduct all or a percentage of sheet metal, lubricants, labour, building costs, maintenance, entertainment, and other expenses in producing the end product, completed automobiles. A corporate executive and his party may dine on the most sumptuous meal and it becomes "cost of doing business" in the production of its goods and services.

For individuals, income is the monies collected from ones' employer, less the pittance of tax credits allowed by the government tax department. However, an individual is not allowed to deduct the cost, or any significant portion thereof, he uses to produce his product, physical and intellectual labour. A management consultant uses mostly intellectual labour; the mechanic uses about equal parts physical and intellectual labour while a construction worker uses mostly physical labour. In all cases, the production of physical and intellectual labour requires resources for the human body to function. Food, clothing, and shelter are required raw materials for physical and intellectual labour. Unlike the corporation, the individual who dines at the finest of restaurants must pay the full cost of the meal, with no chance of the cost allowed as a "cost of doing business," in the production one's physical and intellectual labour.

For centuries, we have relied on some form of levy to finance government operations. As the centuries have passed and the population increased, the provision of services became more complex as needs became greater, particularly due to urbanization. There was a time when the population had a sizable plot of land on which could be grown food to feed the family, with some left over to sell for hard currency. Urbanization of our lifestyle has prevented the ownership of enough land to grow food to feed our families, forcing us into employment to earn cash to feed, clothe, and house our families. Reliance on the land is not an option anymore and without employment, many would starve, go naked, and be homeless. The very few horse and buggy of generations ago did not require many roads, whether of the dirt or paved variety. Many people relied on homemade remedies to cure basic ailments and births were at home, supervised by a midwife or a relative. The simpler life of time gone by did not demand a structured delivery of services.

Urbanization created the need for the structured delivery of services by government and private corporations. Social services were born with the intention of being a helping hand in tough times. Corporations and governments have been using social services as a crutch to abuse employees and citizens, respectively. The cost of providing government services grew as the population grew and as the degree of urbanization increased. It is no longer viable to rely on our present form of revenue collection, namely the various taxes levied by our governments. The cost of policing our present revenue collection systems, with all its loopholes and caveats, is costing billions of dollars. Our present revenue collection system, being voluntary in many respects, encourages evaders and cheaters. Billions of dollars go uncollected each year and the government is incapable of properly policing the many taxation systems. It is more likely governments are unwilling to police the tax system for fear of being perceived as wasting "good money" going after "bad money" and accused of harassing its citizens.

Like banks, real estate agents, stockbrokers, telephone, cable and other utility companies, government must collect fees for services provided. Every person and corporation use government services; whether it is the regulatory framework; roadways, highways, railways, waterways and airways; the judicial system, or the services of those that defend, protect, and serve. Even foreign visitors and foreign corporations use services provided by Canadian governments. The revenue collection system must undergo a paradigm shift from a "tax" system, which encourages the population to believe the money collected by the government really belongs to the population, to a "Government Services Fee" system where it will be quite clear that monies collected by governments pays for providing a multitude of government services. The Government Services Fee, as a percentage of total cost of goods and service procured, would generate substantial revenues for the government while at the same time ensuring the population and corporations pay for the cost of government services used. The costs of government services are not equitably borne by all Canadians with some paying more and others paying less for the services used.

The paradigm shift in financing governments should be based on the least amount of collection points; not on the present method of every person, every employer, and every retailer as a point of collection. Reducing the collection points would dramatically reduce losses for the government. Reports in several forums suggest tens of billions of dollars in tax revenues are lost every year in the underground economy, mostly from consumers avoiding retail sales tax and corporations failing to pay income taxes and failing to remit or properly remit retail sales taxes collected. Revenue collection must concentrate on the minimum number of collection points necessary and having the greatest impact on all Canadians and corporations. Three sectors of the economy have the greatest impact on Canadian lives and offer fewest number of collection points. These sectors are the financial, utilities and energy. Every person and corporation uses a financial institution, a hydro, natural gas, heating oil, and water as well as a refueling station.

Providing and paying for government services from these three sectors would be accomplished by eliminating all forms of taxation and levies that now form our system of taxation. In one Canada, there would not be "tax deductions" for corporations or individuals. Instead, all corporations and individuals will pay a Government Services Fee for the government services used.

Financing the National Government

Government Services Fee – The Amount

Canadians are said to have many bank accounts. Corporations probably also have many bank accounts. Government revenues would be collected on transactions processed by the financial institutions, levies on utilities and fossil fuels. The total number of banks, utilities, and oil companies in Canada may number less than one thousand. The number of collection points will thus be reduced from millions to less than one thousand, representing a very efficient and enforceable fee collection system.

The Government Services Fee, set at twenty percent (20%), would be collected on every financial transaction constituting the movements of money from one bank account to another and the transfers of assets from on individual or corporation to another individual or corporation. Deposits of monetary instruments, other than cash, would not incur a transaction fee. However, cash deposits would incur a 20% transaction fee to minimize the temptation to conduct business with cash as the principal form of payment, a principal reason for the thriving underground economy and the criminal element, which sucks revenues out of all governments. A withdrawal is the movement of funds from the account of one person or corporation to another person or corporation. Movement of funds between accounts of the same person would not be considered a withdrawal, only if the name and address are identical on each account. However, movement of funds between corporations owned by the same parent corporation is a withdrawal of funds and subjected to the transaction charge. The Government Service Fee on financial transactions would be collected by the banks and forwarded to the government.

The collection of Government Services Fee would be the responsibility of the national government, which shall endeavour to consult the local governments before modifying such fee. The national government would collect all fees and proportionately distribute to the regions, keeping thirty percent for general uses, transferring fifty percent to local governments, with the remaining twenty percent distributed nationally, by need, as a means of ensuring the quality and level of government services in all regions. Levies on electricity would be equal to one and one half of one cent per kilowatt-hour of consumption. This fee would be divided into three parts, with each part used to fund general revenues, research, and development of renewable energy and upgrade current infrastructure of publicly owned electric unities. On fossil fuels, a levy of one dollar on each liter of fuel, collected by the refiners and remitted to the national government treasury. The levies collected would be distributed to general revenues of the national government (20%), municipal government funding (10%), fund research and development of renewable energy (15%), highway and road maintenance and construction (35%), public transit (15%), and replacing all self-serve gas stations by hiring full-time attendants(5%). Levies on water, oil, and natural gas would be similar to that on fossil fuels, with funds earmarked for governments and programs specific to water conservation, the environment and research and development of renewable energy.

The lessening of our dependence on bank notes would lessen or eliminate the major problem of counterfeiting. Periodically, the government devises bank notes it thinks would be harder to counterfeit. Yet, the newest of bank notes are widely counterfeited. Our most heavily used bank note, the $20 bill, is widely counterfeited and many establishments are not accepting the $100 bill. A good friend of mine is a senior manager with a company that produces money-processing machines, including machines that scan for counterfeited bills. In conversations, he indicated serious concerns his company have in dealing with the rapid pace of counterfeiters producing their wares so soon after the government introduces new bills. His biggest concern was the quality of the counterfeited bills that are almost impossible to detect without sophisticated machinery or the knowledge of well-trained persons. Counterfeiters have a direct impact on the economy causing losses to individuals, corporations, and governments, leading to demand for increased wages, increased prices, and increased taxes. These increases lead to higher inflation and an erosion of our purchasing power and value of our savings. Consumers are very much aware of counterfeiting, and its impact on our every day lives. More and more merchants are installing scanners to detect counterfeit bills. Increasingly, cashiers are routinely scanning all bills before accepting these bills for payment. Proof the counterfeiting bank notes are a major problem lies with the regular re-issue of bank notes by the national government. With each re-issue are added security features to thwart counterfeiters. The problem of banknote counterfeiting will be forever with us, unless we move towards a society that pays an extra premium for making cash purchases.

With the introduction of the Government Services Fee, a worker would be taking home a significantly larger pay cheque on payday. Imagine a worker taking home his full pay cheque, with the exception of a few deductions, and the feeling of self-worth this would generate. Imagine the worker and his family having extra money to spend on vacations and big-ticket items such as automobiles and appliances.

Financing Local Government

The financing for local governments must be equitable across our large and diverse country. A method must be developed that will consider the physical area of the dwelling, land area owned, overall value of the property , and the location of the property in urban or rural areas. In urban areas, local government provides many services not available to rural residents. The Local Government Services Fee must reflect the level of services provided and desired in both urban and rural areas. No attempt should be made to implement any "special" local government services fee to cater to the interests of rural areas and farms. Once a parcel of land is brought under the municipal's Official Plan, the municipal services fee for urban area will automatically apply.

Local Government Services Fee – Property Value

Local government fees will be calculated on:

(i)   Area of Dwelling;

(ii) Area of Land;

(iii) Purchase price of property.

Municipalities now assess the sale price of a dwelling and, using a multiplying factor, determine the municipal tax for the property. This method penalizes the owner for improvements to his property and forces the owner to pay taxes on an imaginary price for his property. During the 1980's mortgage rate reached into the high teens and beyond, house price almost bottomed out with owners were walking away from the property yet municipalities collected property taxes based on a higher assessed value set when house prices were at normal market levels. Conversely, in a hot market, house prices move up rapidly and assessed value for municipal tax value remained whatever it was set at the time of valuation. Market value assessment does not reflect reality, but rather speculation on the value of the property. The best determining value of property is the actual sale price. It is real and documented in an Agreement of Sale between the seller and buyer. The new value for property taxation purpose will be the purchased fetched on the property's next sale. The municipality will determine any change to the actual yearly property tax due by each owner. The municipal government would keep the entire amount of Municipal Government Services Fee, adding it to general revenues used to provide the myriad of municipal services.

Local Government Services Fee – Automobile

Further funding for municipalities would be from vehicle registration fees. Fossil-fueled internal combustion engines generate tonnes of pollutants into the atmosphere and are one of the generally acceptable causes for the deterioration in our biosphere. The calculation of vehicle registration must be according to vehicle weight, age and engine displacement, three important factors contributing to the amount of pollutants each vehicle generates. Accordingly, a reasonable annual vehicle registration fee would be calculated as follows:

1. Engine displacement - assessed and billed in increments of one hundred milliliters, or part thereof;

2. Gross vehicle weight - assessed and billed in increments of one hundred kilograms, or part thereof;

3. Age of vehicle - with registration fees adjusted doubling on every fifth anniversary of the date of manufacture.

The administration of vehicle registration will be the sole responsibility of Local Governments whom would collect this fee, distributing 20% to its general account, and 40% for the municipal Road Construction and Maintenance and 15% for financing public transit. The National Government would get 25% for its general account.

Financial Reporting

The collection of a Government Services Fee does not preclude corporations and individuals filing a report of earnings and Government Services Fees paid. Given the opportunity to circumvent the law, many will gladly take advantage for their benefit. As with every society between the fascist and communist, there are those who believe they have a right to live off the fruits of labour of others. They will avail themselves of chattels and laurels of others without conscience.

It is therefore imperative that accountability not be sacrificed because the implementation of a Government Services Fee has reduced the opportunity for dishonesty and manipulation of the collection system. Every individual and every corporation must file a Financial Statement showing, income, expenses, assets, and Government Fees Paid. By filing a financial report, Canadians will have a clearer picture of their net worth at the end of each calendar year, which will probably help most prepare for their future needs.

The Economy

It is hard not to hear someone on the radio or television talking about the "economy." The newspapers have stories on the economy. We read about companies doing well or losing business and the Canadian dollar going up or going down. You will hear about the economy booming or busting, expanding or shrinking, performing or underperforming and many more adjectives. The economic experts talk about the "leading indicators" as they make their predictions about Canada's economic performance. The government of Canada's agency, Statistics Canada, will tell us the inflation rate is up or down; productivity increased or decreased and many other indicators of the economy's performance at specific periods. Statistics Canada collects vital information on almost all aspects of Canadians' lives. It regularly takes "snapshots" of the Canadian economy, reporting on productivity, employment, business startups, and failures, individual and corporate spending, and a host of other information.

What is the economy?

The reference to "the economy" is really a reference to a system of production, distribution, and consumption. There are economists, persons who are experts in the science of economics, who could give a very technical explanation of the economy. Most of us might have a difficult time understanding these explanations. My simplest understanding of the economy **is it is about buying and selling.** Everyone buys and sells something. Every nation, company, and individual has an economy. We all produce, distribute, and consume. The economy of a nation is the sum of the production, distribution, and consumption of goods and services of all its people and companies. A company's economy is the products it consumed in manufacturing the products it offers for sale. The economy of an individual is the one product he has to sell, labour, and the many products and services he buys. Companies sell raw materials to other companies that are turned into finished products bought by other companies and people. People sell labour so they may buy food, cars, gasoline, houses, shoes, clothing, sports equipment, and the countless number of goods on the market. Someone must be ready to buy before someone is able to sell something.

The economy is one big circle of buying and selling.

The economy will begin to expand as more people buy more goods. When demand increases, production is increased and more labour must be bought, more workers required, for manufacturing goods. The faster the pace of consumer demands, the bigger the "boom" in the economy. Governments then make more money from various taxes, as the economy booms. When the economy is expanding, corporate profits are likely to rise and the valuation of the corporation assets increases. As an example, whenever the economy grows, more cars are sold and there is a demand for tires, wiper blades, glass, seats, gauges and all the other components that goes into a fully assembled car. The increased demand for cars forces an increase demand on the tire, glass, and seats manufacturers. They, in turn, make greater demand for raw materials and labour to fabricate their products to sell to the car manufacturers. Now, do you see the huge circle of buying and selling? The economy cannot continue to grow ad infinitum. There are side effects to an unchecked economic boom. One dangerous side effect is inflation, an increase in the general price level of goods and services, caused by increasing demands. Left unchecked inflation will wreck the economy. As the rate of inflation grows higher, it takes more money to buy the same goods and services, and you will be crying in your beer as you bemoan the loss of buying power of your money. High inflation rates are not desirable in an economy.

If you buy, you must sell. It is that simple!

The strength of the economy depends on the strength of the buyers and sellers. What will happen when one buyer is unable to sell? Somewhere on the economic circle, one person or corporation will encounter some form of financial difficulties. It usually starts with a corporation, since workers are only able to sell labour, if a corporation is willing to buy. Maybe the fictitious AMZ Corporation overextended itself during the economic boom and is now buying more than it is selling. Thus begins the road to financial difficulties. Faced with declining revenues, and the same amount of expenses, the AMZ Corporation begins to reduce costs, buying less, as it tries to get back to profitability. Buying less includes buying less labour in the form of employee layoffs. AMZ's act of reduced buying traverses around the economic circle, causing a domino effect of reduced buying by every other person and corporation on the circle. Thus begins the downward spiral in the economy. Continued economic decline will cause a recession and deflation, a decline in the general price level of goods and services. With deflation, you will be able to buy more with the same amount of money and you will enjoy the increased buying power of your money. You might think deflation is desirable. Just like inflation, deflation is an undesirable in every economy. The economic boom that caused inflation might put you into, or help you keep, a job. The economic recession that caused deflation will most certainly put you out of a job.

Everyone wants stability and predictability in life. Companies want to know they have a steady stream of revenues to meet known expenses. Canadians want the stability of an income from a job to meet their expenses. It seems the economy is an uncertain beast with its cyclical booms and busts. The cyclical nature and instability of the economy is due to induced distortions. Government subsidies, tax breaks, and exemptions here and there, are used to satisfy special interests and win political favour for the governing political party. Distortions in the real buying power of Canadians have the single greatest impact on the economy. Distortions in the economy are introduced through speculation, manipulation, and unrealistic demands for return on investments. There is speculation on currencies and farm products, called commodities and futures, where one guesses the relative values of one currency versus another or the price of farm products at specified dates. Distortions are introduced by commission payment on the sale of many products. Commission payments are economic distortions, as they do not accurately reflect the value added to the transaction. Big-ticket items such as homes, automobiles, and furniture are areas where commission payments do not reflect the value added to the transaction. Fixed fees or a salary must replace commission payments. Additional distortions in the economy are the daily fluctuation in prices for gasoline, electricity and other products sold on the "open market" of greed. The manipulations of the economy are reported in the news as insider trading, companies misreporting their financial position or corporate executives diverting money out of their corporation.

As consumers, we drive the economy by our buying habits and buying power. A worker's buying power was, at one time, equal to the amount of his take home pay. The workers of the 21st century earn their keep from a regular income, have a home mortgage payment, loans, lines of credit, and credit cards to meet daily purchasing needs and to buy cars, furniture and even take an all-inclusive vacation. We increased our purchasing power to many times more than our take home pay, by borrowing against our future earnings. Corporations also borrow against future earning, sometimes to expand operations or just to keep the corporation alive. Borrowing creates an artificial demand for goods and services and contributes to the instability of the economy, clearly demonstrated by the actions of the Bank of Canada. If the leading economic indicators are indicative of an approaching economic slowdown, the Bank of Canada lowers it interest rate to stave off the slowdown. The idea is to lower the cost of borrowing money to encourage Canadians to borrow and buy more goods. With any luck, we will borrow and buy our way out of a recession. Once enough people are suckered into borrowing to the hilt, the Bank of Canada will step in again, increasing interest rates to slow borrowing. If the leading economic indicators suggest the economy is heating up and on the verge of busting loose, the Bank of Canada increases its interest rate. This action increases the cost of borrowing money, forcing Canadians to reduce borrowing and buying, cooling down the economy.

This yo-yo effect of manipulating the economy creates uncertainties for businesses and individuals. As individuals are the driving force behind the economy, they worry about increased mortgage payments, food, and gasoline costs, putting a damper on any new spending that might be under consideration. The uncertainties of the economy will only be eradicated when the artificial distortions are eliminated. This will only be achieved whenever every person and corporation pay the full cost of government services used. That will only be achieved in One Canada.

Economists who would want to convince me the economy is much more complex, will most certainly challenge my simplified understanding of the economy.

Every person has his or her own economy to manage, which is a microcosm of the larger Canadian economy. We have one product to sell - labour. We buy many products for consumption. Whenever we sell less labour, in the form of reduced paid work time, we must reduce our purchases and the less we will have to distribute among our family. If the small economies of Canadian families begin to falter, the greater Canadian economy will also falter. Workers are consumers and if they cannot buy, companies cannot sell. This is a fundamental fact many corporate executives have forgotten, in their zeal to bolster profits and share prices, by continually resorting to employee layoffs.

The Election Processes

> **"Politics will eventually be replaced by imagery. The politician will be only too happy to abdicate in favor of his image, because the image will be much more powerful than he could ever be."** *Marshall McLuhan.*

Charisma has replaced intellect as the main qualification for public office. Many politicians and aspiring politician cannot effective articulate their positions and have turned to the imagery created and presented by image consultants, now a part of every campaign team. The television image and the five-second radio "sound bite" is the determining factor whenever a politician appears in public or open his mouth to say something. Looking good and saying very little is a surefire way of increasing ones success at the polls. Politicians are afraid of taking positions on issues for fear of being held accountable, projecting an image of being "spineless," "wishy-washy" and being "slippery as an eel." Common refrains from politicians when the heat is on are "I was misquoted", "that is not what I meant", "you are putting words in my mouth" as they furiously backpedal on any positions taken or recorded utterances.

Permanent Voters' List

At the federal level, a taxpayer may chose to authorize the income tax department to inform Elections Canada of the taxpayers desire to be added to the list of eligible electors. At election time, in many jurisdictions, tens of thousands of enumerators fan out across the country to ensure every eligible Canadian is registered to vote. While the election-time enumeration creates short-term, low-paying jobs, the process must be replaced by a national and centrally located permanent voters list. Initially setting up a permanent voters list would require a thorough enumeration process, issuing a permanent voter identity number and renewable voter picture identification card. Maintenance would be by the local government and the responsibility to keep the voters list up-to-date will rest with the voter. In our current system, a person may show up at a polling station and, with proper identification, be added to the voters' list then be permitted to vote. The responsibility for being on the list of eligible voters must rest with the voter and not with the election representatives on Election Day. Persons would not be permitted to be added to the voters list if less than fourteen days remain before Election Day. Being left off the voters list is the price one pays for not being responsible enough to make an effort to be a registered voter.

One Vote, Two Parts

Many of us believe by voting at election time we have fulfilled our civic duty as citizens. However, voting on Election Day is a culmination of a process to elect a government and we will most certainly get the government we deserve if this was the only act in our civic duties. Voting is not just about electing a government; it is choosing the governance model we desire. There is machinery that goes into getting the name of a candidate on the ballot. The vote we cast on Election Day is the second part of a two-part voting process. If you belonged to a political party, you had an opportunity to cast your vote by selecting a candidate who will carry the party's banner into the upcoming general election. That is the first part of your vote; you have chosen a candidate to represent your views in the election. You now have the second part of your vote to cast; voting for your party's choice on Election Day to ensure your party becomes the government and will implement the governance model you desire. If you belonged to a political party and voted on Election Day, you have exercised both parts of your vote. If you did not belong to a political party and voted on Election Day, then you exercised only the second part of your vote. Someone else exercised the first part of your vote, forcing you to vote for a candidate of their choosing. If you did not vote on Election Day, you failed at you civic duty and the present crop of politicians will love you for it. The lower the number of people voting, the better the chances of getting elected as only the vocal, fed up, decided and a few undecided voters up will go to the polls. It is imperative you belong to a political party, participate in the candidate nomination process, and vote on Election Day. Only then, will you fully exercise your democratic rights as a citizen of Canada and only then will we get better government and accountability in governance.

At election time, the political candidate or his representative subjects us to print and electronic advertising, door-to-door flyers, and possibly a personal visit. This is the public part of the election process. I call it the Election Process, Part II. Why is this Part II? Whatever happened to

Part I? The Election Process, Part I is a private and internal nomination process to select a candidate and is open only to members of a political party. This election process is conducted under the rules of the party's constitution.

The Party's Candidate

Long before a person becomes the party's candidate in an election, with his name appearing on a ballot and in the public view, a private election campaign machinery worked to get that person nominated as the party's candidate for the general election. Carrying the party's banner into an election campaign might be considered lucky or fortunate. While luck might play a part, the process is filled with every emotion from a "love-in" to passionate hate; every action from backstabbing and betrayal to embracing; from obeying the rules to completely flouting the laws. The internal party nomination process is fraught with backstabbing, name-calling, behind-the-scenes manipulation, signing dead persons and dogs as members, providing membership for people living on vacant lots and other shenanigans that will disgust you. These devious tactics are usually part of a hotly contested nomination where many hundreds and possibly thousands of members are signed as "instant" members, referred to by many as "rent a member." However, those are the rules of the game and the methods employed in seeking the nomination, while frowned upon by some, are a "family matter" with most party members turning a blind eye. Occasionally, one or more members will challenge the rules and methods used and come out with a victory, bringing a small sense of decency to internal party politics. With more than twenty-five years of attending party political nomination meetings, I have held my nose and voted, primarily because I wanted my choice, and my party's choice, appearing on the Election ballot. "It's all politics" is a phrase I have often heard when someone feels they have been wronged in the workplace and in business. Look around at your workplace and in businesses, you will see many things that are possibly unethical and dishonest. The party members I referred to are your coworkers, friends, relatives, and business associates. I am not deterred by the nastiness of the party's internal political process and you should not be. It is politics and it is all around us. We keep it honest or make it dishonest only by getting involved and making changes from inside. The more people participating in the political process, the more honest it will be and the more likely we will get better governments.

The Election Process, Part One - Private

You have decided to serve your country by publicly representing the area you live in. What is the next step? First, contact the party you wish to represent, apply for membership and becoming a member after successfully meeting eligibility rules. Filing nomination papers signals your intention to carry the party's banner into the next general election. Others may do the same and the party's internal election campaign, the nomination, is underway. Each candidate must then sign up as many members as possible up to a "cut-off" date. Membership rules differ from party to party, as does the nomination process. Even with legitimate candidates, the party may choose its own prominent figure as its standard-bearer, bypassing the nomination process. Called "parachuting," this happens whenever the party feels a high profile candidate, or a loyal party worker, has a better chance of winning the seat, than the current registered candidates. Many arbitrary rules and actions are obstacles on the road to obtaining a nomination. Membership cut-off dates are arbitrarily fixed, nomination dates are not fixed, limits on access to membership forms, lack of access to members signed by opposing candidates and limitless spending, are the major arbitrary rules I have encountered. With an arbitrary cut-off date, the candidate may find himself with a stack of membership forms signed, but ineligible to vote, as the forms were not submitted before cut-off date.

With limitless spending, everything goes; you may spend your own money or solicit non-tax deductible donations from supporters. With enough money, you may out-market the other candidates. These obstacles contribute to the fewer women and minorities in our parliaments. After all the machination by the party hierarchy, the candidates and their supporters, a nomination (election) date is set, members vote and the victor will carry the party's banner into the coming general election. That was easy! Think again!

> **"Ninety percent of politicians give the other ten percent a bad reputation."** *U.S. Secretary of State, Henry Kissinger.*

If you are a political animal, then you have already made your choice to be a member of a political party. If you are apolitical, it is time to reconsider your choice. I urge you to explore the political parties, try to find one that closely matches your views and join it. Politics has become a gutter fight, "knock 'em down," dragged out affair, perceived as sleazy by the population. Most of the expletives used to describe politics and politicians are well earned, mostly because of a few bad apples. Most are perceived as honest, hard working people. Help them out by joining their cause to make Canada better. You would be surprised the speed at which the sleazy ones disappear when challenged by the membership.

The Election Process, Part II - Public

After securing the party's nomination, the nominee is now very proud to carry his party's banner into a public election battle. Marketing the candidate and the party begins, even though the general election date is unknown. Fundraising is now the highest priority, replacing signing more party members. Friends, relatives, and corporations are now in the crosshairs as sources of election financing. The largest source of financing will be corporations, and you may need to promise something in return for a sizeable donation, which is partly tax deductible to the corporation. It takes a lot of people and money to run an election campaign, which is really marketing "you," the candidate. Once an election is called, Elections Canada's strict rules governing election spending comes into effect. Part II of the Election Process is marketing yourself and your party's platform to the general voting population, during an election campaign, and competing for votes with candidates with other political affiliations. At this point, your fortunes depend on your stature in your community and may very well depend on the public's perception of the party, it promises and performance of the party leader.

Simple Majority

Politicians, notoriously held in low regard, have contributed to the growth of antipathy towards understanding and participating in the electoral process. The apathetic voter have been carefully cultivated by politicians, over many decades. In our Simple Majority electoral system, the political party winning the most seats, even though the party might have received a lesser number of votes than the combined opposition parties, forms a government. The result is a population that has lost respect for the government and feeling they are powerless to effect meaningful change to governance. The people' sense of powerlessness stems from the ineffectiveness of their elected representative in our legislatures rendered impotent by the government and the governing party, which is a part of our adversarial governance structure. Remember, the government is not the governing party; it is the leader, ministers and the "inner circle" of the governing party. The impotent representatives include the legislators who are the "back-benchers" of the governing party as well as the opposition parties.

The present "Simple Majority" electoral system, sometimes referred to as "first past the post," declares the winner as the person with one more vote than the nearest competitor. This process brought us winners with as little as 34% of the votes cast in an election, even with the combined opposition parties garnering 66% of the votes. Election results indicate as little as 25% of eligible voters elect municipal governments. Low voter turnout, as low as 52% of eligible voters, contributed to a situation where 25% of Canadians decided the type of government for the other 75%. Critics have vehemently complained about the "first past the post" process and have suggested other forms of election. One such process, often been cited as a workable alternative to our present "simple majority" process, is Proportional Representation.

Recalling Politicians

Over the year, as voter turnout decreases, there has been a clamour from disgruntled Canadians to "recall" their elected representatives. The argument for recalling politicians is based on the perception politicians make promises and then fail to keep these promises when elected. Every candidate in an election, along with their party, develops and platform that is sold to the electorate. If we fail our due diligence to investigate all political parties' platforms, and to know the local candidate, then we have only ourselves to blame for electing a person whose position is contrary to his position before Election Day. The proponents of recalling politicians feel that the threat of a recall vote will force elected officials to be more responsible. In fact, any person who aspires to elected office, in a jurisdiction where recall exists, likely will become even more noncommittal during an election campaign.

How would a recall work? How would a recall vote be triggered? Will we need a petition with 1%, 5%, 10%, or some other percentage of electors or voting-age residents in a given constituency? Who would eligible to participate in the recall vote? Will it be only electors who voted in the previous election, or will it be every voter, even those who did not bother to vote? Would voting be restricted to those who voted for the winning candidate, with the exclusion of electors who voted for the loosing candidates? Would we need another enumeration process prior to the recall vote? The clamour for a recall vote is rooted in the misconception that votes are wasted if cast for the losers; rooted in the fragmentation of Canadian politics into parochialism and the belief that we must hold politicians to a higher level of accountability than that of other persons in similar high profile positions. Our own shortcomings of believing, and expecting, government will solve all our problems are the main causes for dissatisfaction with politicians. In our party political process and governance model, an inner circle control the power within the party and government. This inner circle makes policies and develops platforms that the multitude of political candidates and members of the legislatures must follow. Many factors beyond the control of a single member of the legislature will prevent him from keeping his promise. If the governing party choose to renege on election promises, should we be punishing the individual member of the legislature who had very little input and almost no influence in the decision making process? A Recall vote exists. It is Election Day. The electors have the time between elections to learn and observe the actions of the governing party, learn about the opposition parties and vote, and vote accordingly. On Election Day, we have the opportunity to dump an entire party, including the inner circle of the party and government. Some government members will pay the price by being defected and others will pay a different price by being "recalled" to the opposition benches. Many a political party has been turfed from government for failing to live up to the people's expectations. Several years later, the same political party is re-elected to government and the see-saw continue as the electorate's love/ hate relationship with political parties shift to whichever "hot button" issues are favoured. Let us get onto a bandwagon of holding politicians accountable by becoming members of political parties. Let us swell the ranks of party memberships, giving the members more choices of candidates during the party's candidate nomination process. Let us put our efforts to weeding out undesirable party candidates, long before the party's standard-bearer's name appear on a general election ballot. Democracy will be better served if we keep the self-serving politicians out of our legislatures instead of trying to remove them for underperforming.

The Election Campaign

Political parties desiring to form the next government create platforms or "sales pitches" to convince voters to vote for the political party that will best manage the country. Political parties have a product to sell the population. That product is a collection of ideas, a philosophy, programs and rewards that best suit the political party's objective of forming a majority government and not the population' objective of a better Quality of Life in the ensuing years between elections. Many promises are made; some are outrageous, deceptive, and maybe even lies. We believe the promises made and become disappointed and disillusioned whenever the governing political party backtracks on promise. We call politicians liars and brand them, and their political party as dishonest, whenever they fail to deliver on their promises. Yet they are no different than individuals and corporations who, with slick marketing and advertising campaigns, promise the world and deliver much less.

In their zeal to be elected, each political party paints the others as demons who will rip the heart and soul out of the country, subjecting the population to misery and poverty. Politicians tell the population their vote is wasted if it is cast for one of the smaller parties not expected to form a government. We have fallen for that argument and are now demanding our vote be counted and represented in the legislatures in some proportional form. Votes are wasted whenever they are spoiled, not cast, or declined. **A vote is never wasted, no matter for which political party it is exercised.**

During an election campaign, Canadians believe they will be "changing the system" if they changed the government. Nothing could be further from the truth! The morning after a general election, the needs of Canadians remain the same. Healthcare must be delivered; children must be educated; a transportation system must be in place to move people and goods from place to place; social services are required for the less fortunate and the security and defense of our person and country must be in top form. On Election Day, we are not changing the system; we are merely opting for a different political philosophy; a different group of managers who will deliver government services. The quality, quantity, and method of delivery will change with a change in government. A new set of special interest will crop up; new groups will find favour with the government as others fall out of favour. The constitutional structure of governance will be there the morning after an election. Western alienation, Quebec separatists, and the neglect of other regions of Canada will be perpetuated under a new government, as the focus of the new government will be its re-election in the next general election many years away. Regardless of the method of electing our representatives, the politicking will ensure the interest of the political party supersedes the interests of the people.

What is Proportional Representation?

A number of Canadians and political parties have called for a different method of determining the winner in a general election. In our present multi-party electoral system, the person receiving the "simple majority" of votes is declared the winner. Fuelling the call for a new process is low voter turnout that elected majority governments, even when the total number of votes cast for the winning party is below 50%. Majority governments have been formed with a low as 38% of the popular vote, with the combined opposition receiving 62% of the popular vote. This latter point is the crux of the call for "Proportional Representation."

There are several variations to proportional representation. However, proponents' believe political parties should receive a number of seats in our parliaments, representing the percentage of popular votes received by a political party or group. If proportional representation were in place, the representation in the House of Commons would be greatly different from the current standing. Opposition parties would certainly have more seats than they presently have. Over several elections, voter turnout has been declining with recorded turnouts of 25%, 53%, and 65% at the municipal, provincial, and federal levels, respectively. These low voter turnouts have been cited as reasons to change the present simple majority election method to proportional representation. People are fed up with the actions of politicians and governments and are choosing not to vote, resulting in the declining voter turnout. Voter apathy is the real cause for low voter turnout and no other voting method will cause an increase. While it is the democratic right of eligible Canadian to exercise the voting franchise, we must always remember that not voting give us the government we voted for - incompetent, uncaring, and partisan.

Proportional representation will not solve the problems of voter apathy; rather it will reward lazy (non-) voters and politicians with representation in our legislatures. When a political party fails to win a seat, anywhere across Canada, it is because it failed to convince the majority of Canadians its programs and policies will be beneficial to all Canadians. It is irrelevant that the combined opposition received more votes than the victorious political party did. That the opposition parties campaigned on their respective political platforms and failed to cross the victory line proves they do not deserve seats in parliament. Rewarding political parties with proportional seats in our parliaments based on a percentage of votes received, across the country or in a particular region, will skewer the representative process. Proportional Representation is alive and active in every constituency; the winner receives a proportion of the votes cast in that constituency which is reflective of the issues and concerns of the resident in that particular constituency.

The clamor for proportional representation gained momentum in Canada from the fractious nature of our national political parties, who have narrowed their political focus and have consistently failed to gain widespread support from sea to shining sea. The cries for proportional representation are from those who blindly follow political dogma, failing to recognize the changing needs and attitudes of people in our land and around the world.

Re-engaging Canadians in the Political & Democratic process

There are no compelling reasons to replace our "simple majority" method of declaring the winning candidate, to one of proportional representation. It is incumbent upon all political parties to re-engage Canadians in the political and democratic process. This is easier said than done, as those who would be charged with re-engaging Canadians are the ones who caused the disengagement in the first place. Promises, promises, and more promises by politicians prior to an election almost always lead to broken promises after victory is achieved, followed by "blame the previous government," "the cupboard is bare" for the present government not being able to live up to their election campaign promises.

The political process, from the party level to the public level, must change to instill integrity and confidence from Canadians. Change at the party level must require standard membership criteria for all political parties; standard rules for nominating a candidate, and strict political financing rules. The entire membership, nomination, election, and financing rules must fall under the auspices of Elections Canada. Re-engaging Canadians in the political and democratic process requires a change in our electoral process, at the party and public level. The malaise of our present political process arose from the "balkanization" of Canada into political blocks. Political parties consider themselves a "national party" even though they do not contest all the ridings in the country. Being eligible for recognition as a National Party, political parties must be required to contest at least 80% of all electoral districts in national general elections, even though winning seats in a particular region might be impossible. After years of belonging to, working and voting for, my political party, I found myself torn between my desire to support the party, and the displeasure of voting for its candidate whom I felt would be a self-serving politician, I became an undecided voter for the first time in my voting-life. I penned my dilemma for the Mississauga News, published in September 2003, during the campaign period for the October 2, 2003 Ontario provincial election. Here is the article:

The Undecided Voter

Ever since I became eligible to vote, I did so in every election. In the thirty years since, I have been a card-carrying member of a political party. I have met prime ministers, ministers, MP and councilors, in formal and informal sessions. I have met people aspiring to hold a seat in one of our legislative chambers; very partisan people and people who did not care about any political party and the role or actions of the government.

I believe in democracy and our political process and participates every step of the way. I have had direct influence on the candidate's name appearing on elections ballots and had my name on one ballot in 1991 municipal election. I have signed members for political parties, campaigned on behalf of persons seeking party nominations, and campaigned for candidates in general elections. I have been a candidate's scrutineer and an election poll clerk, to get a better understanding of "democracy at work."

Since my first vote, there have been countless polls referring to the "undecided voter." How does one become an "undecided voter?" I never understood the term and the disposition of any person in that category. Having thorough knowledge of the electoral process at the political party and general election levels, I could not sympathize with the "undecided voter." I never understood my friends' comments "Who are these people on the ballot?" as I always had a "say" on one name, before it made it to the ballot paper. I knew whom I was voting for many months before Election Day. My party's choice may not have been my personal choice; I would be voting for my party's choice, anyway.

Our personal lives, busy as it is, consumes most of our time, leaving little for involvement in politics and activities outside "normal living." We have so little time to learn and understand the political process, we leave ourselves at the mercy of the political "spin doctors." Hearing differing political views massaged into "truth" creates doubts in our minds. Partisans are unconvinced about the other parties' messages. The apathetic citizen, paying little or no attention to politics between elections, becomes the undecided voter, sometimes having a significant influence on the outcome of a general election. The non-voter, whose mantra is "they are all the same anyway," denies himself the opportunity to make changes he wants and lets others make the change for him. He can then continue to say "they are all the same anyway" becoming more ignorant of the control governments have over our life.

With the campaign underway, I have paid attention to the messages from all sides. None have an all-encompassing plan to resolve the ailments of our province. Our confrontational style of politics prevents government and the opposition cooperating for the betterment of the population. Not getting the best from all our MPP's makes us all losers. Too bad! We stumble like a drunkard towards the greatness that awaits our province. Living in Mississauga West for many years, do I "choose change" and vote for my party's choice?; look forward to the rocky "Road Ahead" or hope "Public Power" will give us a government that listens to, and work for, the betterment of everyone? They are not all the same. It is a tough choice; I may choose my party's choice, despite my misgivings about the candidate or I may make my decision as the pen is about to strike the ballot paper.

For the first time, I understand the "undecided voter"; I am now one. I will be voting; that is a certainty. It is my democratic right. I hope, you too, will vote.

Preferential Balloting

Is your vote wasted after voting for a political party that failed to win enough seats to form the government? Far from it! In past elections, political leaders have asked Canadians to vote "strategically." Near as I am able to surmise, "strategic voting" implores the voter to take a hard look at each candidate, look for the likely winner, and vote for that person in order to stop the least desirable candidate, even if that candidate is your party's standard-bearer. What the politicians are saying is it does not matter what you believe in or what your principles are, just vote for that party because it is more likely to win the election. We are told doing otherwise will be wasting our vote. The only wasted vote is one deliberately spoiled, purposely declined, or not cast on Election Day. If victory eluded your chosen candidate, it simply means you and your chosen political party did not have strong support in enough constituencies to win more seats. It is time to re-double your efforts and work harder in convincing Canadians your party's position is in the best interest of Canadians and deserving of their support. Regardless of our political leanings, we all have a preference of candidates on the ballot.

From passionately supporting our first choice to complete and utter revulsion for one or all of the others, each of us cannot be defined in "black and white." Obviously, as a member, we will agree with our party's platform, even if we disagree with some portions. Inevitably, we will find portions of the opposition's platform that matches our beliefs. Non-members might find pieces of all the platforms to like or dislike and may choose the "better of all the evils" or might just decide, "Better the devil you know than the one you don't." Voter preference follows present and historical family voting patterns, influences from employers or just plain guessing. Less than 10% of voting-age Canadians belong to an organized political party, and are expected to support that party every step of the way up to and including a general election. The majority of voters decide the voting preference from various spheres of influences. In a preferential balloting system, the party will continue to field candidates under its banner. However, voters would rank each candidate in order of preference. On a preferential ballot, you simply rank the candidates you would consider voting for, in order of preference; first choice, second choice, and so on. A ballot would only be valid if you voted once for each candidate, voting for at least one candidate and not necessarily voting for all the candidates on the ballot, and indicating a single preference for each candidate. Each preference would be weighted according to the following ranking with the winning candidate required to tally at least 67% of preferential votes received. Here is the suggested weighting:

1. Five (5) votes for being the First Choice candidate
2. Four (4) votes for being the Second Choice;
3. Three (3) votes for being the Third choice;
4. Two (2) votes for being the Fourth Choice;
5. One (1) vote for being Fifth and subsequent choices;

Election Day

Low voter turnout wounds democracy and a wounded democracy will die or come charging back like a wounded tiger. The wounded democracy will either deteriorate into anarchy or charge back as a totalitarian state. For the leaders so inclined, totalitarianism offers power by terror and intimidation, without regard for human life, prosperity, and freedom. In the latter half of the twentieth century, severely oppressed, millions died under totalitarian regimes around the world.

To encourage voter participation, employers will pay their employees one additional day of pay, upon proof of his voting, even if that employee had a scheduled day off. For both the National and Local elections, Elections Canada would provide the voter with the proof required to facilitate this payment. Employers would not be reimbursed for these extra payments. Employees falsely claiming this extra day's pay would be subjected to a five hundred dollar ($500.00) fine. Employers denying payment of the extra day's pay would be subjected to a five hundred dollar ($500. 00) fine, for each affected employee. By encouraging eligible voters to cast a ballot on Election Day, using a financial reward, we may stem voter apathy and increase voter turnout. Making voting mandatory, as some countries have done, is contrary to democracy, where the freedom to chose is paramount.

Election Spending Limits

Elections Canada shall prescribe spending limits for each Senate constituency and the positions of Prime Minister, Deputy Prime Minister, and Governor General. The Senate make into law, the recommendations of Elections Canada, with any amendments it desires. A Senate Election Committee shall revise the spending limits not less than one year prior to every general election.

Government Political Financing

Fundraising for political purposes is a daunting task. Large contributions from organizations beg two questions, "What do they want?" and "What are they getting in return?" Not enough citizens contribute to political parties to maintain their financial viability. After every election, there is the inevitable news story of one or more political parties being badly in debt, hoping to fundraise and pay off its debt before the next election rolls around. Being constantly in debt, political parties are vulnerable to manipulation by their largest contributors. Governments not only manage the affairs of registered voters, it manages the affairs of all Canada's residents. The National government must create a pool of election funds, administered by Elections Canada, for financially reimbursing candidates and political parties for participating in the election process both at the local and national levels. The fund will an amount determined by an independent Election Financing Commission of the people, and allocated per capita, based on the latest national census compiled by Statistics Canada. After each election, the Election Financing Commission shall review the amount allocated for government political financing to ensure all candidates receive equal treatment and the level of financing meet the meet the needs of a political campaign.

At the national level, sixty percent of the pool of funds shall be allocated to reimbursing individual candidates' elections expenses. The formula for disbursement will take the total number of votes recorded nationally and dividing it into pool of money, generating a monetary value for each vote. Reimbursement will then be calculated by multiplying the monetary value by the number of votes received by each candidate. The amount reimbursed shall not exceed the amount spent by the candidate. The remaining forty percent of the financial pool will be divided between the registered political parties based on the overall percentage of the national votes received. This funding formula will encourage regional political parties, wanting to become the Government of Canada, to develop national political platforms that will gather more votes and, therefore, more funding from the national pool of funds. At the local level, the pool of funds would be equal to the national level. However, since political parties are not present at the local level, one hundred percent of the pool funds will go directly to reimbursing candidates' expenses. The government shall establish a similar pool of funds to finance the political campaign of persons seeking the position of Governor General and a similar formula shall apply for the distribution of funds.

Government political financing, based on voter turnout, place the onus on political parties and politicians to "get out the vote." Any monies received from corporations and individuals will be subtracted from the eligible amount of reimbursement. Any monies remaining in the national political financing pool must be returned to the National Treasury.

Democracy, Freedom and Justice are not free or inexpensive. All three go hand in hand and easily manipulated to suit the needs of the manipulators, as it is now. Those affording to purchase them, best enjoy democracy, freedom, and justice. Credibility and respect for politicians are absent from our political processes. Distrust of government and its institutions are commonplace in our society. Perception that "politics" is everywhere numbs the populace's sense of duty to country. The sense of hopelessness to effect meaningful change in the behemoth that is government and the large Canadian and multi-national conglomerate of companies prevents us from ever trying to make changes.

Bringing back respectability to government, politician and political parties require election financing predominantly from government funds through reimbursements to the candidates and with minor contributions from corporations and the population. If we want good government, we must be willing to pay for it; elect it; fight for it; defend it.

For Senators

Individual candidates for Senatorial seats, regardless of affiliation, may spend up to the amount prescribed by law. National Political parties may not spend any monies in individual Senate constituency.

For Prime Minister and Deputy Prime Minister

Individual candidates for Prime Minister and Deputy Prime Minister, regardless of party affiliation, may spend up to the amount prescribed by law. National Political parties may spend an additional amount prescribed by law.

For Governor General

Individual candidates for Governor General may spend up to the amount prescribed by law. Political parties shall be prevented from spending on behalf of any person seeking this office.

Political Contribution

For Corporations

Corporations, Unions, or any associations representing groups of individuals shall not be permitted to campaign on behalf of, or contribute any goods or services to, any candidate or political party. Corporation, unions and other representative associations cannot vote, therefore they must not be allowed to contribute any monies, goods, and services to any election campaign.

For Individuals

Every individual shall be allowed a political financial contribution not exceeding one thousand dollars ($1000.00) to an individual candidate or political party but not both. Since we will not have a "system of taxation" in One Canada, there will be no "tax deduction" for political contributions.

Declaring Political Contribution

The people believe wealthier individuals and corporations have been buying the government and politicians via political contributions. The perception this is happening, in some backroom way, have painted all politicians with a tarred brush, with honest politicians needlessly cast as dishonest. To ensure the people have an accurate picture of a politicians' and political parties' obligation to any one individual, group or corporation, the political contribution process must be transparent and free from any perception of "favour or access buying". It is imperative people know the names of political contributors by compelling candidates to publicly release that information, with all local and national print news media compelled to report on the release of all political contributions. Each candidate seeking an office shall, not less than seven days before Election Day, publish a preliminary list of his largest one hundred contributors and the amount of each contribution. Within ninety days of the election, each candidate shall publish a complete financial statement and a list of all contributors and the amount of each contribution.

The Departments

Every organization requires a division of responsibility in areas that best suit the overall objective and management of the organization. Government must be organized into departments that afford the efficient development of programs and delivery of service to its citizens and to better utilize the intellect of all the peoples' elected representatives.

The Departments

Having observed our political process for more than a quarter of a century, I am constantly flabbergasted by the willy-nilly manner in which departments were reorganized, consolidated, and disbanded. From time to time, Departments are consolidated into super-ministries to bolster a pet peeve of the Prime Minister and headed by a Minister finding favour with the Prime Minister. At other times, consolidating departments into the hands of fewer ministers are sold as a cost reduction measures. How could this be a cost saving measure when the functions of the newly, amalgamated department are equal to the functions of the individual departments? Any financial savings from the consolidation in ministries are insignificant in the scheme of the entire government expenditure. However, the degradation of service to the public is real and efficiency of government solving its problems has certainly suffered after consolidation. After an election, we may be governed by the same political party, or by a previous opposition party. Regardless of who forms the government, the needs and priorities of our people rarely change as we must continue farming to feed our people and protect our farmers; clean up the environment and reduce pollutants; fund science and technology; manage labour, immigration, consumer protection and maintain law and order and security. The entire government structures are important to all Canadians with each department serving a specific segment of the population. Areas such as Human Services, Trade, International Relations, Immigration, National and Internal Security, are extremely important functions of governments and must be separated into distinct ministries, giving detailed attention to their functional needs. The larger the government department, the easier it is to hide inefficiency and incompetence; the easier to hide patronage programs designed to help politicians and their supporters. Consolidating government into fewer ministries deny Canadians the best government services to which they are entitled. Consolidation denies qualified Members of Parliament the ability to function as the people's representative and to be a meaningful contributor to the management team collectively elected. Consolidation also limits ideas to a few, preferred Members of Parliament, stifling ideas and confining a majority of our Members of Parliament to playing marginal roles. Consolidation overburdens the responsible ministers and imposes the ideas of a single person on a host of government programs. Every person has a different opinion on each subject, which is requisite for good debate. Government is about debate, compromise, and consensus. The number of Departments best suited for efficiently managing Canada's affairs must enable the broadest opinions from members of the Senate and involve every member as ministers, committee chairpersons, and committee members. Only then will the Canadian people receive full value of the intellectual capacity of our managers, the members of the Senate and Governing Council.

Every department must have a permanent committee of Senators. With three hundred and fifty Senators and thirty-five permanent committees, there will be ten Senators on every committee. Today's House committees are nothing more that stalling tactics for the government. From time to time, government matters are referred (deferred?) to committee for debate. More often than not, committee recommendations are ignored and "shelved" for review at a future date, regardless of the importance of the matter to the people. Committees shall have the authority to frame laws, as does the Governing Council, and present to the Senate for its consideration. It would become imperative for the Governing Council and Committees to work closely to move forth an agenda that benefits the people. From time to time special hearings are required, which would otherwise burden existing committees. The Senate would create as many ad-hoc committees and sub-committees necessary to develop and implement programs beneficial to the people, affording a speedier implementation of programs. By creating smaller departments, ministers and their staff will better understand the scope of services needed by the people and allowing for the development and efficient delivery of government services to the people. I suggest the following thirty-five departments:

1. **Agriculture and Food** – Responsible for the protection of farmland, food production and supervising the feeding of the nation;

2. **Arts and Culture** – Promotion of film, music, theatre and Art; protection and promotion of our Native, English and French cultures and our multicultural heritage;

3. **Attorney General** – chief law officer of the Executive Council and the Senate; represents the government in any legal action brought against it;

4. **Canadian Heritage** – Protection and Promotion our past, unique to the land that is now Canada;

5. **Communications** – Responsible for all communication mediums, including electronic and print.

6. **Consumer Relations** – Responsible for the protection of consumer rights;

7. **Education** – Develop, implement and evaluate educational programs from Early Childhood Education to University and Skills Training; Training and evaluation education professionals;

8. **Energy** – Secure present energy sources; monitor energy consumption; develop energy conservation program; search for new conventional and renewable energy sources;

9. **Environment** – Monitor environmental pollution; empowered to

revoke any programs that harm the environment and prosecute violators;

10. **Finance** – Develop the national budget and monitor the expenses of all government departments;

11. **Health** – Manage Canadians' health and nutritional needs; ensure the health care is universally available to everyone; develop a sustainable, long term health care plan;

12. **Housing** – Housing is the most essential and basic need of life; create affordable public housing;

13. **Human Resources** – Manage financial assistance, accommodation, childcare, pension and ensuring the availability of the basic necessities of life for those in need;

14. **Immigration** – Develop the criteria for accepting immigrants and refugees, set quotas and develop a plan to educate immigrants about Canada and the Canadians;

15. **Industry** – Manage Canada's transition to a knowledge economy. Ensure continued industrialization of the traditional sectors of steel, automobile, mining, and pulp and paper;

16. **Intergovernmental Relations** – Government to government liaison; act as mediator when local governments disagree;

17. **International Relations** – Responsible for diplomatic and political relations with other countries; promote the benefits of a peaceful, free, open, and just society having a free market with a social conscience;

18. **Internal Security** – Law enforcement by the national RCMP and local police forces;

19. **International Commerce** – Promote Canadian products, and

secure markets for our goods and services; remove barriers to freer and fairer trade and monitor trade practices of other countries;

20. **Justice** – The government's law firm, develops and maintains the legal infrastructure, policy and reforms laws;

21. **Labour** – Develop and implement a national apprenticeship program; act as a job placement agency and, in conjunction, with the Education and Training Department, act as retraining agency;

22. **National Defense** – Responsible for the armed forces and defend the national interest from external forces; assist the Internal Security forces in times of insurrection and disasters;

23. **Natural Resources** – Management and protection of our naturally occurring resources such and forests, animals, minerals and water;

24. **Prisons and Corrections** – Ensure incarcerated persons serve their sentence in humane manner while undergoing rehabilitation before their return to society;

25. **Public Information** – Responsible for the dissemination of government information, public education on government services and public broadcasting;

26. **Public Safety and Emergency Management** – Ensure that all goods are safe for public consumption and use; ensures the readiness and availability of emergency services to respond large-scale man-made and natural threats;

27. **Revenue** – Collect all monies payable to the government;

28. **Science** – Science will lead the way to Canada's greatness;

29. **Solicitor General** – Prosecution of lawbreakers by applying the laws forming the legal infrastructure;

30. **Sports and Recreation** – Manage sports and recreational program

for educational institutions, community sports groups and the National sports program;

31. **Supply and Services** – Government procurement agency;

32. **Technology** – Technological advances we have not yet dream of will change the world of the 21st century. Prepare for Canada's participation in these technological developments;

33. **Travel and Tourism** – Promote Canada and Canadians to the world and to Canadians;

34. **Transportation** – Land, sea and air transportation; ensure these infrastructures are meeting the demands;

35. **Veterans Affairs** – Ensure services are available to assist military services personnel in adjusting to physical and psychological trauma sustained during wars and armed conflicts.

Department of Agriculture and Food

The primary purpose of the department would be to ensure the production of food to feed the nation and for export. The protection of farmers' well-being and farmland would receive one of the highest priorities from this department. Ensure food sold to Canadians meet strict standards by monitoring and enforcing these standards; research the long-term effects of genetically modified foods; conduct Agricultural research.

Department of Arts & Culture

> **"In a world darkened by ethnic conflicts that tear nations apart, Canada stands as a model of how people of different cultures can live and work together in peace, prosperity, and mutual respect."** *Bill Clinton, President of the USA*

Our culture is now a blend of First Peoples, English, French, and the cultures from peoples of the world. We can no longer afford to live in isolation from other cultures. Our actions are now governed by the expectations of every culture; therefore, cultural knowledge must become an integral part of our educational curriculum and decision-making process. People seeking a new life in Canada must be educated about Canada and it cultural diversity.

The Canadian Handbook

> "Canadians know little about their achievements in the past. They don't even teach them in their schools."
> *American Independent Presidential Candidate, Ralph Nader, Dec. 9, 1992, CBC Television interview.*

Who is a Canadian? What are his expectations from Canada? What may Canada expect from its citizen and residents? Who are the men and women that built the Canada we know? What are Canadians' achievements?

Long time ago, American culture began to overrun Canadian culture. We copy everything American; movies, soap operas, and talk and reality shows. Our movie theatres are filled with American made films depicting violence, rape, murder, gun crimes and gangs, and other denigrating scenes. The monstrous size and the financial muscle of the American film and movie industries make it difficult for Canadian producers to compete in film and movie production. Canada is major center for American film and television productions, with several blockbuster movies and television series filmed in our major cities. Unfortunately, these productions depict American cities and culture, with the generous help of the Canadian taxpayer. Our hard-earned tax dollars are used to fund Canadian films, movies and television shows that depict and indoctrinate our children to the American way of life.

Canadians know more about the colonial American, British, and French history and heritage than the history of the men and women that built this great land. Canadians are more in tune with American history and current events than with their own history, culture, and heritage. Canadians know more about American political institutions than their own. Many Canadian post secondary students go to American post-secondary institutions on American scholarships, learning about America, bringing those values back to Canada to "Americanize" us, eroding Canadian values, culture, and heritage.

Canadian culture is exotic, made up of the rich cultures of the world. The greater culture, by virtue of its multilingual, multicultural, and multinational composition, offers us the world in our backyards.

The national government must embark upon a program to create a "Handbook for Canadians," to be distributed to all households in Canada and be given to all prospective immigrants. The Department of Education should develop and teach a history and cultural curriculum, in all grades, beginning at grade one. We must know who we are; that identity is crucial to building a great nation. The handbook would include biographies on all the great men and women, who contributed to our proud nation. Over the last half of a millennium, many Canadians made immense contribution to building Canada, Prime Ministers, Sir John A. MacDonald and Rt. Hon. Pierre Trudeau, First Peoples' activist Louis Riel and Chief Dan George; hockey greats Maurice "The Rocket" Richard and "The Great One" Wayne Gretzsky; First Canadian born Governor General, Rt. Hon. Vincent Massey and First black Lieutenant-Governor, The Rt. Hon. Lincoln Alexander; Astronauts Marc Garneau, Dr. Roberta Bondar and Chris Hadfield; Actors Donald Sutherland, Christopher Plummer, Michael J. Fox and Actress and Producer Mary Pickford; War of 1812 Heroine, Laura Secord; Quebec Premiers Rene Leveque and Lucien Bouchard; Leaders in Battle on the

Plains of Abraham, English General James Wolfe and French General Louis Joseph Montcalm; First Woman Governor General Madame Jeanne Sauve; First Asian-born Premier in Canada, Hon. Ujjal Dosanjh; Creators of insulin, Dr. Frederick Banting and Dr. Charles Best; Writer and TV personality and author Pierre Berton, writer Lucy Maude Montgomery, singers Anne Murray, Gordon Lightfoot and Sarah McLachlan and many more Canadian heroes. We must be proud of our achievements. The only way to be proud is to know of these achievements and their effects on Canada and the world. The Canadian Handbook would educate Canadians on the cultures of Canada and harness the best of these cultures to create the greater, exotic Canadian culture. Canadians define themselves in terms of what Americans are not.

- "We are Canadians because we do not have the crime rate of the Americans"
- "We are Canadians because we do not engage in the American chest thumping ritual whenever we are victorious"
- "We are Canadians because we have a Prime Minister not a President like the Americans"

These phrases make a mockery of being Canadian and Canadian citizenship.

We are Canadians because we put Canada first!

That should be the reason we are proud to be Canadians. We must define ourselves, our nation, and our people. We must "brand" our country for all to see, appreciate, and emulate. Canadians must stand tall and be felt around the world. Working with other departments, Arts and Culture must promote Canada internally and around the world.

National Holidays

Every year Canadians work many hours at a job and at volunteering in order to build our country. While we are rewarded with pay from a job and satisfaction from volunteering, we need the recognition and appreciation of our fellow Canadians for our hard work. Many of us die while on duty; die because of violence and die in the service of our country. Many of us would like to remember our heritage, faith, heroes, and mentors, and recognize our great leaders. The National government should enact the following statutory holidays to recognize Canadians and their contributions to nation building.

January - New Years Day

Beginning of a new year.

February - National Leaders Day, second Monday

Every day we think of the Prime Minister, Premiers, Mayors, and Corporate Executives as leaders, mainly for the high profile they command in the media. There are many leaders in our community and the business world, toiling very hard in building their organizations and our country. These leaders are in government, political parties, corporations, volunteer organizations and our families. We need to recognize these men and women for providing leadership in their organizations and to their people. Many work in their chosen areas without remuneration and, at times, without a "thank you" from those not directly affected. A national holiday offers a day of rest and recognition for their leadership in building the many parts of Canadian society.

March - National Faith Day, third Monday of March

Given the multi-faith composition of Canada, the traditional Christian holidays celebrate one faith, partially excluding peoples of other faiths. We should recognized and respect the faith of all our peoples with a national holiday. In addition to the traditional Christian holidays, this day will be set aside for all to take time to celebrate our individual faith, even if we do not belong to any organized religious group. Even the agnostic will appreciate a day for his own reflection.

April - National Heroes Day, third Monday

The unselfish efforts of individual Canadians have contributed to the strength of our country. These heroes were here before the first Europeans arrived and are in our midst today. Many well-known Canadians, Sir John A. MacDonald, Louis Riel, Pierre Elliot Trudeau, Dr. Frederick Banting & Dr. Charles Best, changed the lives of all Canadians, for the better. The men and women who gave exceptional service to the country deserve recognition as heroes and their memory honoured with a National holiday.

May - National Labour Day, second Monday

Around the world, the majority of nations celebrate Labour Day in the month of May. On this day, we will remember the working people who toil each day to build Canada. Traditionally, Labour Day marked the achievements of the organized labour movement. The majority of Canadians do not belong to a trade union or any organized labour movement. Nevertheless, these workers toil everyday to build a strong and prosperous Canada. Whether it is the Prime Minister, Premiers, Mayors, Corporate Executives, auto mechanics, or a homemaker, we are firstly workers, toiling to improve out lot in life. Recognition of every working man and woman is best served with a national holiday and day of rest.

June - National Civic Holiday, first Monday

Each jurisdiction will recognize this day in honour of its resident's contribution.

July - Canada Day, celebrated on July 1st

This, our most recognized and celebrated holiday, marks the day on which several regions came together to create the Canadian federation. It ignores the contribution of peoples before 1867. Canada Day should be a celebration of our country by all peoples. It should be celebration of Canada as it is today; celebrating the contribution of its people, of all-time.

August - National Heritage Day, first Monday

Each of us is a descendant of one of the many cultures of the world, regardless of the length of time we have been here. On this day, First Peoples, Jews, Muslims, Jamaicans, English, Irish, Italians, and the many other cultures celebrate their heritage and culture. On National Heritage Day, we encourage all peoples to display their heritage and culture for others to see, participate in, and appreciate. Summer is the best time for this holiday, as it would afford us good weather to have parades, picnics and other summer-time activities.

September - National Volunteers Day, first Monday

Millions of Canadians volunteer in so many areas to help build our country. Our society depends on these volunteers to provide key assistance. They should be nationally recognized and praised for their efforts with a National holiday.

October – Thanksgiving, second Monday

Regardless of our lot in life, we have many things for which we must be thankful. Thanksgiving is the day where all fortunate Canadians, mindful of their good fortunes and the abundance of food and wealth remember to help the less fortunate in our society. For Christians, Thanksgiving is a day to give thanks to the Almighty God for the bountiful harvest with which Canada has been blessed.

November - Remembrance Day, November 11th

Proclaimed after World War 1, on Remembrance Day we commemorate those who sacrificed their lives in military service to defend the freedom of our country and of all freedom-loving peoples of the world. Many

Canadians died in the line of duty to protect Canadians while others have died at the hands of violence. Many are forgotten for their bravery and courage and for being victims. During National Remembrance Day, we will honour the memory and contributions of our soldiers and veterans of war, firefighters, peace, and security officers and victims of violence. We will also remember the wrongfully convicted or those who suffered some other injustice. In recognition of the fallen, one minute of silence will be observed in all workplaces, broadcast radio, and television, as is the current practice.

December - Christmas Day

This traditional Christian holiday, observed on the 25th day, celebrates the birth of Jesus. As a multi-cultural, multi-denominational society and with the diminishing importance of Christianity, Christmas has become a time for over indulgence in eating, drinking, partying, and shopping. Nevertheless, it should be celebrated as common day for the majority Christian faiths.

Observing Other Religious Holidays

The multi-cultural and multi-faith mix of Canada demands recognition of various holidays and religious observances. Christians celebrate Easter and Christmas, with workers receiving time off and pay for these holidays. Non-Christians workers also receive time off and pay for these Christian holidays, even though it is a meaningless observance for them.

While Canada is a people of majority Christians denying non-Christians observance of their meaningful religious holidays diminishes a significant group of Canadians for being of different religious belief. Religion is a centrepiece to who we are as person and a people. Helping to form the core values and defining our character, religion is the guidepost of our lives. I am a catholic Christian, which gives special meaning to Good Friday and Christmas Day. On these are days I do nothing except to relax and reflect on my life, past present and future. Hindus celebrate Diwali. For Muslims, Eid follows the holy month of Ramadan; Jews have Hanukah and Rosh Hashanah. Holy days for non-Christians do not necessarily coincide with Christian religious holidays. Provision should be made in law to allow non-Christians observance of two religious holidays, as time off without pay and without repercussion from employers.

Focus on the Family

The family unit is an integral part of the development and evolution of society. It is a compact of the larger world. The affairs, trials, and tribulations of family life are similar to those of the larger society. Being able to manage a family's resources, assets, and members is of significant benefit to the family unit, the neighbourhood, city, country, and world. If we fail to keep a small family unit operating in harmony, we will most certainly fail at keeping our larger world in harmony. A good family life enables adults and children to become more responsible in their actions, learning to take of themselves and each other. The family is a workgroup where all members develop a caring and cooperative relationship that is carried into the greater society. The family is responsible for teaching good manners, respect, caring, deportment, and the many other behaviours that contributes to the building of a strong family and even stronger society. The family is under attack from divorce, work, stress, homosexuality, television, video games, and our growing individualistic and selfish attitude. The dysfunction in the Canadian federation is a direct consequence of the dysfunction in the family unit.

Marriage

The sanctity of marriage is a holy bond between three people, the bride, groom, and the spiritual being of Jesus Christ, for creating the simplest building block of our society, the family unit. A man and a woman make a decision to share and build a life as one unit, procreating, build a family and extend the human species. Marriage is a big gamble with two unique individuals deciding to merge their independent lives, hoping for happiness and prosperity for the rest of their lives. Sadly, many marriages do not last forever, with almost 25% failing to past four years. Even after thirty years of marriage, more than 35% of marriage ends in divorce. At times, every one in two marriages were expected to end in divorce. *(Source: Statistics Canada, 2000).*

Marriage is the most challenging task I have ever undertaken. While the love is strong, the challenge is from the efforts required to learn, understand, and respect my wife and to ensure I behave in a manner that is expected of me. I am sure marriage is also a challenge for my wife as I, too, has expectations of her. Marriage is a lifetime of hard work, and difficult choices, and after 26 years, it is the most rewarding experience of my life. I know not why marriages end in divorce nor do I really know why mine has lasted more than a quarter century. I do know a commitment to working very hard to ensure the relationship last "until death do us part" is certainly one of the main ingredients of a long and happy marriage.

While the causes for divorce are many and varied, the effect lingers on for many years. Children of divorced parents suffer the loss of love, guidance, togetherness of both parents regardless of the amicability of any divorce. Many female spouses end up in poverty, unable to find jobs because they must take care of the children. Children spend more time by themselves and with their parent, often being shuffled across town or between cities to meet custodial requirements of a separation or divorce agreement. Friendships with others, flourished while married, become strained and may end after divorce. At a most vulnerable time, separating or divorcing couples may loose friends, family, and financial stability, picking up a huge load of stress in the process.

Several years ago, a young friend of mine decided to have a live-in relationship with her beau. At the time I learned of her decision, I enquired why a live-in relationship and not marriage. She told me her parents were divorced after years of quarreling and she did not want a marriage that would end in divorce. She gave up on marriage in favour of a relationship that could be ended very easily instead of one that needed a legal solution. Is society giving up on marriage instead of trying harder in making it work?

A few days before my wedding to her daughter, my future mother-in-law offered me some words of wisdom. The first was for me to remember that no two people are alike and no two marriages are a like, therefore, never compare my marriage to any other marriage. The second piece of advice was to remember that "only two fools will not quarrel" and even if her daughter and I were to quarrel, never go to bed angry at one another. After a quarter century married to her daughter, I am glad for the advice because it helped put my relationship in perspective of what's important to me.

Marriage is an attempt to build a stable relationship, which in turn will build a stable society. A few divorces are not a guarantee we will fail to build a stable society. The strong bonds of marriage will ensure a stronger society that functions in harmony.

Homosexual Relationships

Since the dawn of time, homosexual relationships have existed. Revolting a practice as it is, homosexuality is gaining widespread acceptance in our society. Political correctness and the homosexual community's practice of branding opponents as bigots have contributed to silencing the majority. Persons in homosexual relationships are now demanding the sanctity of marriage be extended to their relationship. Homosexuality is an attack of family life, the very foundation of society. Homosexuals are making demands for the right to adopt children, despite the impossibility of a homosexual relationship producing a child. Homosexuals must not be allowed to adopt children. Being a mother or father is not limited to the biological connection between a woman or man and a child. A Mother is woman who conceives and gives birth to, or raises and nurtures a child. A Father is a man who creates, or raises or nurtures a child. Motherhood is the empathic and nurturing relationships existing between an offspring and the mother while Fatherhood bears the same relationship with the child and his father. Society have recognized and accepted the differences in viewpoints of a man and woman on any particular subject.

There is no doubt that perspectives on life differ between the genders and there are numerous studies that confirms these differences. By having a child exposed to the singular perspective of "two mommies" or "two daddies" denies the full development of that child and developing an adult with a singular perspective on life. Looking into ourselves, we see the influences of our parents. If we grew up with both parents, we see the influences, perspective and gain the knowledge of both. Conversely, growing up with a single parent, we gain the knowledge, influence, and perspective of one person. Allowing homosexuals to adopt and raise children would place those children in a situation lacking sexual complimentarity, denying the proper development of the child.

> "In the last few years, the American people have gotten to know me. They know my blunt way of speaking. I get that from Mother. They know that I occasionally mangle the English language. I get that from my father." *George W. Bush, President of the Unites States of America.*

Homosexuals are demanding extended benefits to their partners in homosexual relationships. More and more corporations and governments, fearing lawsuits, have begun to cave-in to the demands of homosexuals and have extended benefits to people in homosexual relationships. It appears the demands for formal recognition of homosexual relationships, whether a marriage or civil union, is rooted in money. Legal recognition would grant many benefits, CPP, OAS, family dental, health and more, to homosexual spouses, a practice now reserved for spouses of the opposite gender.

It is quite clear that the male and female genitalia complements each other and it is very clear that men and women copulate to produce offspring. Homosexuals would have us believe their attraction to the same gender and engaging in sexual activity is a genetic defect. Those issues have been debated and there are significant disagreements on the cause of homosexuality. Homosexuality is an anomaly, not a genetic defect. That one person chooses to engage in sexual acts with a consenting person of the same gender does not legitimize homosexuality, and society should not be shamed into accepting a behaviour that is unacceptable to the majority of Canadians.

Television, Film, Movies, and books are now portraying homosexual activity as acceptable, everyday lifestyle. In our parliaments, homosexuals are pushing laws to promote their cause, trampling on the rights of the majority. Human Rights Commissions have taken up homosexual's cause and have wrongly labeled opponents of homosexuality as bigots and supporters of hate crimes. Provincial courts decided homosexuality is an acceptable behaviour and failing to recognize homosexual relations as a union and any opposition is discriminatory and violates our Charter of Rights and Freedoms. Politicians have now equated opposition to homosexuality as a violation of one's human rights. Governments have not challenged the court rulings and are actively accommodating the homosexuals, with complete disregard for the rights of the majority. The National government abdicated its responsibility by not challenging lower court rulings to the Supreme Court of Canada. Provincial governments also abdicated their responsibility by not invoking the "notwithstanding" clause in our constitution. We are on the verge of legitimizing homosexual relationship in the form of a marriage or civil union contrary to the laws surrounding the sanctity of male/female relationship and marriage. It is illegal for a man to have more than one wife and a woman to have more than one husband. This is also a product of the sanctity of male/female relationship and marriage of our Christian culture and our religious beliefs. If we are prepared to legitimize homosexual relationships, them we must also be prepared to legitimize polygamy and allow a man to have more than one wife and a woman to have more than one husband.

We must carefully consider the implications, on our society, of legitimizing homosexuality with a civil union or marriage. Do we want to teach our children "Donny has two mothers or two fathers"? We know this is a lie; one can never have two mothers or fathers. Do we want homosexual teachers educating our children on the merits of homosexuality over our genetically programmed sexuality of a man and a woman complimenting each other? We cannot, no should we prevent, homosexual acts between adults. As a society, we have the authority and obligation to promote the views of the majority, if only our leaders would act accordingly. We must never allow homosexual marriages or civil unions and cease the practice of allowing homosexual couples adopting and raising children. Homosexuals accuse opponents of using fear and hate to keep them closeted; to deny them the right to marry and benefits accorded to married persons; to deny their human rights. These are the same fears and hate homosexuals direct at their opponents. Proponents of homosexuality have seized upon society's acceptance of genetic disorder as the cause in many disabilities plaguing the human race. This attempt is politically motivated and aimed at convincing politicians and lawmakers to accept, and more positively respond to, a lifestyle that homosexuals claim is genetically determined and unchangeable.

The majority must standup and prevent the colonization of basic human instinct, and the destruction of the family, with the learned actions and choices of homosexual lifestyle.

Prostitution

In relation to sex, prostitution is an act or practice of engaging in sex acts for hire. This does not only apply to women selling, and men, buying sexual favours, although this is the most common form of prostitution. Women have been known to buy sexual favours from men, although possibly to a lesser extent than men buying sexual favours from women do. As homosexual acts are becoming more prevalent and accepted in our society, we are learning of more and more men and women selling themselves to members of the same gender. Prostitution is not really considered a crime in Canada. Over time, it has been considered an immoral behaviour contrary to the laws of God. At times, prostitutes have been considered victims of the sex trade. Sex for money is taboo in our society. Consequently, our laws are enforced using communication and procurement avenues. If a man was to say to a woman "I would like to have sex with you and I'll pay you $100," and she agreed, that would be communicating and procuring sex for money. That is against the

Criminal Code. However if the question was rephrased to "May I take you out for dinner and a movie and then go to bed with you?" with the woman answering "yes", followed by the dinner and movie and sex, that would not be communicating and procuring sex for money. What is the difference here? Both traded sexual favours, yet the first pair would be subjected to criminal charges and the second pair would not.

Many aspects of the sex trade must be made illegal and the perpetrators severely punished. Firstly, society must determine the age where it is acceptable for a person, male, and female, to engage in sexual acts. It is my view it should be the age society considers the Age of Majority, twenty years as recommended in One Canada. Many in the sex trade are teenagers that are being exploited or otherwise forced to perform sexual acts for money, out of personal financial need or by coercion by others. Adults are forced into prostitution by others seeking to profit from the sex trade. Drugs are used as a controlling tool to ensure many unwilling participants in the sex trade remain servants and slaves of the sex trade. In parts of the world, children as young as eight years are being forced to perform sexual acts while parents and governments turn a blind eye.

Any action to force another to engage in any sexual acts must be a criminal offence with the severity of the punishment increasing, as the age of the victim gets younger. Sex for money between a willing man and woman should not be a crime. However, engaging in actions, where one party is on public property, to get customers must be a punishable offence. A public place would be defined as a place where any member of the general population would be permitted to attend with or without an entrance fee. There are many risks involved in an uncontrolled sex for money trade. Most notable is sexually transmitted diseases and sex slaves. The sex trade is an industry that requires corporate and health regulations. The corporate regulation will ensure a stream of revenue to pay for government services and the health regulations will ensure and environment free from diseases via a regimen of regular health tests. Regulations will ensure properly constituted businesses are established in the Sex industry and would allow sex trade professionals protection of labour laws and the right to organize a workers union if they so desire. By properly regulating the sex industry, government will ensure an avenue exists to reduce exploitation of mostly women in the sex industry. While we are on the verge of legalizing homosexual marriages, we prosecute consenting men and women for trading sex between them, for money.

Department of the Attorney General

The Attorney General, chief law officer of the Executive Council and the Senate, represents the government in any legal action brought against it. The Attorney General shall ensure the intent of government legislations are defended in the courts and its defenses are in the best interest of the majority of the people.

Department of Canadian Heritage

Heritage is important qualities, customs, and traditions that have been part of a society for a very long time with which its members identify. Analyses of heritage reveal who we were at specific points in time. Over the past five hundred years, an abundance of cultures created Canada. That heritage is our guide to the future and to be truly Canadian we must learn and understand our heritage so that we may create a better future. Development of a heritage curriculum for inclusion in our education system is of paramount importance to building the best place and greatest nation on earth to live.

Department of Communication

Communication, whether by pictograph, hand and smoke signals, or electronic audio and video transmissions, is the most important tool to understanding each other. The message and, manner in which, we communicate affects our development as a people and stability as a nation. Communicating a message of guns, gangs, violence, killings, racism, or hate will transform these behaviours into accepted societal standards. Why then do we allow behaviours, in films and video games and on television, which would break the law, were they to be conducted in our streets? Portrayed as 'artistic freedoms" or "freedom of the press" we allow our children to be desensitized to violence, rape, killings, hooliganism, gangsters and robbery portrayed by television, films, computer and video games. Bloody fights in some professional sports are marketed as part of the game. Early Childhood Development professional have expressed concerns with the amount and level of violence in computer and video games. Parents are concerned about the overly aggressive nature of children, and bullying which is now an increasing part of school life. We should never allow portrayal of any action or imagery in our media and on our store shelves that virtually violate our laws.

Broadcast Television

Stretching across six time zones and with a time difference of four and one half hours, some Canadians go to bed while others are arriving home from a hard day's work. A national system of broadcasting should be created that allows Newfoundlanders to watch programs from British Columbia, giving British Colombians' perspective on the news, and vice versa. The Canadian Broadcasting Corporation have attempted this feat, but with the savaging of its budget over the several years, barely manages to provide the minimum coverage. The National government should instruct the Canadian Radio Television Commission (CRTC) to create a set of three hundred and fifty local stations, whose carriage is mandated on cable and satellite delivery systems. The mandate of local stations will be to ensure its broadcasting content is least 60% directly relates to the area served; 25% for national programming and the remaining 15%

covering international programming. Local stations will establish a connection between the peoples of each region and form an important link for Canadians to learn and understand about the distinctness of each region. Local stations will allow for the promotion of local athletes, actors, theater productions, and cultural events. The three hundred and fifty local stations, with the division of programming into a majority local and equal national and international programming will complement the existing national television networks whose broadcasting focus will be on national and international events. The CRTC shall also license at least ten regional super stations whose mandate is broadcasting 40% Canadian content, 30% local content and 30% international content.

The Canadian Broadcasting Corporation should be the vehicle to promote Canadian culture and artists in Canadian-made movies, films, documentaries, sports history, and geography. Public, government-owned broadcasting is very essential to the development of a country and to the dissemination of government and public service information. The public broadcaster has a duty to ensure the views of qualified political parties receive equal broadcast transmission time, regardless of parties' financial position. Four separate CBC and Radio-Canada television broadcasting services should be created, CBC LeisureWorld, CBC SportsWorld, CBC Education, and CBC NewsWorld. CBC Radio would complement the four CBC television networks, in both official languages. An international version of the CBC Radio and Television are vital communication medium to promote Canada to the world. The government must increase funding to Radio Canada International and ensure CBC Television is carried on major satellite and cable system around the world.

CBC LeisureWorld

CBC LeisureWorld would concentrate on Culture, History, Drama, Movies, Plays, Comedies, Documentaries, and Entertainment programming. Advertising-free and having 90% Canadian content, CBC LeisureWorld will be the primary broadcast medium to promote Canada. Canadian content defined as having 50% of the leading roles played by Canadians, 50% of the production takes place on Canadian soil and 50% of the production crew are Canadians residents. CBC LeisureWorld would be supported through government financing and public donations.

CBC SportsWorld

CBC SportsWorld, created by either purchasing a major Canadian all-sports network or from the ground up would concentrate on live and recorded sporting events, sports related movies, sports comedy, profiles of Canadian athletes as well leading world athletes and world events. Separating sports into its own channel will afford more airtime to amateur and professional sports currently having lower exposure. Semi- and professional soccer, women's hockey, rugby, and lacrosse, are growing sports requiring national exposure. Our university, collegiate, and high school athletes need more national exposure to the population and advertisers. The mandate of CBC SportsWorld would be to concentrate on sporting events in which Canadian teams and individual Canadians are participants. Funding for CBC SportsWorld would be derived from a nominal subscription fee, public funds and advertising revenues.

CBC Education

Educational television plays an important part in our lives. Programs for children and adults on one dedicated educational channel, supplemented by privately broadcasted educational programming, would greatly benefit the population. Funding would be entirely from public funds. CBC Education would be created by amalgamating existing provincial educational authorities.

CBC NewsWorld

CBC NewsWorld exists today, and is a premiere source of the latest news, documentaries, and features from all parts of the world. In 1994, the CBC created NewsWorld International (NWI) available in a few foreign countries, including the USA. In 2000, CBC sold NWI to an American company, with a contract to operate NWI on behalf of its new American owners. The paltry onetime cash infusion the CBC received from the sale of NewsWorld International pales in comparison to the role NWI could have played for Canada around the world. It is imperative for the CBC to broadcast television signal in other countries of the world. The National government must create CBC International to promote Canada, its people, culture, and a Canadian perspective of international news and current events. Funding for CBC International would be derived from public funds and advertising revenues.

To be a leader in the world, our voices and images must be heard and seen around the world. The best images and voices are those of CBC Television (English), Radio Canada (French), CBC Radio and Radio Canada International.

Cable and Satellite Systems

The growth of cable and satellite television industry is such that more than 90% of Canadian households have access to both. The television antenna mounted on roof-tops to receive over-the-air signals are mostly used in rural areas and are very important access points for many Canadian to stay informed and entertained by television. Subscription to satellite and cable television systems with digital set-top boxes, offers a multitude of channels for our viewing pleasures. Many more will come as technology makes it possible to compress and transmit many more channels in the same bandwidth as a single television channel. As a subscriber to cable and satellite television systems, I am disappointed with the Canadian content on both systems which seems to concentrate on providing its subscribers with a multitude of American channels, a majority of which carry the same programming. Having 300 channels to choose from is really like having a television reception system with about 50 channels. Despite programming similarity across many channels, I enjoy watching local programs from many Canadian cities, available on the Canadian satellite system. Many Canadians use legally available satellite systems equipment to pirate American satellite programming at the expense of Canadian satellite systems and to a lesser extent, our cable television systems. These American systems do not carry Canadian television stations, depriving the pirates of quality Canadian programming and further indoctrinating the pirates to the American way of life. If receiving and decrypting American satellite programming with modified equipment is illegal, why is it legal to sell the equipment in Canadian stores or allowed across our borders by our customs agents?

Television is a medium that allows us to visit far away places, attend classes, and entertain ourselves from the comfort of our homes. What better way to travel to Ireland, Jamaica, Barbados, Switzerland, South Africa, Russia, India, Japan, China and all the other countries of the world than to have local television channels available on our satellite and cable television systems. The satellite and cable television system owners and the CRTC must rise to the challenge of offering uncensored broadcasts from as many countries into Canadian homes. In One Canada, the first five hundred channels on satellite and cable television systems would be reserved for local and national Canadian broadcasters. Cable and satellite providers would be allowed to carry as many network and specialty channels from any part of the world their subscribers' desire.

Canadian Film and Television Productions Fund

The Canadian Film and Television Production Fund would collect a broadcasting fee equal to five percent of the total bill per subscriber, per month, from each delivery system. Monies collected would be allocated to all aspects of the development and productions of film and television reflecting Canadian culture and values, including multicultural productions.

National Telephone System

Each day, the telephone system grows at an overwhelming rate with the addition of voice and fax telephone numbers for home and business, voice and fax telephone for small office/home office, pagers, cellular telephones, and telephone numbers for bus stops and so on. With our busy lives, many parents provide cellular phones and pagers to children as young as twelve years. The demand will continue to grow, necessitating the introduction of new area codes, splitting large urban areas into two or more area codes. Since the mid 1990's, new area codes are being added to large urban areas in an "overlay" manner. Requesting a new telephone number may mean having a new area code in your house to go with the existing telephone number. Eventually this will cause confusion and prevent people from identifying the area served by any particular code. Canada is part of the North American Numbering Plan (NANP) with the United States of America, its territories, and Caribbean islands. The NAPN assigned a country code of "1" to this entire region, stretching from Trinidad and Tobago in the Eastern Caribbean Sea and the Cayman Islands in the west and Canada and the USA in the north-south direction. An area code used in one country, precludes its use in any of the other countries. It is time Canada move away from the constraints of sharing one common country code with the U. S. A., its territories and the Caribbean Islands.

Having its own, unique country code affords Canada the assignment of at least two telephone areas codes to each of the three hundred and fifty regions. However, with a lesser population, some jurisdiction may require a single area code for many years into the future. Larger metropolitan areas may require more than two area codes to meet its needs. The uniform assignment of area code beginning in Newfoundland and increasing in number until Vancouver Island is assigned the largest number area code would be far better than the random and haphazard assignment of area codes than begs the question " Where is area code XXX"?. With twenty nine million telephone numbers in Canada, in a numbering system having the capacity to serve billions of telephone numbers, never again would corporations and individuals be required to change area codes, update stationery, inform friends, or learn new dialing instructions, all at our own expense. The telephone companies would also save on advertising costs to promote new area codes and dialing instructions.

One of the biggest problems plaguing the public switched telephone system is unsolicited telephone calls from polling organization, research companies, charities and marketers and a host of other organizations. While some of these calls are beneficial to our society, the majority are unwanted, unwelcome, a nuisance and an invasion of our privacy. Since we pay for our telephone service, we must have the right to restrict or authorize the use of, and access to, our telephone number. We have the right not to be harassed or solicited by any unwanted caller. All unsolicited calls must be banned and a national registry must be established wherein the owner of the telephone number grants permission for unsolicited calls, by category and by individual organization.

Post Mail

Annually, Canada Post delivers tens of hundreds of millions pieces of mail across Canada. Using its six character postal codes, mail is identified for delivery to a particular city block or rural area. In the 1980's, Canada Post, a corporation owned by our federal government, embarked on a program to create two classes of customers. The first-class, the full service customer, is in existing residential areas and business parks who continue to receive door-to-door mail delivery. The second-class, partial service customers, are in newer residential neighbourhoods and corporate business parks who must pickup mail from "super mailboxes" located some distance from their residence or business location. For the same price of postage, one set of customers receives full service and another receives partial service. No longer are Canada Post customers equal, despite paying the same price for a postage stamp. Canada Post has partially disenfranchised many Canadians. This practice must stop and full door-to-door delivery of mail must be restored, affording equal treatment to all Canadians.

Unsolicited Mail

A flood of unsolicited mail reaches our door or super mail boxes every day. Referred to as "junk mail," these generally unwanted mail causes frustration and revulsion amongst many in the population. At Super Mailboxes these junk mail collects as garbage as recipients ditch the pieces instead of taking them home. Junk mail uses valuable natural resources and creates paper waste, some of which ends up in landfill and some recycled. Direct mail marketers purchase Canada Post's list of postal addresses specifically for the purpose of sending unsolicited addressed mail. If we choose to stop this unsolicited mail, we must contact direct mail marketers and request removal of our addresses from the list. Since Canada Post needs the revenue generated, its practice of selling its mailing address list to direct marketers must be augmented with a provision mandating Canada Post to remove the name of any person not wishing unsolicited, addressed mail delivery. There must also be provisions to accommodate persons wishing unsolicited addressed mail from specified industry sector. Canada Post's practice of discount rate for bulk mail must also cease, with full postage applied to all mail. It is unthinkable that a corporation owned by our government, by us, encourages and participates in activities that aggravates and harasses us and even offers a price discount to the perpetrators.

National Voice and Data Distribution Conduit

Fiber Optic Cable

A top priority for the government should be the installation of fiber optic cable to every house in Canada by the year 2015. We live in a society where our technological advances have reconditioned our expectations to be instantaneous. We want results now, if not yesterday. The technological and information permeated our lives, providing us with instant access to almost everything. The Internet has so deeply woven itself into our lives the need for faster and reliable access to accurate information becomes more critical every day. The internet offers our government an opportunity to deliver a greater amount of services to the people, and at significantly reduced costs. The delivery of Government Services On-Line will require high-speed internet access. The best medium for data transmission is Fiber Optic cables, with it almost unlimited bandwidth facilitating movement of large volumes of voice and data at very high speeds.

In our cities, towns, villages and hamlets, the distribution of television and telephone services are by separate, competing mediums and technologies. Fiber optic technology will allow the creation of a national distribution "conduit" for voice and data. The almost unlimited bandwidth of fiber optics affords the construction of a national distribution medium. Digital technologies afford transmission of "packets" along the transmission medium, even if those packets belong to television, telephone and data control signals. Internet technology is shifting to Internet Protocol Version Six (IPv6) which offers about 340 Undecillion individual digital addresses (340×10^{36}, or 340 followed by 36 zeros). This vast number of Internet Protocol (IP) addresses affords every person on the planet to have a large assignment of IP addresses for their personal use. Assigning a group of 1000 dedicated IP addresses, with many left over for governments and corporations of all sizes would be more than adequate for every person on the planet.

This vast pool of Internet Addresses, when combined with a fiber optic national distribution medium, allows a "connected" Canadian the flexibility to assign her one thousand individual addresses to every piece of electrical/electronic equipment owned. Imagine every automobile, television, radio, VCR, DVD player, computer, refrigerator, stove, air conditioner, MP3 player, PDA, telephone, security system, and light fixture having a unique address and connected to the internet. The automation and communications possibilities are endless. Imagine being able to transfer large computer files between friends, relatives, and corporations, without the limits imposed by the local Internet Service Provider. Imagine being able to receive the latest traffic, news and weather information on your car computer display. Imagine being able to create a peer-to-peer network with friends and relatives around the block and across the world. Imagine being able to stream movies and songs to your entertainment system, commercial free, and at a time of ones' choosing. Imagine being able to adjust the air conditioner or furnace temperature from your office. Imagine being able to view surveillance videos of your home and cottage from your car, office or your friends place. Imaging the possibilities of a 'connected" Canadian! While some of these functions are possible, it is not very easy for the technologically challenged Canadian to implement, nor is it cost effective.

The greatest mass deployment of technology is the internet, becoming a lifeline for many sectors of our economy. The ability to send electronic mails, messages and files have tremendously increased our ability to communicate. Connection to the internet varies from slow dialup telephone lines and high-speed telephone and cable services to business-class high capacity fiber optic cable. The time is upon us to create a national fiber optic distribution conduit allowing digital voice and data transmission, over the same medium, to all homes and businesses, replacing telephone and cable wires and other wireless modes of transmission. With a national distribution conduit, telephone, television and data-acquisition service providers would "pipe" their respective signals into the single conduit for delivery to their subscribers. Billing for services would be by the Gigabits (Gb) received, paying for only the services used and the amount used. We now pay flat fees for cable and satellite television channels, telephone services and features, bundled in a manner to extract as much fees from the consumer even though we may not need or rarely watch some television channels or the telephone sits idle for many hours of each day.

Our electricity, water and natural gas providers use people to walk from house to house and business to business to physically read their respective metering devices. With a national fiber optic conduit, and the development of electronic metering devices, computers located in every business and home will carry out these functions. The resultant savings would benefit the customer and the meter reading personnel would be retrained for a skilled position, such a installing, and repairing metering devices.

The government, telephone, and cable companies will ask the inevitable question of who owns the national distribution conduit. My suggestion is it will be a cooperative ownership by the three parties as a non-profit venture, paid for from user fees billed to those customer "piping" information into the conduit.

Department of Consumer Relations

"The more the data banks record about each one of us, the less we exist." *Marshall McLuhan*

It seems there is a computer database for everything these days. Collecting information is not a new phenomenon. Once, data banks were filing cabinets with paper copy of completed forms and reports, with accessibility more tedious than today's data banks. Modern data banks are electronic is nature and are readily accessible. With a few keystrokes, ones entire life may pop up on a computer display in an instant. In these computer data banks we no longer exists a persons but mere account numbers with our names attached as the account holder. The impersonal nature of data banks makes us less significant as persons and elevates the computer to a more prominent place. Users believe the computer data banks, even if the information is inaccurate. More and more merchants want our names, home and e-mail addresses, and home and business telephone numbers, for their records. The gathered information is stored in computer data banks somewhere, maybe in Canada or some third world country, where labour is cheap and security is not a big concern. Nevertheless, each of us exists in a multitude of databases at the banks, credit card companies, electronics stores, department stores, car dealerships, government agencies and probably in many unknown places in Canada and around the world. Our news media have reported stolen computers and hard drives containing extremely private client information. Private and confidential information have been posted on corporate web sites. The multitudes of databases pose a privacy risk for every one of us. There is no need for a merchant to know our personal information when buying a telephone jack, washing machine, or stereo equipment. If paying by cash, the transaction only needs a receipt for the purchase. If payment is by credit/debit card, our personal information is already in the credit/debit card company's database. If we choose to pay by cheque, where the risk of "Not Sufficient Funds," NSF, is a real possibility, then the merchant have an expectation to garner detailed personal information in the event a cheque is returned NSF.

We must stop the wanton collection of personal and private information by anyone and everyone. We must also centralize record keeping of personal and private information in a National Central Records, under tight military-style security, supervised by watchful eye of a Privacy Commissioner. Persons and organizations needing personal and private information on any person must make a formal request to National Central Records, detailing the reason for the request and providing proof of authorized access to the requested person's private and confidential files. Personal and private information represent the integrity of the person and must be kept confidential at all times, requiring most stringent of safeguards. No matter how stringent the security measures, failures in security are ultimately the responsibility of a human being. Unfortunately, the weakest link in any security measure is the human factor, with our greatest security failures traceable to human errors, negligence, and criminal activity. If charged with protecting data, we must be vigilant in that regard. As corporations try to increase their profits, more and more work is outsourced to low wage foreign countries, increasing the security risk to our private information. Identity security will be a major problem for many years into the future. Identity theft is recognized as the fastest growing crime in the technologically advanced countries of Europe, North America, and the Far East. Identity theft will become the greatest security threat to our country and our person. Imagine a foreign power or terrorist organization determined to inflict harm on another nation. Infiltration of that nation will be much easier after assuming the identity of a local person. Reducing the chances of identity theft require simple steps that are mostly under our direct control. I have taken the following steps to reduce the chances of my identity being compromised. To people or organizations for which I am unfamiliar, I never give out personal information such as home address, home and cell telephone numbers, driver's license number, credit card number, bank name and branch, spouse and children names. I do not provide my Social Insurance Number to any one, except to a Government of Canada department. I do not make purchases with personal cheque, preferring to use credit cards. I minimize my use of bank machines. Everyday I scan my computer for spyware and keyboard loggers and delete any detected. (Spyware are little pieces of software download unto a computer unbeknownst to the computer user/owner. Keyboard loggers record keystrokes. Both might send information to someone, somewhere in the world to use for whatever purpose suits them). I shred all paper that has any of my personal information on them. I also shred any documents, including envelopes, that identifies companies or individuals with whom I have business or personal relations. I recognize it is impossible to go through life without providing some personal information to a merchant or supplier of services. It is a question of trust versus need. Each time I am confronted with request for personal information I ask myself two questions. Do I trust the person or company requesting the information? Do I really need the goods or services in exchange for my personal information? If I have doubts, I walk away.

Personal information is your integrity. Protect it at all cost.

If a person successfully assumes another persons identity, he will be able to access bank accounts, driver's record, and credit history and have access every other piece of personal information; in effect, the identity thief will become the person whose identity was stolen. The perpetrator will steal or destroy the integrity of the person whose identity was stolen.

As consumers of government services, we will be subjected to much more detailed personal information gathering by the tentacles of government, under the guise of personal safety and national security. Government will force us to surrender personal information if we want to use government services. Large corporations are following the lead of government, demanding detailed personal information from us, and forcing us to sign service contracts before providing services. Governments will force corporations to collect personal information on their clients and turn that information over to the government. As **government is the most powerful institution in the land, capable of creating everything except life and destroying everything including life,** we will have no choice but to turn over our personal information to government and its surrogates. Those of us who believe in the teachings of the Holy Bible will recall a prediction in Revelations about the number 666, the mark of the Beast. In essence, the Bible teaches every person will need this number to live on Earth. Is surrendering our personal information to government the beginnings of the mark of the Beast? If we surrender our freedom and rights in the name of safety and security, it will lead to the prediction in the Holy Bible's Book of Revelations.

Consumer Credit Reports

I remember my parents purchasing goods at the village shop, usually paying in cash. I also remember my mother asking the shopkeeper to "trust" her with food, noticing she would receive the food and not giving the shopkeeper any money in return. I also noticed other villagers were not as lucky as the shopkeeper would not "trust" them with food. My mother later explained that the "trust" is her owing money for the food because she did not have the money to pay at the time we needed food. She explained payment to the shopkeeper would be made on her payday. The other villagers were not able to "trust" food because they did not pay on time, for the last time they were "trusted" with food.

After I began to work in Jamaica, I discovered the "lay-away" plan to purchase a product, pay for it over time, while the merchant held the product until full payment was received. I paid cash for most of my purchases, with one or two on lay-away. I never knew what a credit card was, until I came to Canada. When I came to Canada, my co-workers told me to "build up your credit" as a means of "establishing" myself in Canada. Baffled, I finally asked about credit from one who became my friend. I learned that buying a car, furniture, or renting an apartment all depended on one's credit history. I got into the game; I had my first store credit card, then I began to "collect" credit cards and had more than twenty in my first three years in Canada. My wife made her purchases by cheque and I made mine on credit cards. I preferred credit cards because I did not like supplying every merchant with my personal information, usually written on the back of the cheque. Like many other Canadians, I am aware of the collection of financial information by organizations. However, I was never aware of the quantity, quality, and type of the information collected, and the retention period for the collected information. Neither was I aware that this information was collected, recorded and stored in Canada and possible in foreign countries. Recently, I discovered the Credit Bureau, the people who collect, store, and disseminate Canadians' personal financial information. These people provide merchants with a credit report on all Canadians and rate our "credit worthiness" by giving each of us "Credit Score."

Every month we pay our bills, mostly on time, and maybe a few late throughout the year and, for the most part, have a good sense of our creditworthiness. Therefore, we applied for a personal or business loan and was turned down, or given the published interest rate, once approved. Your credit history and credit score may be the answer. Credit Bureaus maintain files on our financial private lives. Lenders have access to, and use, this information to asses our suitability as a client. Every time you open a bank account, apply for a loan, or a credit card, take advantage of one of these "buy now, pay later" promotions, unbeknownst to you, an enquiry is made to the Credit Bureaus. Every time you are late in making a loan, mortgage, or credit card payment, a report is filed with the credit bureaus. These enquiries and reports are kept on file for as long as seven years. The number of enquiries, reports and the amount of debt you carry are factors affecting your Credit Score, the number lenders consider an objective measure of your creditworthiness. A higher Credit Score may get you a lower interest rate loan, with the converse being true for a poor Credit Score. Your credit file is window on the financial side of your life. The accuracy of its contents may be the difference of thousands of dollars in your bank account. It is your responsibility to ensure it is very accurate. Companies making enquiries and filing reports on you do so at their pleasure, without notifying you. They make mistakes and these mistakes will stay in your credit file for seven years, if not corrected by you. Federal and Provincial laws provide for you to receive a free credit report from credit bureaus if you make the request in writing and provide acceptable photo identification. The two largest credit bureaus in Canada are Equifax and Trans Union. Look them up in your telephone book or the internet. Request your free credit report by mail or receive instant access via the internet, for a fee.

Federal and provincial privacy and credit reporting regulations grant consumers important rights regarding credit files and related matters. Generally, by law you have the right to:

- Know the contents of your credit file;

- Know the sources, nature, and substance of the information collected by the credit reporting agency;
- Have unverifiable information deleted from your file;
- Receive a free copy of your credit file by mail;
- Have derogatory, credit-related information deleted after seven years;
- Review your credit file in person ;
- Know who has received your credit file in the past year
- Review your file in the presence of a person of your choosing;
- Add a brief written statement as a part of your credit file;
- Have disputed information investigated at your request;
- Know the name and address of the credit reporting agency responsible for preparing a credit file used to make a decision regarding your credit, insurance, or employment.

Get your report twice each year, carefully review, and confirm this information:

- Name (including prefix and suffix) , must match your birth certificate name or current legal name;
- Address (former and current);
- Social Insurance Number (if available);
- Date of Birth;
- All accounts listed as your own are currently, or was once, a valid account in your name;
- Outstanding balances/limits on the accounts are correct, as of the dates shown;
- Payment histories are correct;
- Derogatory credit information has been deleted after seven years;

- All listed inquiries are legitimate.

It is a very time consuming task to correct or eradicate any inaccurate information in your credit file. In this regard, we get very little help from our government on such an important part of our lives.

The government must require every person or corporation making an enquiry on our credit file to notify us in writing within thirty days of making the enquiry, and stating the reason for the enquiry. The government must further require every company submitting a report to credit bureaus to notify the consumer at least thirty days in advance of any such report being submitted. The consumer will have the option to file a written objection to the report and attempt to remedy any negative effects.

One of the few areas of life for which we have direct control is our financial affairs. We must be in control of our borrowing, and spending and, as everything in life, knowledge, and its use, is power and "Prevention is better than Cure." We must ensure:

1. bills are paid on time;
2. manage debt to income ratio (debt payment must be less than 20% of your take-home pay);
3. limit the number of loan and credit card application you submit;
4. Guard your personal information such as Social Insurance Number, bank account and credit card numbers;
5. Give information on a "Need to Know" basis;
6. Check your credit file at least twice each year.

Our society is built on consumerism. The more goods and services consumed, the more profits earned and maybe the more jobs created. Or so the thinking goes. In reality, our consumerism is based on indebtedness. Traditionally, our power to purchase was based on the size of our pay cheque. As loans, credit cards and lines of credit became more readily available and acceptable our means to "buy now and pay later" became greater. Thus our purchasing power was artificially increased and our consumer mentality was change from "I must save to buy it" to "I must have it now."

Our newfound borrowing and purchasing power distorted our reality and perspectives on our net worth as individuals. Borrowing has become the most important aspect of our lives. Our burrowing has artificially driven up the prices for homes, automobiles, household appliances, post secondary education and almost every other product or services we purchase. Our increased debt is a mortgage on future income and lifestyle.

The importance of Credit History and Credit Score in ones Quality of Life cannot be overemphasized. As we move into a society governed by fear and deceit, supplemented by denials, greed and selfishness any and every conceivable statistics will be manipulated to extract more money from the majority. A case in point, some automobile insurance companies in the United States of America is using Credit History/Credit Score to determine insurance premiums. As reported in the Toronto Star of August 26th and 28th, 2004, a number of Canadian automobile insurance companies have copied the American method and others are studying the method and observing the current practitioners. Canadians tend to copy American business practices, typically about five years after implementation in America. We can be sure, if there is profit to be made, the insurance companies will all start using our credit score and credit history as an important determining factor in setting premiums, not just for automobile, but could include life, supplemental health, critical illness, disability, and all forms of insurance.

Buy Now before the Price Goes Up

This is the cleverest marketing slogan I have seen and heard since I have been making my own decisions to purchase goods and services. Inflation conditioned us to believe prices will always go up. We are consumers and we fear price increases. We are workers and we fear job losses. Both have the potential to be devastating to our lives and that of our families. These fears are the basis for "Buy now before the price goes up" sales pitch. In reality, if you do not buy now, the price will most certainly go down. Price increases are a result of consumers bidding against one another for goods and services. The marketplace is one big auction where every purchaser is bidding against other purchasers. It is the goal of every seller to separate the buyer from his money, regardless of what is for sale. It is our responsibility to part with our monies when we are receiving good value for money. My father-in-law once told his grandsons "You must love money, to keep money," explaining it is not the love of the currency itself, but the love of the feeling of freedom and independence money brings. Our society conditions us to believe the accumulation of money is evil, must be shunned and spent as soon as we have a little. We are taught at an early age to Buy, Buy, Buy. This ploy ensures we spend all we earn, never saving for the "rainy day" ahead. Who will help if we run out of money? Not the companies that helped us spend our money. Certainly not the financial institutions or the government, they are always looking to take money off us. Maybe you will get some help from a company looking to make a few bucks from our predicament, hitting us harder, financially, while we are down, most often with no other place to turn for help.

Save as much of your money as possible, you are ultimately responsible for your financial position.

Being a shrewd consumer requires vigilance in getting good value for price paid in relation to ones earnings. We must define our needs and wants. A need is something we cannot live without; food, clothing, shelter, water, heat, electricity, a television set and a radio are items I consider a "need." Everything else is a "want" and that we could live without them. You must determine you needs and that of your family, then decide how much money you will spend and how much will be saved for the rainy day that is coming. If you fall in the 70% of employees struggling to make ends meet, you have very little chance of receiving a substantial pay raise from your employer as consumer prices rise. Therefore, your only recourse as a consumer is to reduce spending, and if we collectively reduce our purchases, and be frugal whenever we purchase goods and services, prices will inevitably fall. The economic circle will be affected with the majority of prices falling to match our reduced spending.

Coupons, Mail-Rebates, and Bill Credits

The schemes merchants will create to separate us from our money are very creative and tempting. Often a coupon will get us a discount at the cash register, giving us instant savings on our purchase. How much did it cost the merchant to print, promote and process the discount coupon? Did these expenses not increase the retail cost of the good or service? Did the consumer benefit or was this a part of a merchant's ploy to increase sales? The mail-in rebate is an extremely clever scheme that puts the onus on the purchaser to take an action to ensure they receive the price discount. Have you ever bought a product that had a $1.00 mail-in rebate? How much time, envelope and stamp did it cost you to send in that mail-in rebate request? Have you ever bought a product and forgotten to mail in the "mail-in" rebate claim form? I consider the mail-in rebate a clever means of increasing the product retail price, and revenues for merchants, in a backhanded manner that forces the buyer to request the rebate. Failing to request the rebate means we paid a higher price than the merchant believe his product is actually worth. Is just "marketing" or is it dishonesty on the merchants' part?

Another cleaver ploy is the "bill credit" which forces us to spend our money up front, and then wait a long period before the credit appears on our bills. The bill credit forces us to spend additional monies with a merchant to ensure we received the promised credit. Have you purchased products and waited months for the credit to appear on your bill. How many times did you call the merchant to enquire why the credit did not appear on your current bill? For the months you did not get the bill-credit, the merchant earned interest on your money and kept it for himself! Isn't that clever? The merchant forced us to buy something from him, take our money, kept it for a few months, earned interest and then gave us a rebate. It did not cost the merchant very much to get our business because we put up the money in the first place. With many merchants and tens of thousands of buyers participating in the discount coupons, mail-in rebate and bill-credit programs, it is not hard to see the merchants smiling all the way to the bank. With the "mail-in" rebate and "bill-credit" schemes, merchants know that a large percentage of purchasers will simply forget or neglect to take action to receive the promised benefits in a timely manner.

The Department of Consumer Relations must ensure these three practices are discontinued. Merchants offering price discounts on their products must do so at the cash register and not force buyers to take any other action to obtain these discounts. The buyer will realize an instant savings that may be applied to additional purchases, further stimulating the economy.

Department of Education

> "Keep your thoughts positive because your thoughts become your words; Keep your words positive because your words become your behaviours; Keep your behaviours positive because your behaviours become your habits;
> Keep your habits positive because your habits become your values; Keep your values positive because your values become your destiny." *Mohandas K. Gandhi*

Education is a right, not a privilege, yet our governments treat post-secondary education a luxury. Looking back on the past quarter century, we see the massive reduction in funding for educational intuitions and social services as government wrestle with runaway costs and deficits. At the same time, the generous tax advantages enjoyed by large corporations, wealthy Canadians and foreigners have increased. While our bloated bureaucracy is the main cause of runaway government costs and deficits, governments have been unwilling to reduce costs by amalgamating levels of government, reduce the bureaucracy and grant greater autonomy to local governments to manage their affairs. Why do governments reduce financial support for education and social services? Is it because there is a lack of money or is there a sinister motive? Is it possible the governments attack these areas as a means of keeping the populace un-educated, poor and ignorant, and susceptible to corporate and political manipulation? There is sinister motive for reducing funding to education and social services. By reducing financial support to social services and education, the government creates a large pool of lower educated, poor, desperate, and disadvantaged people who are easy prey for labour exploitation. Our society teaches that the accumulation of "chattels and laurels" is a measure of ones success. Therefore, our motivation is to accumulate as much wealth as possible in our lifetime. Inevitably, the accumulation of wealth is a direct result of exploitation, which is achieved by having a steady supply of cheap labour. By reducing the funding of education and social services, the government creates this steady supply of cheap labour. What benefit is there to the government keeping a large number of the population average or lower educated? A lower educated person might be susceptible to manipulation and most likely gullible to the electioneering promises of politicians. Our politicians have promised "to wrestle inflation to the ground," to give us "mortgage interest tax deductibility", ensure there are "jobs, jobs, jobs" for everyone, proclaimed "free trade is the cause of my life", and to "eliminate the deficit and debt". Many politicians were elected after making these banal promises. We did not wrestle inflation to the ground. Even after promising jobs, jobs, jobs, Canada suffered high unemployment rates. Deficits exist in our governments and many are carrying crippling debts. How much longer are we prepared to accept the winning political party claiming the "cupboard is bare," "the books are in worse shape than we anticipated?"

Creating a multitude of lower educated people benefits the politicians as it is easier for them to "pull the wool over the eyes" of the lower educated population, who might be incapable of properly analyzing election promises. Political spin-doctors perceive less educated people as more gullible, easily manipulated and capable of reprogramming to accept the views of the manipulator. The strength of a people and of a country is reflected in the educational level of the populace. Sadly, education has been allowed to deteriorate in the past quarter century. Post secondary education is rapidly becoming a luxury item for many Canadians. Those who brave the ever-rising costs, end up with a debt load as large as a home mortgage. Post secondary education is gradually being priced out of reach of the majority and one day will be the domain of the wealthy and very wealthy. Two levels of government will free up billions of dollars, allowing more money for quality day-care, kindergarten, primary, secondary and post secondary education.

Our educational infrastructure and their providers are constantly asked to provide more services, educate more students and with less money. The result is the elimination or curtailment of programs deemed of no benefit to society. Extra-curricular activities have seen the most severe cuts or elimination. Sports and arts programs have suffered. The collection of programs making up these two areas contributes the most to our cultural and physical wellbeing. The intellectual capacity of an individual is a direct result of his physical fitness and appreciation of his culture. We have sacrificed the health and culture of all Canadians by continuing to spend on bloated bureaucracy instead of the betterment of our people and education in particular. Healthy children are athletic, technical, and artistic by nature. Only as children get older do their individual disciplines become evident and nurtured into a vocational field to earn a living as an adult. At the younger ages, sports and the arts offers a fun and exciting way to teach children the basics of life; appreciation and understanding of our humanity, discipline, respect for people and property, competition, camaraderie, cooperation and deportment. Getting children interested in sports and exercise, at an early age, increase the chances of a continued physical fitness regimen into adulthood. A physical activity regimen, lasting for about sixty years, would increase the health of our people, increasing their contribution to society, allowing our "golden citizens" a sense of belonging to our society. A physical activity regimen would help to reduce our national healthcare cost. Our educational institutions must concentrate on the development of every person, as a whole. We cannot train each person to be an engineer, doctor, dentist, computer technician, or other professional while ignoring financial management and people skills. In teaching our people to manage their finances, we will increase their financial stability and that of the country. In teaching our people the art of interacting with his fellow man, we increase cooperation with and respect for one other, probably with a corresponding decrease in crime and assault of a bodily nature.

Life Long Learning

Many of us have never been back to high school, college or university since we graduated. Leaving the educational system between ages nineteen and twenty-eight, we spend our entire life in the work force. For some forty years, while the world around us changed every day, we plod along in our job, caught up with "living life," whether to the fullest or just eking out a living. Institutions of higher learning provide us with a basic education to enter the real and working world. After we enter the real world, we are retrained for a job, where gain our experiences from real life situations, which changes from day to day, year to year, and decade to decade. We change as society change; we discover ourselves as our knowledge grows. We do not stop learning at the time we graduated from secondary or post-secondary institutions, although, from time to time, we might attend classes in job-specific subject matter. Therefore, we must embark on a path of life-long learning for our own benefit. Ever dynamic, our world is uncertain at best. Plant closings, declining profits, divorce, and death change our lives as they occur. A path of life-long learning will afford us the opportunity to prepare for the future while we earn our keep from a job. If we constantly remember that a job is a means to earn money required to live the life we want, them we must not allow that job to be the "ball and chain" of our life. We must diversify our education and lifestyle in order to succeed and enjoy life to the fullest. Learning another profession; invest and manage our finances or get a hobby by learning something new, could all enrich our lives from graduation through retirement to death.

Educational Development

A person's self-esteem is a product of the environment created from the earnings of a good paying job, having a loving family, caring friends good health, self-respect and freedom. It is human nature to form a matrimonial relationship with another of the opposite gender. Inevitably, procreation produces offspring, creating a larger family with increased expenses. An able-bodied person, unable to provide the necessities of life for himself and his family will be at the mercy of governments of the day, predatory employers and accumulated debt. The lack of self-esteem usually cause a person to spiral down to the depths of poverty and depression, putting further demand on our social and healthcare services. Knowledge, and its use, is the key to improving ones lot in life. A post-secondary education is a right, not a privilege, even though it will not guarantee good citizenship. We must provide our people with the educational opportunities and tools needed to build and lead a productive and rewarding life. The cost to educate a person will be less in the long-term when compared to providing social services to those who are unable to provide for themselves, over many decades. The new national government must embark upon a program to build many more universities and colleges. Canada is home to many prestigious universities; Universities of Toronto, McGill, and McMaster, Simon Fraser, are probably the most well known. Building more community colleges would ensure there is a place for every student that wishes to pursue post secondary education in Canada

The National government must expand the national cadet program as a means of providing good education to our children. Every secondary school, college and university would become a cadet core station, with civilian and military instructors implementing the cadet program and core values. Every Canadian between the ages of 12 and 25 years would be encouraged to join one of the Air, Army and Naval cadet corps. In return, the government would provide one year of free post secondary education to every cadet who spends two consecutives years in a cadet corps. The cadet corps builds character by teaching discipline, respect for people and property, competition, camaraderie, cooperation, deportment, and other traits of good citizenship. A national volunteer program, called Katamivik, offers Canadians the opportunity to earn a small sum of money in return for nine months of service to communities across Canada. From all accounts, this program has been beneficial to the volunteer and the areas served. We should support the expansion of this program to complement the cadet program.

Our provincial and federal governments offer loans and grants to eligible students. In 2000-2001, the federal government, through the Canada Student Loan Program, provided $1.57 billion to over 350,000 eligible students. The Canada Study Grant provided $81 million to over 55,000 eligible students in the same period. Both parents and students recipients are all grateful for the assistance of the various student loans and grant programs as it eases the financial burden in the pursuit of post secondary education. As education becomes more expensive, more and more student will be carrying very large debts upon graduation. Not only are students graduating with a degree or diploma, they receive a loan contract as part of their graduation.

We are having a major problem with children in the ten to eighteen year age groups, and adults up to twenty-five years, many having lost respect for adults, property and generally lack of discipline. The breakdown of moral values has resulted in more crime, more divorces, increased number of adults and children in poverty. Governments are spending billions on policing, prisons, the courts, and community supervision, yet continuing its massive financial cutbacks to social and educational services that will keep people from a life of poverty and crime. We must arrest these problems in their incubating stages, at the impressionable ages of a child's life. Arresting these problems will reduce disrespect, crime, vandalism, and encourage respect for life and property and the many traits of gentlemanly behaviour. In the longer term, the taxpayers will save billions of dollars, society will be safer, and people will be more caring.

Teachers

> **"A teacher affects eternity; he can never tell where his influence stops."** *Henry Brooks Adams*

A teacher is one that teaches, especially one whose occupation is to instruct, to guide, instruct by precept, example, or experience. Remembering my days in primary and secondary school and in college, teachers were influential in my life. They were someone I looked up to and respected even if I doubted their commitment to the students. Sometimes I even took their preaching as gospel. Back in Jamaica, a math teacher once told our class if they were going to be engineers, they must be the best and if they were going to be thieves, they must be the best. That was 1970, and as a fifteen year old, that made a significant impression on me; you must be the best at everything you do.

Once upon a time, teachers were well respected in schools and the community for their knowledge of subject matter and dedication to the children and to the profession. Times have changed. Teachers do not get the respect they deserve from parents, children and politicians and, along with their unions, have become the punching bag for every constituency. Blamed for all the ills of society, failing to educate our children and instilling values in them, teachers are perceived as overpaid, under-worked and having too much time off during the summer. With tens of thousands of teachers across our land, there are definitely many bad apples, as it is with every profession and every facet of society. Yet, we do not blame the legal profession for a few sleazy lawyers or the medical profession for a few botched operations by incompetent surgeons. Why then, do we lump all teachers into same category of incompetent, over-paid, and under-worked professionals?

As parents, we perceive teachers working from nine to three, five days a week. We assume teachers work six hours each day, five days each week for forty weeks each year. For this very easy job, teachers receive vacation at Christmas, Easter and all summer. We work eight to twelve hours each day, five days each week for about fifty weeks each year. For this yearly service to our employer, we receive two to four week's vacation while teachers receive about twelve weeks. We are jealous of a profession we perceive as having it easy at our expense; after all, we pay their wages and benefits negotiated by strong unions. We consider teaching as secure job, protected by greedy unions and we, therefore, become more jealous of teachers as our employers over-burden us with more work, threaten layoff and reduced wages as we struggle to make ends meet without a dental or drug benefit plan. Our politicians, sensing a vote to gain, play to our misconceptions of the teaching profession. Governments constantly attack teachers as the cause of all our societal and educational problems. Inadequate spaces in our schools, colleges and university are a direct result of chronic under funding from governments and politicians who want to create a steady supply of under-educated people. Throwing money at the problem, as opposition politicians have suggested, will not solve the problem. The first part of solving the problems in our educational system is to create the environment where teachers are respected and trusted and are able to work in dignity. That well placed trust and respect and feeling of self-worth will bring back the dedication of teachers and the commitment to teach our children.

While our children were in school, I hoped their teachers were guiding them as I would when they were under my personal supervision.

Teachers have the attention of our children more hours per day than parents do. We should be treating teachers with dignity and holding them in high regard. This one profession, more than any other, moulds the lives of our most impressionable members of society. With their influences over our children, teachers prepare children to be the adults and leaders of tomorrow, affecting the development and direction of our society for generations to come. Teachers are one of the most important people in the life of a child and in our lives as parents. Children believe teachers! Remember your child coming home, saying "Mommy, teacher said…" Do your remember yourself saying the same phrase to your parents? The importance of teachers in our lives has not changed since man figured out how to teach something to his fellow man.

What should we be teaching our Children?

National Curriculum

Canada has become what we have taught our people over generations and will become whatever we teach descendants in generations to come. Our culture is representative of our teaching in the classroom, television programming, books and music and the arts. Education, being under provincial jurisdiction, does not have a national curriculum. Even within provinces, the educational curriculum differs between school boards. We must create a national curriculum of core subjects consisting of English, French, Math, Physical Education, Science, Environment, History, Politics, Arts and Social Studies for primary and secondary scholars, constituting 70% of a full curriculum. From region to region, Canada is a diverse country, requiring the remaining 30% of the curriculum be customized to meet regional requirements. A partially customized curriculum would allow regions to add additional language studies, farming, tourism and any other subjects deemed in the best interest of the regional population. With a national curriculum, every child and teacher would be assessed equally and that a certificate awarded in one region has the same value as one awarded in any of the other regions. Schools must become part of a Learning Campus, the centre of the community served and be a Centre of Activity.

The School - A Centre of Activity

A school should be the centre of activity in a child's education. We have segregated our primary schools, secondary schools, libraries, community centres, arenas and recreational fields (soccer, baseball etc) from one another. We should move to create a community spirit by building schools, libraries, community centres, arenas, and recreational fields in the same structure and on the same compound, creating a learning campus. Visitors and patrons would eventually develop a cooperative community relationship as opposed to the detached community atmosphere of today. Schools should be an incubator of the real world. We cannot continue to shelter our children from the realities of life. Today, schools are nothing more than fashion runways for the major apparel, makeup and jewelry brands. Schoolchildren should be wearing uniforms to school at all ages with deportment and behavioral rules strictly enforced. In the real world, dress codes are in effect and failure to comply will result in disciplinary action and even dismissal or some other form of covert management action that will stifle one's career growth.

The School Day

Our school system was devised long ago, in a time when people and society depended on agriculture to earn a living. Our school breaks coincide with the Christian holidays and the agricultural harvest. The school year must be readjusted to balance the ratio of schooling days to holiday breaks. The long summer break at the primary, secondary and post secondary levels is not conducive to continued educational development. Schooling must be continuous all-year round with a two-week break for every six weeks of schooling. With longer school days and year-round schooling, we must relieve the any stress that may be placed upon our students shortening the schooling periods and having shorter and more frequent breaks. Our Christian society would suggest that the first break be the last week of December and the first week of January every year, followed by six weeks of schooling, then a two-week break; the cycle repeating for the entire year. While there are many summer camps and child care services available, parents of younger children are constantly struggling to engage their children in meaningful endevours during the long summer breaks. By shortening the schooling period and having frequent breaks, we will allow our students to relieve stress throughout the year and reinvigorate themselves, quite possibly increasing their capacity to learn. We will also allow parents more opportunities to take vacations with their children, themed to winter, spring, summer and fall. In many corporations, prime vacation periods are rare and often enjoyed by the most senior employees, forcing many junior employees to be on vacation while their children are in school.

The hours of school should be increased to nine hours at the primary and secondary levels, with the school day segmented into three mandatory sessions of three-hours and one optional session of extra-curricular activities, according to the following schedule:

1. 8:00AM to 11:00AM – Classroom instructions;
2. 11:00AM to 2:00PM - Students report to teacher-supervised study rooms for lunch; complete or receive help with homework assignments.
3. 2:00PM to 5:00PM – Classroom instructions.
4. 4:00PM to 9:00PM - Extra curricular activities that includes sports,

drama, Cadet Core commitments, and community volunteer service. With a majority of families having two working parents, and single parenting on the rise, parents are away from home for more than twelve hours each day, with some working on weekends. Parents, having themselves been out of school for many years, are challenged by the assignments brought home by their children. It is necessary to provide a supervised environment for children to receive expert help with homework assignments. Therefore, the allocation of three hours at the middle third of the school day, from 11:00AM to 2:00PM, will provide expert help for students; provide supervised area for completion of assignments and for having lunch. Teachers from all disciplines would be assigned to providing help and supervision as needed.

Religious education is very important in building society and the development of our moral values. Intrinsic to humankind is a set of core values. Humankind is full of reference points that form our core values; love and hate, good or bad, rich and poor, religious and atheists, and so on. Our reference points are learned from our interaction with others. Our understanding and application of these core values, and effect on people, will determine our behaviour in society. As our core values mature, they become our ethics. Whether we are devout believers in a deity or atheists, our ethics is our guidepost to living a wonderful life. The multitudes of denominations in Canada require religious choice in educational institutions. Having publicly funded denominational schools is not in the best interest of equality in One Canada. The interaction of children of different faiths in a school setting will create a better understanding of each other's faiths and begin to tear down the walls of bigotry. It is imperative we allow for students and teachers to conduct religious educational classes in the middle three-hour period. The right to choose was granted to man by God and it is our choice to worship him or not.

In the adult world, we are constantly rushing to get to and from our jobs. Some of us face long commute by private cars or public transit. Our rushed day at work continues as we take our children to after school recreational programs from hockey to soccer, swimming to ballet, and dancing to karate. Evening programs offered at every school will help to reduce our rushed life after a hard day at work.

Financial Management

Woefully lacking in our education system is Financial Management courses. I am referring to information on setting up bank accounts and the different types available; credit cards and their uses; interest rates and their effects, managing debt and calculating and knowing ones financial position. The banks are very good at sending out credit card information and application to high school, college, and university graduates, many of whom are graduating with large student loans. My sons, upon graduation from high school, received credit card information and application forms, touting low introductory interest rates that were about quarter the normal interest rate on credit cards. Both our sons considered applying for these credit cards, however, with good counseling from their parents, they chose the "pay-as-you" method to purchases their goods and services. The credit card issuers are merely trying to "rope in" young and impressionable into a life of revolving credit financing, to increase their profits. Business is business and profit is their motive, however the manner they may make it.

While our society is geared to consumption and to encouraging people to buy, buy, buy, debt is stifling prosperity of our people. The marketing hype of "buy today before the price goes up" or "why wait until tomorrow, when you can have it today" or "buy now, pay later" have caught most of us in the never-ending cycle of debt. I am no stranger to being suckered by the marketing hype. Not all debts are bad. Financial advisors will tell you there are good debts, such as mortgage on the house and investment loans. They will also tell you credit card debt, car loans, furniture loans, and vacation loans are all bad debts to carry. These messages need to be taught to our children before they graduate from high school, giving them the knowledge to borrow money, responsibly. When debt-laden, we are unable to purchase new goods and services, as most of our pay cheque services the current debt. Teaching our children to responsibly borrow and manage debt will not risk economic growth but will sustain it.

Sexual Health

Should we be promoting sex education in our educational institutions and mass media? Is it society's responsibility or is it the responsibility of parents to teach sexual health to their children and for us as adults to learn on our own? Sex education is not about intercourse alone, as some of my adult friends think. It is about teaching young adults to appreciate their biological reality and their interaction with members of the opposite gender. Many adults would benefit from sexual health education. Sex education must encompass sexuality and sexual health. Sexual health education is concerned with the well-being of individuals and is what we ought to teach in our educational institutions. Sexuality is the central aspect about being human and being the highest form of intelligent of life on Earth. Sexuality is sexual intercourse; gender identities and roles in society; sexual preference and orientation. Sexual health is about understanding human reproduction and its responsibilities, eroticism, pleasure, and intimacy. We experience our sexuality through thoughts, fantasies, desires and behaviours. Our culture, a composition of our beliefs, attitudes, values, practices, roles, and relationships, offer an insight into our sexuality. Our sexual experiences and expressions of sexuality are influenced by the interaction of physiological and biological capabilities, psychological well being, social status, economic position, cultural heritage, racial group, religious beliefs and spiritual factors. Our sexual health is defined by our physical, emotional, and mental state, combined with the absence of disease, dysfunction, or infirmity. Excellent sexual health requires a positive and respectful approach to sexuality and sexual relationships, pleasurable and safe sexual experiences, free of coercion, discrimination, and violence. The sexual health of individuals demands personal and societal responsibilities that are affected by each other and by the social environment in which we live. If we are to educate our people about vibrant, sexual health, we must engage educational, medical, public health, social welfare, and legal systems in our society. In our culturally diverse society, sex education is an almost sacred topic. One's personal, family, religious, and social values are very important factors in understanding and making decisions about sexual behaviour. Expressions of sexuality in some cultures are forbidden, while it is openly discussed in others. Sexual health education will equip our maturing adults with knowledge of teenage pregnancies, sexual transmitted diseases, family planning and the merits, or not, of prostitution.

As we approach the teenage years, our bodies are undergoing rapid physical, biological, and mental changes. The changes in our young bodies produce additional feelings we are unaccustomed to, causing stress in our lives. Puberty brings about the biggest change in our bodies as it prepares for adulthood and its primary role, reproduction. Human reproduction and child rearing demands long-term personal and financial commitments, therefore, it is important for society to educate teenagers about pregnancies and the long-term consequences.

Teenage Pregnancy

Teenage pregnancies are a sad fact of everyday life, and every effort must be made to reduce its occurrence. Sexual health education at the beginning teen years is of utmost importance to stemming the continued increase in teenage pregnancies. Stressing unwanted pregnancies and sexually transmitted diseases, a mandated curriculum would teach teenagers to understand their bodies, the sexual emotions of puberty, safer sexual intercourse, the reproductive process and a planned family life. We will not be able to achieve 100% abstinence from sexual intercourse in teenage and young adult years. It is therefore imperative that sexual health education continue throughout high school and into college and university. An unwanted pregnancy could destroy the life of a young woman, while having little effect on a young man's life. Too often, the mother is left to fend for herself and the baby she did not create alone. Often, society must pick up the cost of maintenance of mother and child through social assistance. Quite possibly, mother and child live in poverty, the mother never having the financial resources to continue her education after childbirth. This could be the beginning of perpetual adult and child poverty!

Political Education

What would politics be without people? Politics is not something that just happens! It is a plan by determined men and women working to make social and political changes. Politics is people working to change legislation and other official political matters. Politics is ordinary people wanting to make a difference in their lives and in the lives of their fellow citizens, working with government from outside the Legislatures to get the results they want. Politics is activism by people determined to make change happen. If the activism goes against the "establishment," the activists are branded "a special interest group" with a stigma attached to the group. Often special interest groups are dismissed as "saber rattlers" and 'shit disturbers" garnering little respect from the population, no matter ho noble the cause. The most effective and widely accepted special interest group is the political party, most famous for practicing politics.

> **People are not separate from the political process, they *are* the political process!**

"I don't care about politics," "I am not interested in politicians," "Politicians are all liars," "I don't trust politicians," and "I am not joining a political party." If I received a Loonie for every time I heard one of these phrases, I would be a very rich man today. Politics control every aspect of our life. Governments are formed out of political parties whose sole purpose for being is to control and manipulate people and processes. It is therefore imperative that all of us, from our early teenage years to the end of our lives, learn and understand politics, its machinations and its effect on our lives. "From the bedroom to the boardroom, politics affect everything we do," is a message I have tried to convey to every Canadian I have come across. Our civic duty is not just to vote at election time; it is also to make sure we get the best person to manage public affairs. Politics is a duty to country and to our fellow man. Political education must include an understanding of our constitution, Charter of Rights and Freedoms, judicial system and the operation of governments and political parties. Our lack of in-depth knowledge of politics and importance of governments in our lives are the causes of our present dilemma of political apathy and ever decreasing voter turnout at the polls.

Cultural Education

Bigotry and stereotypes are products of ignorance and fear. Millennia ago, First Peoples culture and languages in North America numbered more than fifty. Every country, and even regions within a country, has their own cultures. Canada has welcomed millions of immigrants, with their rich and varied cultures and religions, to add to the English, French and First People's culture. Culture is not just food, dancing and clothing. It is an understanding of the meaning behind the dress, dance, food, religion, and belief of a people. In our western culture, we wear a suit and tie to signify authority and professionalism, while a $1500 bottle of wine or a particular make of automobile signifying affluence. Christmas and Easter are symbols of Christian religious beliefs. Other cultures have equally important symbolisms and we must learn, understand and respect them. It is imperative we provide cultural education to our children from early ages through college and university. Bigotry, stereotype, and prejudices are learned from our peers and our parents. The defeat of these vices rests squarely in education at a young age.

History

"History is the version of past events that people have decided to agree upon." *Napoleon Bonaparte, Born 1769 – Died 1821, (Napoleon I, Emperor of the French, 1804-1814)*

The rich history of Canada and its First Peoples must be taught in all our schools. History (His Story or Her Story) is a record of the author's perception of events witnessed; was passed by word of mouth, written text or pictograph. History is composed of facts and hearsay. History has been recorded to bolster a cause, demean and demoralize the vanquished, and to provoke and antagonize the foes of the author and his supporters. History has been used to control a people; to prolong a conflict and to sow the seeds of hatred and reverence. Recorded history have been debated, revisited and revised as newer information come to our attention. History must never be forgotten nor should it be our hitching post. History must be our guidepost to the future.

"Those who do not remember the past are condemned to repeat it." *George Santayana, (Born 1863 – Died 11952), Philosopher, poet, literary and cultural critic.*

In our zeal to be politically correct, some amongst us have called for revising Canadian history to correct a wrong, or to remedy an injustice. Others have called for apologies for the wrongs of society on their kin of the past. Still others have demanded financial compensation for actions of past peoples and governments. We must strive to learn from and prevent a repeat of history. Canadian history must be taught in all our primary and secondary schools. Today's Canadians need not apologize to, or compensate, anyone for the actions of governments of the past, if the government was acting within the laws of the day. Where past governments broke the law or engaged in deceptive practices, governments must compensate and apologize to the wronged, no matter how long ago the occurrence.

Social Studies

As a twenty-year soccer coach and a community volunteer for more than thirty years, I have witnessed the deterioration of social interaction between one another, at very early ages. In our busy lives, time for socializing have been significantly reduced, transforming us into an extremely competitive, "me-first" society of increasingly selfish people, putting more strains on social relationships. The advent of longer parental work hours and commutes, advanced technologies such as computers, the internet and video games have pushed adults and children out of communal gatherings and into separate "spaces." This "cocooning" forces a reduction in social interaction and increases anti-social behaviour, now being blamed for increased bullying and violence among school-aged children. We have redefined obnoxious behaviour as an "in-your-face" attitude and have now accepted that type of behaviour as a mark of a "go-getter," when in reality the person displaying this "in-your-face" attitude is nothing more than a bully. Our isolation from one another brings a sense of total individuality, diminishing or eliminating our societal reference points, forcing us to believe our actions, opinions and thoughts are always correct, regardless of the boarder societal values. Our individuality is paramount to defining our values, our goals and aspirations. Our communal spirit and deeds project our commitment to society. We cannot live a life of total individuality nor can we display never ending communal spirit. A balanced combination of individuality and communal spirit and deeds will propel our nation to being the Greatest Country on Earth.

Age of Majority

When does a human being become an adult? Is it at fourteen years old, when consensual sexual intercourse is legal? In some provinces, a sixteen-year-old person is legally eligible to apply for a driver's permit; maybe that is the age of majority. Could it be at eighteen years old when they are able to vote? In some jurisdiction, a nineteen-year-old person may legally consume alcohol. This, the age we are permitted to be intoxicated, must be the age of majority. A rental car company will not rent a car to person under the age of twenty-five. Regardless of the jurisdiction one lives in, the myriad of laws restricting the age at which a human being may engage in a variety of activities is unacceptable and creates a bureaucracy that is difficult to manage. Why is that we have enough sense to vote at eighteen years but not have enough to drink alcohol? Is it because it gets the politicians in touch with young impressionable minds that might be gullible to political promises and thus voting for the politicians? At fourteen years, teenagers do not know enough about Sexual health, and about their developing bodies to engage in safe sexual intercourse, yet is it legal to have sex at fourteen years; a time when an unwanted pregnancy could destroy the young lives of the teenage mother father, their parents and, more importantly, the child.

Equality means setting the age of majority at the same level for all activities, whether it is engaging in sex acts, consuming alcohol, or voting. While young people mature at different ages, it would be prudent to set the age of majority to begin, and achieving adulthood, on the twenty birthday of a person, the end of the of the teenage years. Just as there is no definitive age when children become a youths, there is not a magic age when a teenager switches over to adulthood. With careful nurturing of parents, a teenager grows into adulthood over many years. As a parent, watching my children and their friends grow into young adults I concluded that twenty is probably the best Age of Majority indicator. Observing our friends children grow up further convinces me this is the correct age for the demarcation between adulthood and Youth, just as I believe thirteen years is the correct demarcation children and youths. My observations indicate young adults in the neighbourhood of age twenty years change their youthful perspective and begin to mature and develop an awareness and acceptance of responsibility for their actions as they transform themselves into adulthood. At twenty years old, sex, marriage, alcohol consumption, having a full driver's license and voting would be permitted. It would not be in the best interest of society to criminalizing any of these activities; however, parents must be held accountable, at a higher level of responsibility, for the actions of their children, while these children are below the age of twenty years.

Youth offenders are treated with "kid gloves," receiving a "slap on the wrist" as punishment for crimes committed. Our perception is the law gives "carte blanche" to teenagers to commit crimes. The punishment for the commission of a crime should be independent of age, with the sentence fitting the severity of the crime, the age of the offender and restitution to society. When a person dies at the hands of a teenager, is the loss of life any less significant than the death caused by an adult?

Are the effects of illegal drugs less dangerous when sold by a teenager versus and adult? When a group of teenagers swarms another and beat him to death, is the pain any less for the victims' friends and families and is the death any less significant? It is time to give back the responsibility of parenting to those that brought the offspring into this world. It is time to let parents and guardians take responsibility for children upbringing and moral education, with the help and support of social services, our educational and judicial systems.

The role of government will be to intervene whenever it is determined that a child is the subject of physical and psychological abuse. The government would also intervene if the parents and guardians were failing to provide the necessities of life, including education. The government would work with the parents and guardians to minimize the risk to the child, with removing the child as a last resort. The government must not become the parent because the biological or legal guardians have failed to provide good parenting.

Department of Energy

Energy is available in many different forms on our Earth. The First Law of Thermodynamics states energy cannot be created or destroyed only transformed into other forms of energy. Our world depends on many forms of energy to power the many devices that keep us warm in winter, cool in the summer, gives us light at night, control the flow of traffic that moves us from place to place and keep us in touch with one another. Every product produced today requires some form of energy, whether stored in a battery, delivered by wires or stored in a combustible agent. Our greatest source of energy is derived from fossil fuels, is non-renewable and is a major source of pollution of our planet. Over billions of years, Earth's natural processes created fossil fuel in many parts of the world. Canada is blessed with the largest fossil fuel reserves, mostly tied up in the tar sands of Alberta. Compared to other forms of energy, this very affordable energy produces many harmful gases that are killing our environment. The national government must fund the development of a better, more efficient means of burning fossil fuel in the internal combustion engine, despite the implications on job losses in the oil and gas sector. We have been afraid of job losses in these sectors because their very effective lobby groups have convinced politicians that environmentally safe energy sources will wreak havoc on the national economy. The history of mechanization and industrialization of the world is littered with job displacements from one sector to the other. As new technologies afford us greater efficiencies, jobs were displaced in one sector as jobs were created in other emerging sectors. The displacements of jobs in the fossil fuel energy sector will be no different from those of the late 19th and early 20th centuries. Various governments around the world have forced the price of fossil fuel upward as a means of generating huge profits for themselves. In Canada, we adopted a policy of selling our own fossil fuel to our people at world prices. By driving up the price of fossil fuel energy, produced in our own backyard, we have forced upwards the price of all our Canadian manufactured products. Our fossil fuel energy should be sold to Canadians at prices significantly lower than when sold to other countries of the world as our tax dollars help to finance the search for, and development of new oil fields.

Solar, Wind and Hydro Energy

An abundance of energy is available from the natural sources. The sun, the largest nuclear reactor in our solar system, wind and water sustained life on our planet for billions of years. We have made tremendous progress in development of devices that aids in harnessing these natural resources converting them into electrical power to meet or needs. The rapid pace of introduction of electrically operated devices is outpacing our capacity to generate electricity. Fossil fuels, nuclear fission reaction, and hydroelectric systems generate the bulk of electrical power required to power our way of life. We must replace fossil fuels and nuclear with more natural and renewable energies. In the process, we will reduce pollutants and hazardous materials on our Earth.

Fusion Energy

The sun is a gigantic fusion reactor, generating immeasurable amounts of energy. Nuclear Fusion is the forced combination of atoms in a nuclear reaction in which nuclei combine to form more massive nuclei, releasing energy. Unfortunately, we have not yet succeeded in controlling Nuclear Fusion to make a reactor that will generate more energy than it takes to run, though billions of dollars have been spent in the attempt. We must re-double our efforts and increase funding for research and development of fusion, solar and wind energy, by imposing a research and development charge on present forms on non-renewable energy.

Geothermal Energy

Solar, thermo-chemical and radiogenic energy are all forms of "Thermal" energy. The Earth is a hot planet and a huge storehouse of energy, internally produced by radiogenic heat and externally from the sun. Near the centre of the earth, temperatures are theorized in the thousands of degrees Celsius. The Earth's energy, called "Geothermal Energy," is visible when a volcano or geyser erupts or hot spring bubbles out of the ground. Geo-thermal energy has recreational and commercial uses. Canada's geothermal resources are located mostly in British Columbia and Alberta. An abundance of geothermal energy could contribute significantly to our energy security and provide us with a green "energy source" that could potentially reduce our contribution to greenhouse gas emissions. Canada needs to develop a much larger strategy to explore for geothermal energy to generate electricity and possibly for individual heating and cooling of homes.

Department of Environment

From the dawn of time, man lived in one or another form of shelter. These shelters protected him from the sun, rain and falling objects. The first man, according to the Bible, lived in the Garden of Eden. That may have been millions of years ago. There were no houses or huts for him to live in; he might have lived under a tree or in a cave. Since the creation of the first man, there has been evidence that people have lived in caves, mud huts, some form of solid, sturdy structures, up to the skyscrapers of today. Long before the arrival of man, there was one consistent "shelter" protecting the Earth from the dangers of the Sun. That shelter is the environment – our Biosphere. This home, invisible in parts, has protected and sustained all living things on our planet. The eco-system ensures we have clean, fresh and pure water, poison-free food, the right amounts of rainfall and sunshine to sustain life. The eco-system rejuvenates itself, without the interference of man. It has done so for billions of years and it has done it efficiently and very well. It will continue to protect itself, despite the destructive forces of man, and even out attempts to "help" Mother Nature protect itself. We live in a very large biosphere, a closed-loop system regulated by its creator to maintain life indefinitely. Every living being, from snakes and rats to fishes, birds, trees and humans, depend on the survival of the other being. The Biosphere will be here long after man has disappeared from the Earth, and we will if we continue to abuse the Earth.

Before the industrial revolution, man balanced his need to cultivate the land and construct houses, with the need to protect his "heavenly shelter." Sadly, man became greedy, uncaring and downright hostile to the environment. We dump chemicals into our water supply and on land; pumped billions of tons of pollutants into the air; and clear-cut our forests; all in the name of amassing financial wealth. Less oxygenation, more carbon dioxide and soil erosion, followed by floods and mudslides are the results of clear-cutting forests. The long-term effects of many chemical in use are barely known, yet we continue to use them to generate profits for corporations, without regard to the health of our people and the living organisms of our biosphere. Only now have we begun to see the long-term effects of chemicals whose uses began generations ago, long after corporations took their profits and gone on to develop other chemicals on the road to making even more profits. We have built buildings and roads over most of our arable lands; readjusted and even interrupted the flow of rivers and streams; pumped tonnes of carbon dioxide into the atmosphere, creating a greenhouse effect that is causing a rise in temperature on the planet. We have damaged the ozone layer and are at risk of being fried by ultra-violet rays from the sun. In the pursuit of accumulation massive financial wealth, and the desire in controlling people's lives, we have been abusing Mother Nature, the creator and owner of the environment. The Earth and its biosphere are on loan to us for the time we are alive; it is on a perpetual loan, to present and future inhabitants of the planet. We are charged with protecting the environment and are its custodians for our descendants. We have an obligation to ensure the protection of our "shelter" with the same vigour as we would protect our own individual homes. The parched lands of tropical regions, massive floods and ice storms in the northern hemisphere, ever more powerful hurricanes of the Caribbean, typhoons of the East, huge forest fires, and greater and more frequent earthquakes around the world are testaments to the damage man has inflicted on the Earth. All this have resulted in the loss of tens of thousand of lives, loss of billions of dollars in property and most importantly of all, and the loss of dreams of living a good, prosperous and peaceful life for many, mostly poorer, people of the world. Scientists have reported an increase in temperature on the planet, threatening the frozen polar ice caps. On our present destructive course, global warming will continue for several decades to come resulting in gradual melting of the ice caps. The inevitable rise in water levels in the low-lying areas of the earth will displace millions of people. In areas of the world, much farmland is at or near sea or ocean level. As the polar caps melt, these farmlands will gradually be flooded with saltwater, rendering them useless. The alarm have been raised about the large hole in the ozone layer, which, if continues to grow, will expose us to ultraviolet radiation, leading to increased skin cancer. The waters in rivers and oceans, and the rays of the sun will become a source of fear for inhabitants of the planet. Water is the sustenance of life. Scientific probes to other planets have first searched for water, as proof life might have existed on those planets. Water is scarce and is our most valuable resource that is too easily and frequently squandered. Less than three percent of the Earth's water is fresh, with only three-thousandths available in liquid form, the remainder locked up in glaciers or icecaps or is deep in the earth. Fresh, clean water is scarce and getting more so as we pollute our rivers, lakes, and accessible groundwater, with biological, chemical, and radioactive contaminants. The Industrial Revolution created machinery and mass production methods enabling the exploitation of the seemingly endless supply of natural resources. After one hundred and fifty years of industrializing the world, we are faced with an abundance of people and labour-saving machinery, but diminishing natural resources. The people of the planet have plundered its natural resources and violated its natural laws all in the name of acquiring financial wealth. Over billions of years, the Earth created an abundance of natural resources and ecological systems that provide vital life-support services to all living things. The natural resources are of immense economic value; water sustains life, trees produce wood to build our houses, fossil fuels power our cars and electricity generators. Many of these natural resources and the entire ecological system are literally priceless, with some having no known substitutes.

Current business practices and public policies, based entirely on greed and the need to accumulate massive wealth, are being degraded and liquidated by the wasteful use of energy, materials, water, fiber, topsoil, and ecosystems. Business practices have superseded the need to conserve energy and protect the biosphere.

Only after the last tree has been cut down, only after the last river has been poisoned, only after the last fish has been caught, only then will you realize that money cannot be eaten.
Cree Indian prophecy.

The Earth is the only known biosphere, which we could call Biosphere I, in our solar system. Humans cannot duplicate the functions of Biosphere I, and is completely incapable of replacing any of the Earth's natural resources from our manufacturing capabilities or brought here from another planet. The importance of the Earth's biosphere was clearly demonstrated by man himself in 1991–92 when the $200-million man-made Biosphere II project in Arizona was unable to sustain breathable air for eight people. From the beginning of time Earth - Biosphere I – have been performing this task daily for an increasing number of people, presently nearing six billion, free of charge.

With the advent of the Industrial Revolution, we have abused the environment and its owner, Mother Nature. While there have been minor attempts to reverse some of these abuses, generally, the abuses have continued at an increasing pace. Mother Nature, patient and very forgiving to date, will protect itself from the destructive habits of man. Mother Nature has begun its onslaught on man, returning the abuse it suffered, protecting itself by destroying humans, with ice storms, hurricanes, monsoons, earthquakes, fires, flooding and mudslides. That protection will become more fervent in the decades and centuries to come. The pain and suffering inflicted on us by the devastating forces of Mother Nature are directly related to our abuse of her. Mother

Nature will prevail and the sooner we realize this, the more we will enjoy this beautiful planet. Mother Nature is GOD and GOD will not let us destroy the planet and its inhabitants in our relentless pursuit of instant gratification and accumulation of financial wealth, fueled by our greed and selfishness.

The Kyoto Protocol on Climate change is a starting point in protecting the environment. While Canada and many countries have ratified the Kyoto Protocol, the USA has refused, preferring to continue polluting the environment for short-term accumulation of wealth by corporations and political supporters. We will never be able to develop a protocol or agreement that is acceptable to all; we will only be able to compromise our interests into a minimum set of specifications, which might still not be acceptable to all. Job losses will occur in industries affected by measures to halt the adverse effects of climate change, and just like the industrial revolution, many more jobs will be created in new industries born to address climate change.

Department of Finance

Taxation

Tax - a charge, usually of money, imposed by authority on persons or property for public purposes; a sum levied on members of an organization to defray expenses; a heavy demand.

Income Tax is a tax on the net income of an individual or a business.

In various names and forms, taxation has been the prerogative of Pharaohs, Caesars, Kings, Queens, Presidents, and Parliaments and even members of organized crime. The Income Tax is an early nineteenth century invention in times of emergency to address an economic necessity.

The Birth of Canadian Income Tax

From Confederation until World War I, the major sources of Federal revenue were postal rates, customs and excise taxes and other minor sources. In response to the escalating cost of World War I, Britain and the United States of America introduced a tax on income to help pay these costs. The cost of war for a young Canada was also escalating and draining the resources of Canada. Responding to the imposition of Income Tax on citizens of Britain and the United States of America, Canadian Finance Minister Sir Thomas White, on April 24, 1917, told the House of Commons "it would appear to me that income tax should not be resorted to (in Canada)." Yet on July 25, 1917, the House went into "Committee of the Whole" and Sir Thomas White, Minister of Finance and Representative for Leeds told the committee:

"Mr. Chairman, I desire today to lay before this committee proposals for a national measure of income taxation. Hitherto we have relied upon duties of customs and of excise, postal rates and other miscellaneous sources of revenue. Canada has been, and will continue during the lifetime of those present today, to be a country inviting immigration. I have, therefore, thought it desirable that we should not be known to the outside world as a country of heavy individual taxation. We are, however, confronted with grave conditions arising out of the war. The time has arrived when we must resort to direct taxation. I am confident, Mr. Chairman, that the people of Canada, whose patriotism during this war has been so often and so nobly proven, will, in light of present conditions, which call for it, cheerfully accept the burden and the sacrifice of this additional taxation.

We cannot see very far ahead in these days. We do not know how long this war will last. We do not know what the attitude of the people of this country will be upon the many questions, social, industrial, financial, and fiscal. Therefore, I have placed no time limit upon this measure but merely have placed upon Hansard the suggestion that, a year or two after the war is over, the measure should be reviewed by the minister of finance of the day, with a view of judging whether it is suitable to the conditions which then prevail".

Calling the introduction of income taxation a "War Tax Upon Income," Finance Minister White hoped his tax would not much past the end of the war. Opposition Finance critic Alexander MacLean had his doubts, *"I have no doubt that once we have embarked upon it, the judgment of the country will be that it should be continued for many years to come."*

The "Income War Tax Act' of 1917 was a mere ten pages long. The present Income Tax Act is hundreds times longer. How did the present day Income Tax Act become so large? More and more sections of the Income Tax Act cater to special interests with an exemption here and another there. These special interest provisions and exemptions make it very expensive to regulate the taxation regimes of the eleven countries that make up Canada. For all political parties and politicians, taxation is a political game and a means of getting and staying elected. At the time of its introduction, income tax was envisioned as a means of financing the needs of government, not a means of transferring wealth from the many to a few. The top 10 percent of the population controls the wealth of the country and feeds off the remaining 90 percent of working people. Taxation is also a means of transferring money from small businesses to the few large conglomerate corporations.

Sir Thomas White proclaimed Canadians would *"cheerfully accept the burden and the sacrifice of this additional taxation."* This is hardly the sentiment after more than eighty years suffering under the burden of taxation.

We perceive the proceeds of taxation as belonging to us and not any government entity. Funds collected from the people must be used to provide needed goods and services, not to be wasted by politicians and bureaucrats. Full accountability is demanded of the government. The people created groups, associations and federations that purports to represent taxpayers' interest in holding the government accountable for the manner in which it spends Canadian taxpayers' money. Canadians realize government needs money to provide us with goods and services. While many Canadians voice their objections to paying taxes to government, most really object to the waste in government and the perceived free ride corporations and the wealthy enjoy on the backs of taxpayers. Stories of government waste and corporate handouts are common in our media. Our government seems incapable of eliminating the waste and unwilling to stop handouts to the wealthy and corporations. I do not object to paying taxes. I strenuously object to any individual or corporation whom do not fully pay for the government services consumed. Some years ago I read of a wealthy family transferring one-half billion dollars out of Canada and given a tax exemption by our government. Another free ride on the backs of most Canadians.

Service Charge – fee paid for a particular service.

Centuries, maybe even millennia ago, Kings, Pharaohs, Warlords, and land barons collected taxes from people under their control, without providing goods or service in return. These taxes were to maintain the lifestyle of the supreme leader, the King, Pharaoh and Warlord. This parasitic means of taxing the peasants were carried down through early nineteenth century, even as governments changed to elected representation. Governments now provide a collection of services to its people. The "taxes" collected by government is not the peoples' money, as some would have us believe. Rather, governments collect a fee, a service charge, for services provided. Governments deliver education, health and social services; it builds roads, airports and operates rail services; government builds parks, soccer fields, hockey rinks, museums and other place that preserve and teach our history and culture; governments create and maintain the legal infrastructure that allows us to enjoy a safe and secure environment, generally affording an increasing quality of life. Taxation must be replaced with a "Government Services Charge," which would be payable by all persons and corporations without regard for their financial position. Every person and every corporation use government services and must pay the fees required for providing these services. If one person is not paying for services used, then another is paying too much for these same services. Private corporations collect a fee for services provided, yet as consumers, we do not have the right to dictate the manner in which these corporations spend their revenues. If we are shareholders in these corporations, we have very limited input into such matters. Should we be dissatisfied with the services supplied by private corporations, we may have the option to voice our dissatisfaction or find another supplier of the required services. The people of Canada are not shareholders in their governments; we are consumers of government services and as such may complain or even boycott services provided by the government. We do have, at general election time, the opportunity to hold the governing party accountable for the quality of services the government has provided between elections. Government provides services that cannot be profitably provided by private corporations. In many cases, government provides public services to the people for the betterment of society. In many instance government provide services in a monopoly environment. In this environment, we do not have an option to purchase these services from another supplier. Governments operate in a monopoly because it would be unprofitable for the private sector to provide the required services. Governments cannot be operated as a business, concentrating on the bottom line of profits and return on investment. Many services provided by government do not produce a monetary return on investment, measured in dollars in a fat bank account. What is the return on investment in a highly educated society? What is the return on investment on the availability and affordability of health care for everyone? If we measure return on investment as a tangible product, money in a fat bank account, then government services have no return on investment and never will. The return on investment on government services is in the increase in the "human potential" which will lead to a better Quality of Life for all.

Quality Of Life is defined as:

> **"The product of the interplay among social, health, economic and environmental conditions which affect human and social development."** *Quoted from Government of Ontario document.*

Some politicians would have us believe governments may be operated debt-free while maintaining our quality of life. Others believe government capital expenditures must be paid for in full instead of mortgaged and paid for by present and future benefactors. An investigation of those jurisdictions will reveal reduced amounts of recreational facilities; reduce quality of recreational activities; traffic congestion; mediocre public transit and urban sprawl. Government may have debt but must never be allowed to operate with a deficit. Contrary to political spin doctoring, debt and deficit are not the same monster.

Debt and Deficit

Debt – something owed.

Many Canadians are saddled with debt; homeowners with a mortgage; automobile owners with payments; credit card holders with unpaid balances. Businesses are no exceptions; they have used portions of lines of credit; bank loans and stocks/shares sold to individual and corporate investors. Canadians owe billions of dollars in all forms of debt. We lend each other our money with the help of financial institutions such as banks, insurance companies, and investment houses. Our company and private pensions and personal savings are loaned out to whosoever is qualified to borrow. In weak economic times, companies loose money and are unable to repay debts to financial institutions creating bad and uncollectible loans, resulting in losses to these financial institutions. These financial institutions then raise their service charges to recover theirs losses and repay the monies we lent them in the first place. Effectively, we are charged increased service fees so that we may get back our deposits. This is the best of both worlds for the banks, insurance companies and other financial institutions. They reap huge profits without risking any of their own monies.

Money to operate our governments, and provide government services, is collected from consumers of government services and takes many forms. Personal and corporate income taxes, vehicle registration charges, drivers license registration charge, goods and services tax and provincial sales taxes, are but a few. These tax bases are volatile, fluctuating with economic conditions. Whenever the economy is booming, the taxes collected will be high and conversely in a recession the taxes collected will be reduced. This is the reality of a free market economy. The demands on government services increases in a recession and decreases in the boom times. If you believe the current crop of ultra-right wing politicians, we are better off lowering taxes to the bone and let the adversely affected population survive using their own devices, without any help from government. Sadly, the populace bought these ultra-rightwing policies for the past two decades and is now seeing how wrongheaded these policies were. A gradual shift to the caring society that once was Canada is taking place and the ultra rightwing conservatives will be booted from office. Since the days of "trickle down economics," the merits of tax cuts have been debated with proponents claiming tax cuts stimulate the economy and opponents claiming reduction in the quantity and quality of government services. Proof of reduced government services are everywhere while economic stimulus are almost impossible to see.

In the same manner Canadians borrow money to purchase homes, cars and furniture and to pay for vacations, the government must borrow to finance the cost of its infrastructure and the services provided. Unlike the government, a worker's wages rarely fluctuate with the economy. In bad economic times, workers wages and benefits are frozen or reduced, followed by layoffs. Yet, in boom times, corporations reap and keep the benefits, not sharing any with its workers. A company loosing money may close up shop, leaving workers, suppliers, investors and other creditors holding a bag of debts. Governments cannot just close up shop and move to another province, state, or country. Governments must continue to function whether there is a boom or bust in the economy. It may pile up debt, but is must continue to provide policing, snow clearing, road repairs and all the other services necessary to for the people to enjoy a increasing Quality of Life.

Deficit- an excess of expenditure over revenue

Over many decades our governments spent more money than it received as revenue, with the difference being made up by borrowing or printing more money. Deficit financing of government services is acceptable in times of disaster or wars in order to stimulate the economy. Increasing government expenditures ensure the population do not starve or go without essential services. Deficit financing of government services is a conscious attempt to stimulate the economy by means of lowering tax rates or increasing government expenditures. Unfortunately, in the years our governments practiced deficit financing, we were not at war nor were there any national disasters. At the same time, the wealthy enjoyed their very low tax rate whist the majority struggled with providing the necessities of life for their families. Deficit financing produced a crippling debt load that must be repaid. Once again the benefactors of deficit financing are enjoying their lower tax rates and those that struggled to provide the necessities of life are once more struggling as they are being forced to bear the brunt of government debt reduction, in the form of reduced government services, new and increased user fees, and higher taxes in various forms. In reality, our governments have no money of their own, and all monies collected are derived from some form of levy on each Canadian and every corporation. Governments then provide services it believes the population wants and needs. This is where paying for the cost of government services becomes unfair as some pay more for services used while others become parasitic by not paying for the services they use. Governments, wanting to curry-favour with particular constituents, namely the loudest and richest voters, enact legislations to satisfy these constituents. The patchwork of laws governing the taxation system is a result of these curry-favouring schemes. The inequities that exist in our society are directly related to the actions of governments and the politicians, regardless of their political ideology, that forms these governments. Often times I have heard my friends and colleagues, referring to politicians, "What do they care, it's not their money", whenever the all too familiar colossal waste in government spending are exposed. If it is not the government's money, then why are so many Canadians afraid of demanding everyday accountability from our governments?

It is the government's money, collected for the services sold.

Government Subsidies

Economic development, regional prosperity, diversification, economic stimulation, job-creation projects, and mega-projects are all handouts to business that have proven to be failures. They are a boon to the companies and their owners, politicians and political "bagmen." Government corporate handouts distort the market place, produce a dependency mentality, and become a make-work program, with decision made for political reasons rather than on sound business principles and practices. Wherever there is a handout, there will be a line-up of receivers willing to use and waste the goods and services, because it was "free." Corporate subsidies must cease immediately. If a business cannot survive form its revenues, then it has no business being in business; it must be allowed to fail, even if it means job losses. By eliminating business subsidies, thereby removing distortions in the market place, the government will create a stable business climate. Uncertainty will be removed, business will prosper, consumers will spend, more jobs will be created, and more government services fees will be generated.

Charity

Charity begins at home and it is incumbent on the government to encourage corporate and individual charitable contributions. Charitable donation must be for helping the charity and not another scheme to reduce or avoid paying for government services. I came across charitable donation strategies that purports to the get tax credits for up to six times the amount donated. It appears the main beneficiaries are the donors, donations facilitators and not the Charity. The work of many charities helps countless people across Canada. These organizations work very hard to raise money from individual Canadians and corporations. Sadly, in some charities, more money goes to feeding the bureaucracy than to the benefiting the persons in need. With a Guaranteed Annual Income system, many now supported by charities will be able to support themselves. The death of parasitic and unscrupulous charities and the savings from tax deductions will help to support a Guaranteed Annual Income System.

"Everything cost somebody, something."

I often wondered how a person could get a tax refund if he did not pay any income taxes. I also wondered how it is possible to get a tax refund larger than the income taxes paid. I still wonder how so many Canadians pay huge amounts of taxes through payroll deductions and at the end of the year must send more money to government to cover their tax liability. It is quite simple; some people are living off others! Any person not paying for government services are freely using those services for their own benefit. The deficiency in our present tax system forces the majority to pay for the services freely provided to a minority. We have an obligation to ensure every Canadian pays the full cost of government services used. Since all individuals and corporations use government services, it would not benefit the country to have a system in which any person or corporation would avoid paying the Government Services Fee. The implementation of Government Services Fee, and the elimination of the current antiquated taxation system, would create efficiencies in our system of governance and production that is unheard of around the world. Implementing a Government Services Fee would also attract streams of revenue from every country in the world, adding to the funds required to create the Greatest Country on Earth. Government Service Fees, instead of taxation, would encourage businesses to create, instead of eliminating, jobs. Our present tax system rewards corporations eliminating jobs via tax breaks and rewards laid off workers with employment insurance benefits. Structuring the governance of the country to increase employment would result in increased worker productivity, increased self-worth and better self-esteem for Canadians and larger profits for corporations. It appears our corporate structure benefits from the overly generous tax advantages rather that structured on sound business principles and procedures.

Individual Taxpayer

Under the present tax system, there are differing tax advantages for living single people, living common-law with children, living common law without children, married people with kids, married people with no kids, single people with children. This patchwork of taxation creates inequities and causes a continuing increase in adult and, most disturbingly, child poverty. Each person is an individual and, regardless of age and status in life, should be treated equally. Marital status, age, family size, or co-habitation state should not affect one's responsibility to pay for the government services consumed. The Government Services Fee would ensure every wage earner and corporation pay for the services consumed. Each year my wife files her tax return and must wait until I am ready to file mine. As two individuals, I resent us having to file our tax returns as "dependency" on each other. We both have separate earnings and both have the freedom to spend our money as we each see fit. Every individual must be allowed to file a complete and separate tax return, independent of the earnings of a married or common-law spouse. In our case, entering my income on my wife's tax return, or vice versa, causes the higher wager earner to pay more taxes than if we filed separately, even while married. I must conclude the reason the government wants to know the amount each of us earns is purely to increase the amount it collects from us as married couple.

The Goods and Services Tax, (GST)

In the late 1980's the federal government introduced the Goods and Services Tax (GST) to replace the manufacturers' sales tax. The GST is the greatest achievement for the government of the day, and is now a "cash cow" for the federal government. Since its introduction, the much debated and hated GST forced one Minister's tearful resignation, who in a gimmickry fashion, sought re-election and re-captured her very safe seat. The debate continues on the fairness and the effect of the GST.

One thing is certain; the GST has generated a large portion of the Federal government's revenue. I was passionately against the GST as I saw it not as a 7% federal retail sales tax but as 15% percent retail sales tax when combined with the sales tax in Ontario. We do not care whether the taxes levied are property taxes, alcohol taxes, municipal user fees, provincial taxes or federal taxes. We see them all as "taxes," a heavy burden on our hard-earned monies taken away from our families and us and wasted by our governments. The GST as implemented is a "special interest" sales tax. Certain segments of the economy were exempted to please special interest groups. Collecting and remitting the GST places a very large bureaucratic burden on every business in Canada. If there a ten million businesses in Canada, there are ten million GST collectors. Payment of GST is easily avoided by paying cash for purchase. Even when collected, companies do not remit all GST monies to the federal government. There are GST rebates for lower income people, foreigners and others. There is a huge bureaucracy running the GST.

Government Service Fee – The Amount

The present taxation regime must be eliminated and replaced with a twenty percent Government Services Fee that would apply to every transaction in every sector of the economy, without exception. Transactions such as the sale of stocks, transfer of monies between accounts of two different people, transfer of monies outside of the country, sale of a house, real estate fees, legal and professional fees would all be subjected to the Government Services fee. Eliminating the current taxation regime and replacing it with a Government Services Fee will better serve the people through rationalization of services, and allow each Canadian equitable treatment by their government. With two levels of government, there will be no need for retail sales taxes or any other form of consumption tax or charges. For the first time in history,

Canadians from coast to coast would pay for the cost of government services consumed. The net effect will be a reduction in the amount deducted from one's pay cheque. The underground economy, estimated at up to $60billion, would disappear, and welcomed by governments, law abiding Canadians, and businesses. The addition of more than $60 Billion of legitimate sales to the economy would generate more than $12billion in Government Services Fees. This $12billion in new revenues would offset some of the losses the government might suffer as it moves from a patchwork of taxation schemes to one that distribute costs to all users of government services. Putting more money into the pockets of the wage earners would generate more economic activity, creating many more jobs and generate billions of dollars in new revenues for the governments. Every Canadian and every corporation operating in Canada or doing business in Canada would pay for all government services used. The government would use the Guaranteed Annual Income System to assist lower income earners increase their standard of living.

Government Service Fee - Collection

It will be much easier to collect government service fees from less than ten banks than from millions of employers and their employees. Banks will be required to collect the fee and remit to the government treasury on a monthly basis. Clients' monthly financial statement will list the number and total amounts of debits and credits plus the total amount of government services remitted to the government. For the task of collecting and remitting government services fee, financial institutions will keep one percent of the government services fee collected, providing each institution offers every account holder one each of savings and chequeing accounts and one debit card, free of any bank service charges, with daily interest, calculated as the cumulative average of the Bank of Canada's Prime rate, payable on all monies in each account.

Financial Reporting

The replacement of "taxes" with a government services fee will not preclude any person or corporation from making a financial report to the Department of Revenue. However, the financial report will now provide a snapshot of the corporation's financial position and the net worth of each person, via a balance sheet. The financial statement will allow every individual to detailed knowledge of their assets, liabilities, and equity in their operational entity. For individuals, the financial statement will afford additional knowledge of ones net worth every year, providing an early opportunity to re-adjust ones financial plan many years before retirement. With the help of financial planners and the knowledge gained from financial education in our schools, Canadians may better plan for an enjoyable life after retirement, and having the financial resources to pay for it without depending on government pension plans and other handouts.

Department of Health

National Drug, Dental and Health Plans

Under our constitution, health is a provincial jurisdiction, financed mostly from the tax dollars collected by the Federal government. With ten provinces and three territories, we have thirteen health plans, each covering procedures, and services it deems necessary for its residents. A procedure covered in one jurisdiction might be de-listed in another. Some provincial governments have allowed the operation of privately owned and operated health clinics and privately built hospitals, leased back to the government, and then operated by private entities. By allowing non-government owned and operated health clinics and hospitals, we are destroying universality of healthcare, a fundamental building block of a great society. The role of government in health care is accessibility, affordability and universality; the role of private sector in health care is profit. Both roles are at loggerheads with each other. In short, government's role in funding and operating a comprehensive healthcare system is to prevent sickness and quickly heal the sick while the role of the private sector is to ensure a constant supply of sick people to ensure profitability. Unless the people replace neo-conservative governments with socially conscious governments, we will find ourselves with completely private, for-profit medical care system, jeopardizing the health of Canadians struggling on poverty wages.

If there are a million companies operating in Canada there are probably a million supplementary health plans, all with their attendant bureaucracies and waste, with each plan having a different group of benefits for its participants. It is time to create one national health plan by amalgamating all provincial, territorial, and corporate health plans into one comprehensive, universally accessible, national health plan. Our health care focus must be on prevention rather than cure. Why is it that supplementary health plans do not cover vitamins, minerals, and other products that help keep us healthy? We have an excellent national health care, administered by the provinces. So we think. Provincial governments have butchered their health programs to the point of fragmenting any semblance of a national plan. Health is a provincial responsibility, therefore, the level and quality of services provided by provincial health plans will be at the mercy of the provincial governments of the day. Health care must be the sole responsibility of the national government, with services administered and delivered by local governments, according to national standards crafted by the national government and the Mayors Executive Board.

National Dental Care Plan

A national dental care plan is a required component of a national health plan to ensure the overall health of the population. Dental care is a luxury in our society. Were it not for corporate dental plans, many

Canadians could not afford dental care as services and procedures are priced beyond the means of many Canadians. Facing rising premium costs, many corporations have reduced dental procedures and services covered, with some have increasing premiums paid by employees. The primary reason for rising costs of dental care is a greater awareness and usage of the myriad of dental services and procedures that are available to Canadians. Another contributing factor is the actual service and procedure fees, imposed by dental associations, and charged by dental practitioners. The national government must establish a National Dental Plan, with a fee schedule, to provide all Canadians with basic dental services.

National Drug Plan

Like the many existing company pension plans, drug plans are many and as varied as the corporations in our country. Once more, the bureaucracy to manage the myriad of plans is mind-boggling. Drugs to cure illness are covered in plans yet drugs to prevent illnesses are not. Drugs are expensive. Foreign pharmaceutical corporations hold most the drug patents. These corporations spend hundreds of millions to lobby government to keep drug prices high. We must develop a National Drug Plan to ensure essential drugs are universally available to all Canadians. A national drug plan must be established to benefit all Canadians, regardless of their stature in our society. With the myriad of plans in existence, and with their attendant bureaucracies, one all-encompassing national drug plan would be self-sustaining with the support of the governments and premiums from beneficiaries.

Marijuana – Drug or Medicine?

Marijuana is considered a mood-altering drug that takes control of the user's mind. It is a criminal offence to possess and traffic marijuana in many countries of the world. I saw the mood-altering effects of marijuana on many of my teenage friends in the village of Cornwall, in Jamaica where I grew up, in the surrounding villages and at high school. In Jamaica, marijuana is called "Ganja" or "weed," is frequently used by many in the population, and is exported to Europe and North America. It is also illegal to possess or traffic Ganja in Jamaica, where fines are generally stiffer and prison terms longer than in Canada and the USA. Arguably, the stiffer penalties result from pressures north of the Caribbean Sea. During my years in high school, many of my classmates and other students at my school smoked ganja. I cannot speak of Ganja's effect on girls and women, as I do not know of any who have smoked it. My high school in Jamaica was one for boys only. One could easily identify those who smoked a "joint" at lunchtime or after school. Smokers' facial appearances changed and their demeanor became easy going. We referred to them as "high", "cool" and "mellow." Some boys were smoking a joint at lunchtime everyday. They claimed smoking "weed" placed them is a better frame of mind and helped them to study better. I cannot attest to their conclusions. Surprisingly, their grades and marks were not affected, with the ones in my class averaging "A's" and "A+'s", which translated in marks of 80-89% and 90% and over, respectively. Many years later, I learned some of my ganja-smoking high school classmates became lawyers, doctors, engineers and successful businesspersons. Anyone knowledgeable with Jamaican Reggae music might be familiar with the link between many Reggae singers and ganja. Rumors abound that Jamaica's internationally renowned Reggae King, Bob Marley, was a heavy ganja user. The members of an entire religion in Jamaica, Rastafarians, are devout users of ganja. They are a devoutly religious, easygoing, and peace loving people. I saw the mood-altering effects of ganja on the boys from the village in which I lived. These boys were heavy smokers, and like my high school classmates, were always "high," 'cool," and "mellow." They were never violent and were helpful and respectful to the adults in our village. The mood-altering effects of marijuana were clearly demonstrated to me in a football match (soccer game) between two village teams. More than half of my village teammates smoked marijuana before a match. During the game, a teammate, attempting to play the ball, swung his leg and missed a very easy play. I asked him, "How come you missed the ball?" He said, "Man I'm so high, I'm see three balls coming at me and I swing at one of them." It seems he was swinging at the wrong ball. Despite "hanging" with my boyhood friends for many years, I have never smoked marijuana and cannot testify to the effects of smoking it. Clearly, I have seen its effects as a mood-altering drug.

Growing up in a third world country, homemade medicines and remedies are part of life, either out of financial necessity or the knowledge of, and belief in, local plants and herbs. As a very young child, and up to my early teenage years, I remember suffering debilitating breathing problems that prevented my participation in sports, particularly my favourite sport, football. Even walking up the hills of our village was a difficult task, with frequent stops to catch my breath. I remember feeling the burning sensation in my chest as long as I was awake. I remember continuously coughing in the evenings and continuing into the night and for as long as I was awake. I was regularly sick in primary school and could not participate in sports. Doctors told my parents their young child was suffering from bronchitis. My mother told me that; I did not know what it was; I just knew I was always gasping for air. Marijuana came to the rescue in the form of homemade medicines. My parents made two types of medicines from the leaves of the ganja tree. The first was boiling the leaves in a pot of water to make a beverage we called 'ganja tea." At breakfast, I would drink one mug of this tea before I went to primary school. This was the only way I was able to get relief from my breathing problems allowing me to walk the one mile to primary school. The second type of medicine was made from stuffing ganja leaves in a bottle and filling it with Jamaican White Over Proof rum, the potency of which is known by those who have drank it. This produced a very potent medicine, one teaspoon of which was fed to me before bedtime every night. My mother told me it was the only way to control my constant coughing at night. I have experienced the medicinal effects of marijuana (ganja) and I believe in it.

Canadians with particular ailments have reported relief after smoking marijuana. I believe in the medicinal value of marijuana and do not believe it is any more dangerous a drug than alcohol or cigarettes. I have never smoked cigarettes or marijuana, but have often wondered why cigarettes are legally available, even with its known cancer causing effects. I believe the objection to legalizing the use of marijuana is rooted in the benefits of its medicinal value, which cannot be patented in its natural form. Maybe its natural medicinal value will reduce the need for man-made drugs, reducing the profits of drug companies. In the interim, it is desirable to legalizing the use of marijuana for smoking or used as a medicinal drug, prescribed and supervised by physicians trained in its uses and knowledgeable on its effects. It is time we conduct extensive research into marijuana with a view to producing medicines from its plants. We ought to de-criminalize the possession, smoking, uses and transport of marijuana as long as it does not exceed fifteen grams on the person or outside the person's normal place of residence. Trafficking would be illegal unless a person or corporation is licensed for that endeavour, just like cigarettes and alcohol.

Department of Housing

National programs are required to ensure the housing needs of all Canadians are met. Public and affordable housing must be available for those who cannot afford the market price of a house. Public housing built and operated by local governments and operated on a not-for-profit basis will meet the needs of lower income Canadians. Housing co-operatives, owned by a corporation and managed by the residents, under the watchful eye of the Canada Mortgage and Housing Corporation, will benefit lower and middle income Canadians. For nine years, we lived in one such housing cooperative, Brooks Cooperative Homes, in Mississauga, where I served as President, Vice-President, Treasurer, a director and a member of many of its operational committees. While more than half of the residents did not participate in the cooperative's overall management, we were able to keep the rent well below market rents, allowing my wife and I to save the required down payment for a house. Housing Cooperatives are a stepping-stone to people having ambitions of purchasing their homes. The single and largest purchase a Canadian will make is a house and the most difficult part of home-ownership is saving the down payment. The largest single monthly and cumulative expense in a Canadian's life is the mortgage payment. Our property tax laws treat a home as a speculator's purchase rather than the purchasing of a residence. Property taxes, based on the arbitrarily determined market value of the house, are a cruel means of extracting government fees to pay for government services. Being the largest expense a Canadian will ever have, a home must be priced at an affordable level, with pricing controlled at the rate of inflation. In new subdivisions around my neighbourhood, new house prices seem to increase on a weekly basis, even though all the specifications of the home remain the same. Housing is an essential need and a right of every Canadian, necessitating government intervention by creating affordable housing for lower income Canadians and by regulating house prices and sales agent fees.

Department of Human Services

The National government must create and administer national programs for social services consisting of Guaranteed Annual Income System, National Pension, Dental, Drug, and Child Care Plans, and a National School Breakfast and Lunch Program.

Guaranteed Annual Income (GAIN)

Employment Insurance, Canada Pension Plan, Registered Retirement Savings Plan, Old Age Security, GST Rebate, Child Tax Credit and the many other social benefit programs that are a part of our social safety net were designed to help less fortunate Canadians. The admirable intent of these programs is appreciated by many Canadians, particularly the recipients, and is loathed by corporations and wealthy Canadians. With the management of all these plans comes a very large corporate and government bureaucracy, consuming money and producing very little of value in return. Think of millions of applications for benefits, the millions of cheques mailed out every month and even more millions queries, appeals and denials of benefits. The national government must roll all its social safety net programs into a **G**uaranteed **A**nnual **IN**come **S**ystem (GAINS), which will benefit all Canadians and reduce the government bureaucracies that now administer the social safety net. For each person attaining the Age of Majority, the Guaranteed Annual Income System would pay a fixed income of $20,000 per year. Some would argue the GAINS is over generous, very costly and contribute to a mentality of laziness to a section of the population. Whether we continue the plans we now have, or implement the GAINS, there will always be Canadians attempting to take more than they deserve. We see that in many wealthier Canadians and corporations looking for every conceivable tax deduction that will allow for a reduction in their tax liability. The cost savings from the reduction in the bureaucracy would contribute significant monies to the financing of the GAINS.

An employed Canadian may be earning an income many times more than the proposed GAINS amount. Becoming unemployed, this person would automatically be eligible for the GAINS payment. However, there would be a reduction in his lifestyle because of the differences in employment wages and the lower GAINS benefit. The national government must implement an insurance plan that would allow employed persons to purchase employment insurance in multiples of the GAINS amount and not exceeding their gross base employment pay. The employment insurance premiums will ensure payment of benefits for a period not exceeding two years, after which the GAINS will become the sole source of income for the unemployed. Premiums for this insurance will be the responsibility of the employee and his employer.

National Pension Plan (NPP)

The National Pension Plan would replace the present multitude of corporate pension plans, Registered Retirement Savings Plans (RRSP), Canada Pension Plan (CPP), and Old Age Security (OAS). Retirees will receive the benefits of the GAINS or the NPP, whichever is greater. Since the introduction of the RRSP, millions of Canadians have opened accounts, taking advantage of their tax deferral provisions. Millions have lost billions of dollars in the cyclical boom and bust of the economy. The financial markets have a direct impact on all the monies deposited in RRSP accounts. Unfortunately, a majority of Canadians do not have enough money left over, after living expenses, to make a meaningful RRSP contribution, with some Canadians not making any RRSP contributions. The RRSP is a tool for the wealthy to hide more of their money at the expense of those whom cannot take advantage of the RRSP rules. It is not the role of government to "baby sit" its citizens. Rather it is the role of government to guide its citizens on a path of self-reliance, and to ensure they stay on that path with a monitoring process.

The present system allows for citizens to be negligent in planning their lives and to later become wards of the government or be very dependent on government handouts, falling prey to the governing party's electioneering machinery. Corporate pension plans, the RRSP, CPP and OAS must be rolled in one National Pension Plan (NPP) to benefit all citizens. All persons would make mandatory premium payment into the NPP, based on a percentage of their income. Corporations would make premium payments based on a percentage of their total payroll.

Whenever a corporation finds itself in a financial struggle, inevitable comes reports of the corporation tampering with employee pensions as a means of siphoning money from the corporate pension plans and into company operations. After corporate bankruptcy, corporate pension plans disappear or benefits significantly curtailed at the expense of employees whose "blood, sweat and tears" paid for the plans. After many years of service to a corporation, employees deserve every penny of pension benefits they are entitled to on the day they retire. Denying or reducing these entitlements is tantamount to stealing from the retiree. With the National Pension Plan and the Guaranteed Annual Income System, these unethical behaviours by corporations will never happen. Every Canadian would be offered the opportunity to purchase pension income insurance in multiples of the GAINS, up to an amount equal to gross income, adjusted annually. Realizing there will be Canadians who could not contribute to the NPP for of several reasons, such as chronic employment, being unemployable, seasonal employment, disability, the GAINS and Social Services would provide top-up income.

Working full lifetime, the average worker spends about forty years in service to her country. Over that time, the worker paid Income Tax, Goods and Services Tax, Provincial Sales Tax, Property Tax, Excise Tax, Duties, and more taxes. Hardly any money is available to save for the "Golden Age" years. By removing the bureaucracy from the corporate pension plans, RRSP, CPP, OAS and eliminating the many parasitic tax advantage, more money would go directly into the NPP. By further removing government from the management of the NPP, better rates of return would be realized from prudent investments. The NPP would be become a huge pool of the people's money, earning a rate of return that would help the plan grow. The revenues from continued contributions and the rate of return would allow the plan to provide the lifetime benefits. The management of the NPP would be vested in a Board of Directors of thirty professionals. The composition of the Board would be ten members selected by the National Government, in consultation with the Mayors' Executive Board; ten selected by the Labour Movement and ten selected by the financial sector, (insurance companies, credit unions, banks, investment companies, etc). The Board shall hire the processionals required to carry out the mandate of preserving and growing the members' contributions.

Death of Canada Pension Plan

Time after time, we are bombarded with stories from the "experts" about the death of the Canada Pension Plan. We are told premiums must be regularly increased in the coming years to ensure sufficient funds to pay the "baby boom" retirees. The federal government increased premiums to employees and employers alike to stave off the pending CPP financial shortfall. The experts told us the CPP troubles are a result of increasing number of retirees, decreasing new employees and inadequate premiums. How it is the number of Canadians filing income tax return has increased every year yet CPP is in trouble? One significant contribution to the perceived financial troubles at CPP is contract workers and consultants. As companies declared employees redundant, massive layoff occurred in the latter twenty years of the last millennium. The tens of thousand of laid off employees became lower wage earners, part time employees, self-employed consultants and contract workers, making a lower contribution to CPP. The lower wage earner and part time employees will most certainly contribute less to CPP as their pensionable earnings are lower. While contractors and consultants may gross the same amount of money as prior to being laid off, their self-employed status affords many deductions, thereby reducing taxable and pensionable income and, consequently, CPP contributions. The health of CPP lies in the number of full time employees, earning middle income and the number of employers making regular contributions to the plan. In the new Canada, the CPP would be replaced by the National Pension plan.

National Child Care Plan

Jackie and I were fortunate with providing care for our children. We made the decision to take care of our children as much as we could and with a minimum of care from childcare providers. We believed parents must be the primary source of care for their children but recognized that we need the support of childcare providers. We decided I would work a permanent night shift and she would work permanent day shift. This reduced the need for outside caregivers to about four hours each day. Not all parents are able to make this arrangement as jobs are mostly from 9-5 each day, necessitating children spending long hours each workday with a caregiver, depending on age of child. Our friends with younger children requiring daycare have told us the cost is a very significant portion of their weekly expenses. Childcare and Daycare are provided by mothers at home, trained and untrained childcare providers and for profit daycare centres. Affordable daycare seems to be going the way of the dodo bird, putting a strain on the financial resources of lower paid workers. A National Day Care Plan would use schools, churches and community centres as daycare centres operating on a not-for-profit business model. The daily rate for childcare would be equal twice the hourly rate of pay reflected in the minimum wage. Priority for admission would be given to lower paid workers, verified by employment earnings and net worth statement. Those who prefer to use profit oriented, privately operated daycare centres would have that choice from among licensed centres.

National School Breakfast and Lunch Program

It is well-known in our society that many adults leave home and go off to work without having breakfast. Some confesses to having only a cup of coffee or a glass of juice with a piece of toasted bread. The reasons for not having breakfast are varied, from getting out of bed too late, to being unable to eat so early in the morning. Whatever the reason, the medical community have continually stressed the need to eat in the morning. After all, we are breaking a long overnight fast with this first morning meal, breakfast. If the adults are accustomed to skipping breakfast, it stands to reason their children will also skip breakfast. Educators and educational professional have identified morning hunger as a major problem in children's early morning learning capacity and in children's behaviour. Various reports suggest many children are becoming more fatigued, having trouble concentrating and are more irritable and generally having difficulty learning. Educators are convinced children behave and learn better when they are properly nourished. Parents, themselves skipping breakfast and feeling the effects at work, are now more aware of the children's problems and becoming more anxious to keep their children from becoming hungry in the morning. Teachers and their school boards have identified many children attending school without having breakfast. While financial hardship was part of the problem, parents having to leave early for work, makes it difficult to ensure the kids ate a good breakfast. Across Canada, many schools and their Boards have instituted breakfast programs, either for free or minimal fee. The program must be expanded to include lunch and be available in every primary and secondary school in Canada as part of a comprehensive National Breakfast and Lunch Program, funded by governments and sponsorship from corporate branding and advertising.

Child Poverty

In November 1989, the House of Commons unanimously resolved to "seek to achieve the goal of eliminating poverty among Canadian Children by the year 2000." In 2003, there were more children living in poverty than in 1989. The government failed! It is shameful we have done so very little to arrest and eliminate the sources of child poverty in our rich nation. Child poverty is not the exclusive domain of unemployed adults or single parent families. More than half of all children living in poverty have parents who are in the paid labour force. With Canada having one of the highest levels of low-paid jobs in the industrial world, a job is not a guaranteed escape from poverty. Low-paid jobs do not normally carry benefits, forcing parents to spend sparse cash on drugs, dental procedures and other items middle-income earners would normally have on a benefit plan. Childcare expenses and housing sap the financial resources of lower paid workers having children.

Women bear the brunt of poverty being lower paid then men, are mostly in low-paid and part-time jobs, and usually do not qualify for benefits after becoming unemployed. Even with a mother and father working, a child is likely to live in poverty if both are in low-paid jobs and especially if the mother loses her job. As a top G7 country, it is appalling that more than one million of our children live in poverty. Not only our politicians and fellow Canadians know we are not making a concerted effort to eradicate child poverty, the world and its experts knows it.

"1. 2 million Children in Canada experience poverty. If gathered into one area, they would create Canada's fourth largest city" - *World Vision Canada, Always Among Us, 1995;*

> "16 countries have lower child poverty rates than Canada" - *UNICEF, Child Poverty in Rich Nations, 2000;*
>
> "Canada has the greatest number of children, per capita, living in poverty within the 18 most industrialized countries " -*UNICEF, Child Poverty in Rich Nations, 2000;*
>
> "40% of people being served by Canada's food banks are children under the age of 18" - *The Progress of Canada's Children, 2001;*
>
> "There are more than 1.1 million Canadian children living in poverty" - *Statistics Canada;*
>
> "The average family in Canada spends 35% of its income on housing, clothing, and food" - *Campaign 2000, 2003 Report Card on Child Poverty in Canada;*
>
> "Despite a commitment made in 1989 by the federal government to eradicate child poverty by the year 2000, the number of poor children had increased between 1989 and 1999 by 39%" - *Campaign 2000, 2003 Report Card on Child Poverty in Canada.*

Canada will have perpetual child poverty if we do not break the cycle now, by implementing a guaranteed annual income for every adult Canadian, combined with national drug, dental, and childcare plans and a national breakfast and lunch program. Canada cannot become the Greatest Country on Earth when more than one million of our greatest assets are being prevented from developing their full potential.

Within the one million poverty-stricken children may be the next Dr. Frederick Banting, Dr. Roberta Bondar, Wayne Gretzsky, John Polyani, Hon. Pierre Trudeau, Sir John A. MacDonald, Louis Riel, the engineers and designers of the Avro Arrow, or any one of many other outstanding Canadians, past and present. The quality of our social services reflects our commitment to invest in our people, an investment that continuously pays dividends over more than seven decades.

Department of Immigration

Canada is a country of immigrants; even the native peoples traveled from afar to get here, though many thousands of years ago. We traveled by water, land and air to get here, seeking a better quality of life. We built a better life, contributing to the vibrancy of Canada at the beginning of the twenty first century. As in every other country, there is very small proportion amongst us who advocate closing our borders to all immigrants, especially from the non-European countries. Maybe these proponents of border closings are motivated by racial, colour, ethnic or economic biases, their own selfishness, or greed. Regardless of his or her motivation, we must not let anyone close the Canadian border to any immigrant. A good friend, a Polish-born Canadian, and I were stunned when his Canadian-born son declared Canada should close its borders to immigrants. When his father asked the reasons for his belief, the son replied there were too many immigrants in Canada, living off welfare and contributing to crime. I reminded the young man his life of freedom and abundance is a direct result of Canada's immigration policies. Otherwise, he would have been born in a communist society, without freedoms and living in poverty. I wondered if his pronouncements were directed to all immigrants or just the non-white immigrants. Today, I wonder how his beliefs affect his judgment in his chosen profession of authority. Canada is under populated and increasing the population to double its current level by the middle of the twenty first century should be a priority for every national government. Why would increased immigration benefit Canada?

Immigrants established themselves in the Canadian society, becoming Canadians and adopting the Canadian way of life. That life includes a significant number becoming patriotic Canadians, learning Canadian politics, playing hockey, adopting the best parts of multitude of cultures and weaving their way into the life of Canada. One significant adoption is the reduction in number of children immigrant families are producing, averaging the 1.5 children per household of Canadian families, far less than families in the old country. Numerous reports have suggested the rapidly aging population will not be able to sustain itself without a significant increase in CPP premiums. These reports suggest the decline in birth rate, and consequently the number of employees paying premiums, is the major cause for concern. The solution is to increase the immigration from the nearly two hundred and fifty thousand levels today, to one million per year for the fifteen-year period, followed by five hundred thousand per year for the next fifteen years and lowering the level to two hundred and fifty immigrants per year until such time as new levels are warranted.

Immigration creates a need for houses, apartments, cars, consumable goods and services. Our society is built on "selling something to someone." If few cannot sell, we do not need to build and if we cannot build, we cannot employ people. There is a fear and resentment of immigrants; a fear brought on by ignorance of the new culture, new language, new dress and differing lifestyle. Immigration has never been a threat to Canada and the Canadian way of life. Immigration has helped Canada evolved into the well-respected nation it is today. Life for immigrants has not been easy. Many immigrants are from countries with warmer climates, a slower pace of life, and rural and agrarian societies with a singular culture and language. Adapting to the Canadian climate is trying for the first few years; speeding up to the Canadian pace of life requires significant adjustments; understanding the various cultures is a challenge. After years of living, and adjusting to life in Canada, the rewards are beyond words.

What is Canadian Experience?

Immigrants are often asked for "Canadian experience" when applying for a job, even if they were employed by Canadian or American companies in their native countries. Immigrant professionals such as doctors, engineers, and nurses, are relegated to driving taxicabs, or being security guards by professional certification bodies refusing to recognize the education, training and experiences from the old country in the name of "Canadian Experience." I am a testament to the requirement of "Canadian Experience." In Jamaica, I worked for almost three years with the telephone company maintaining and repairing equipment manufactured and installed by one of Canada's largest telecommunications equipment manufacturers. Canadian telephone companies were using this telephone equipment in their switching centres. My training in the installation, maintenance and repair of this equipment were by Canadians and Jamaican instructors, themselves trained by Canadians. I had my certificates proving I had successfully completed many courses on specific telecommunications equipment. I even had a letter of reference from the District Manager for the area of Jamaica where I was working. I recall four Canadian instructors and installers were from, Fergus and Toronto in Ontario and Montreal and a place called Three Rivers in Quebec. After coming to Canada, I learned Three Rivers was actually Trois Rivere in Quebec. During the Canadian High Commission's processing of my application, the immigration official stressed Canada's need for qualified telecommunication equipment technicians, the category under which I was classified. Within a couple of weeks of arriving in Canada, I was at the employment office of Canada's largest telephone company applying for a technician's job. During the interview, I was praised for my excellent qualifications and good letter of reference while in the same breadth was advised I did not have "Canadian Experience" and therefore would not be offered a job. I asked what exactly is "Canadian Experience?" I was told I did not have any experiences working with Canadians, would need to adjust to Canadian environment and a litany of other "Canadian Experiences" needed to qualify for the job. It did not matter that I lived in Canada for a year. It did not matter that I had my Grade Eleven transcript from my one year at Glendale Secondary School Hamilton, Ontario. It did not matter that I worked with, and was trained by, Canadians. It did not matter that the telephone equipment I was trained to install, maintain and repair were the same telephone equipment used in the telephone exchanges in Mississauga, Toronto and Brampton, among many other cities throughout Canada. It mattered most, in 1976, that I was not "white." The only Canadian experiences I needed for that job was the ability to read a city map, knowledge of the bus route and schedule from my home to the telephone exchange where I would be working and my hours of work. I had my "Canadian Experience," as I had maps of Mississauga and Toronto and their corresponding bus routes and schedules. I was not waiting for the telephone company to call me for a job; I was out looking for a job, any job, traveling by bus to interviews. With my consistent mark of 90% plus in high school Geography, reading an understanding a city map and a bus route schedule has been no problem. "Canadian Experience" is an excuse to exclude newly arrived non-white immigrants from employment and is bigotry. A white immigrant with my experiences, even if he could barely speak English, would have been hired for the job. After seven years of gaining "Canadian Experience" by living and working in Canada, and after graduating from Sheridan College, Brampton Campus with an Electronics Engineering Diploma, I went back to that same telephone company for a job and was promptly told I was "over qualified," proof that the request for Canadian experience is rooted in bigotry. Imagine the non-white immigrant professional whose first language is not English; not born and raised in a British colony; not educated in Canada and you will understand their frustrations of being relegated to jobs where their training and experiences are wasted to fulfill the bureaucratic requirements of professional sanctioning bodies and relegated to menial jobs by corporate human resources departments.

Many highly skilled immigrants are languishing in jobs that are not utilizing there skills and experiences, all in the name of lacking "Canadian Experiences." Certainly, Canadian customs, practices and procedures differ from the old country. The laws of Physics, Chemistry and Biology are the same throughout the world; the biology of human body is the same whether one is Russian, Pakistani, English, French or African. The bulk of an education and experience possessed by an immigrant professional should be recognized by Canadian certification agencies. Immigrant professionals would then be required to attend short course on policy and procedures used in Canadian society. Upon completion and successfully passing the requisite examination, immigrant professionals would be certified to practice his craft in Canada. The vast untapped resource of immigrant professionals, who are ready, willing and able to make meaningful contribution to building Canada, lies dormant as we encounter shortages of the very professionals we refuse to certify.

Immigrants

It is a testament to life in Canada when so many desire to live here, migrating legally and illegally. It is a privilege to be accepted as a legal resident of Canada and an honour to be granted Canadian citizenship. Many peoples of the world seek to start a new life in Canada as immigrants. Some wish to leave their native country, fleeing a life of poverty, persecution and curtailed freedoms, never to return. Others come to Canada to earn a better wage, build up assets and return home; still others want to have the best of both worlds, earn lots of money in Canada and live like a King in the old country after retirement. Regardless of an immigrant's origin, with few exceptions, she is coming to Canada to live in freedom, prosperity and opportunity, knowing fully that ones work ethic will define the lifestyle lived. Being granted the privilege to live in Canada carries responsibilities. Too many immigrants treat Canada as a place to extract a good living as they prepare to retire in a life of luxury back in the old country. Not enough immigrants give back to Canada the respect and obligation it deserves for having given them a life of freedom, opportunity and peace. Whether to Canadian born or immigrants, Canada is not a country to be exploited, grabbing its wealth and running off to some other land to live like a King. Canada is not a country to be raped by immigrant Canadians-of-Convenience, or Canadian-born who prefer to carry on business in Canada while living in tax havens of the world. Above all, immigrants must cherish the goodness that is Canada. We must be "more Canadian" than Canadians by birth or lineage because we have a better perspective on Canadian values and its bounties.

Immigrants to Canada should be granted a non-renewable Canadian Resident and Work Permit, for a seven-year period from the date of arriving in Canada. During that period, every immigrant must be required to attend classes on Canadian values, Culture, Law, Politics, History and Languages. For non-English speaking immigrants, they must learn to speak English or French and for English speaking immigrants, they must learn to speak French. For an immigrant to be eligible for citizenship, he must physically be present on Canadian soil for a period of five years, showing proof of residency, which would include one or many of active bank accounts, property ownership, drivers' license, utilities bill, employment and income record. After five years of Canadian residency, immigrants would be eligible for Canadian citizenship, which would normally be granted before their seven-year Resident and Work Permit expires. It is the right of immigrants to decide if Canadian citizenship is in their best interest. However, immigrants whose Resident and Work Permit have expired will not be permitted to return to Canada, should they choose to visit another country. It must not be the intent of government to punish immigrants for not choosing to apply for Canadian citizenship or to deny any immigrant the privilege of maintaining residency in Canada after their Resident and Work Permit has expired. Accordingly, persons with expired Resident and Work Permit would not be able to purchase international travel tickets and Canadian immigration officials at land border crossings would be instructed to deny re-entry to persons with expired Resident and Work Permits.

Naturalized Canadian Citizens

Sworn in by a Judge, an immigrant is granted citizenship after meeting specified conditions, including security investigations, and swearing allegiance to the Monarch. However, the Minister responsible for Citizenship may revoke that citizenship, at anytime and without cause. That power vested in the Minister may be abused for political gain and must be removed and placed under the control of the Judiciary, with the Minister being the final avenue of an appeal. Anytime the government decides it want to revoke citizenship, the Ministers involved must apply to a court of competent jurisdiction for a revocation order, whereby the Ministers must show cause for requesting the revocation. In my view, the only acceptable cause for revoking of citizenship is provision of false information by the applicant, whether that information is of personal or safety and security nature. Once granted, citizenship must be for life and equal under the law to the rights, privileges and punishment afforded Canadians by birth. No longer would naturalized Canadians be "stripped" of citizenship, should they choose to commit or live a life of crime. Instead, the full weight of the law would be brought to bear, as it would be for a Canadian by birth. Only then will a foreign-born Canadian Citizens be equal to citizen born on Canadian soil.

Citizenship and its Demands

Once born in Canada, a Canadian must never be permitted to relinquish Canadian citizenship and would forever be subjected to Canadian laws, regardless of the length of time that person lived outside Canada and regardless of any other citizenship that might be acquired. Citizenship is much more than being born in a country or having citizenship rights granted through naturalization. Canadian citizens include people born on Canadian soil, foreign-born and granted citizenship, and children born outside of Canada and to Canadian citizens. Is citizenship just a title, duty, or responsibility? It is all three! The title of Canadian citizenship carries prestige around the world and is no more evident by the desire for a Canadian passport by international criminal element and agents of other countries operating in the spy-world. Canadian citizenship is a signature mark of belonging to a country whose people are at peace with one another and the world, represent the voice of fairness around the world, and fighting for and protecting the freedom of others. Citizenship is a duty and a responsibility to a country and its people. It is defending the security of the land and people; upholding the laws of the land; working for the betterment of society and contributing time and effort to those in need. Citizenship is participating in, and defending, the democratic process, the rights and freedoms we must have to live free and pursue our hearts desires. Citizenship is voicing our opinions, having our say, being involved in the community, making things happen, and taking part in decision making within the larger society. Citizenship is obeying the laws, reporting lawbreakers, taking what is rightly ours without exploiting others. Citizenship is being responsible for your actions, by owning up to them and be prepared to pay the price for any misdeeds.

Citizenship demands putting Canada first!

"If you don't think that your country should come before yourself, you can better serve your country by livin' someplace else." *Stompin' Tom Connors, (Born 1936 -) Canadian Singer/songwriter.*

Citizenship is giving back to the country much more than you took out. That includes giving to charity and not expecting the government to do it for us. I challenge every Canadian adult to give one twoonie ($2) each week to a charity of his choice. I challenge every Canadian company to encourage their employees to contribute a twoonie each week to charity, with the company contributing an amount equal to the employees' contributions. With more that fifteen million workers, a twoonie a week would generate more than $30million a week to charity and more than $1.5billion each year, and with matching contributions from corporations, $3billion would be possible. If we all contributed a twoonie, then the government need not use a large bureaucracy to collect money from us and distribute to charities. Charities need not go begging monies from the government or launch telemarketing and print campaigns, or operate lotteries to generate monies to provide food, clothing and shelter for the disadvantaged in our society.

Department of Industry

The Industrial Revolution saw the mechanization of processes that required backbreaking manual labour. The Industrial Revolution, a time of dramatic change from hand tools and handmade items, to mass-produced products, may be defined as the application of power-driven machinery to manufacturing. Workers became more productive; prices dropped as more items were manufactured at a faster pace and at lower cost, making exclusive and hard to make items available to the poor and not only the rich and elite. Life generally improved, but the industrial revolution also proved harmful. Pollution increased, working conditions were harmful, and capitalists employed women and young children, making them work long and hard hours. The industrial revolution was a time for change, for the better, and for the worse.

The mechanization of the world, beginning in the early 1700, gave us the printing press, steam engines, steam ships, planes, trains, automobiles, the telephone and revolutionized manufacturing and gave us the "assembly line." The mechanization of our world has become more sophisticated with the addition of computers and computer controllers. With the increasing levels of automation, from lawn sprinkler systems, to home alarms, and the space shuttle launch control system, automation is more efficiently replacing humans. Up to the period before World War II, industrialization was mostly mechanical and electrical. Since the development of the miniature electrical switching device, the transistor, we began to add "logic" to the industrialization process. Not only do we make things happen faster, and less tedious to humans, we compensate for unexpected developments by using "electrical logic devices," better known as computers.

During the Industrial Revolution, resources seemed inexhaustible with nature viewed as something to be tamed and civilized. We pumped noxious gasses into the air, polluted our waterways, oceans seas and rivers. We believed the Earth would neutralize these poisonous chemical and we could go on collecting profits, living our lives of excesses. One of the greatest tragedies of the Industrial Revolution is the development of the sophisticated war machinery. We now have enough conventional, nuclear, and biological weaponry to destroy every life on Earth many times over. While there have been treaties between countries calling for the destruction of the more dangerous weapons, we are still developing and deploying even more deadly and smarter weapons. Collectively, the countries of our world have spent hundreds of billions of dollars on the development and deployment of deadly weapons while hundreds of millions of people are starving, dying of thirst and starvation and living in squalor. Our leaders talk about fighting terrorists with bombs, guns and imprisonment while neglecting the root cause of terrorism; starvation, homelessness, landlessness, and oppression.

Made In Canada

"Made in Canada" is not a phrase seen on many products anymore, having been mostly replaced by "Made in ..." or "Assembled in Canada" and "Assembled in ...." We are importing more cheaply made products, exporting jobs to foreign countries and contributing to the exploitation of people in poorer countries. As consumers, we constantly demand lower prices on our purchases and an ever increasing demand for our wages. We, the people, demand the exportation of our jobs by demanding ever-lower prices for the goods and services purchased. Corporations respond by having products produced in countries that have lover wages and no benefits, eliminating jobs in Canada. Whether a corporation or a person, we have forgotten that demanding a lower purchase price on goods and services will directly result in lower wages and benefits. In an ideal world, our cash outflow would equal our cash intake, resulting in zero profit. In the free enterprise market, we must have profit, and big ones to boot. Maximizing profit means lowering our costs and increasing revenues. One of the easiest ways is to outsource production to low wage countries of the third world, where the pay is pennies a day and a benefit package is non-existent. Corporations label products as "Made in Canada" or "Assembled in Canada." Several years ago, as President of a soccer club, a supplier of soccer balls approached me, seeking to be the club's supplier for hundreds of soccer balls. My personal goal was to supply one soccer ball for every registered player and six to every coach; saving a few dollars on each good quality ball would make that goal closer to reality. After meeting with the representative, I discovered the balls were substantially cheaper than our current price and queried why the big difference in price on a ball that looked like the same quality as those currently in use. I was told the balls were of the same quality and cost about the same as a couple cups of coffee to make in the far east, yet were being offered at to us at more than ten times manufacturing cost. I sensed exploitation, and, rightly or wrongly, refused the overture of doing business with this company.

"Made in Canada" means that 51% of the total direct cost of producing or manufacturing the goods is Canadian. "Assembled in Canada," means the finished product is "put" together, wholly or in part, from components made elsewhere. The automobile is a product assembled in Canada, from Canadian made parts as well as parts from around the world, and using Canadian labour in final assembly. With a product made or assembled in Canada, Canadians must have provided the labour. Therefore, the definition of "Made in Canada" must be changed to exclude all Canadian labour and a new pictorial be used to forcefully convey Canadians involvement in the production of goods and services. The Maple Leaf has nine points, which could be used to denote percentage Canadian content. A line from each point to the stem, starting on the left, would mark an area, coloured red, denoting a full 10% Canadian content. 0% Canadian content would be represented by an outline of the maple leaf while 100% would be red maple leaf. We must also require pictorial labels on all foreign products indicating no child labour was used in producing the good.

Assembled in Canada

We are a trading nation, buying goods and services from other countries as they are buying from us. When our own companies shift manufacturing to other countries at the expanse of Canadian standard of living, we must be sure to identify the company as Canadian owned or headquartered. Many products are assembled in Canada from components made all over the world. As mentioned above, a pictorial design with the maple leaf would show the percentage of a product "Assembled in Canada" from components assembled outside of Canada. Every job in Canada depends on the other. You may not be a consumer of your company's products but there is someone buying the goods and services produced by your company; otherwise, you would not be employed today. If we want to keep jobs in Canada, afford health care and pensions, and better our standard of living then Canadian consumers must read the label and Buy Canadian. The profits from corporations and the taxes they pay help to maintain our standard of living. If we continue to "Buy Foreign" then corporate profits are sent to foreigners and very little taxes paid in Canada, increasing the standard of living in foreign countries while tearing down ours.

Department of Intergovernmental Relations

Cooperative governance requires the cooperation of all levels of government. Development and deliverance of services require a high level of integration, reduction in inter-jurisdictional squabbles, and end to outright hostilities. The primary purpose of this department would be to strengthen relationship between local government jurisdictions and the national government. The Department of Intergovernmental Relations will be responsible for the management of the political relationships between the national government and the local governments. This department will act a mediator whenever a dispute arises between national government departments and local government departments.

Department of International Relations

We live in a changing world where borders and governments change regularly and the importance of having presence in each country of the world, regardless of the political stripe and beliefs of the government leaders, is critical to creating a better country. Every country in the world needs special attention in understanding and cultivating a relationship with Canada. While countries in all regions of the world have similar needs, each has specific economic, security, and political needs. We must customize our International Relationships for each region and for each country in the region. Special attention must be given to relationships with the United States of America, United Kingdom and France. We have the world-recognized continental regions of North America, South America, Europe, Asia, Africa, Australia and Antarctica. The continents would be further sub-divided into smaller regions. North and Central America and the Caribbean Islands would be divided into the regions of the USA, Mexico, Central America, and Caribbean Islands. Brazil, and the rest of South America (South America). The regions of Europe will be France, Germany, United Kingdom, Scandinavia (Norway, Iceland, Sweden, Denmark, and Finland), Western Europe (Spain, Portugal, Italy, Greece, Turkey, etc) and Eastern Europe. Russia, Eastern Asia, China, India, South Asia, and Southeast Asia will divide the continent of Asia. Australia and New Zealand, Oceania forming the regions of Australia. Even Antarctica deserves special attention. The continent of Africa, the area that will experience the greatest growth in this millennium, will be further subdivided into Eastern Africa, Western Africa, Northern Africa, and Southern Africa.

Canada has longstanding relationships with United States of America, United Kingdom and France, formed from shared colonial links, shared border and mutual security. We have begun developing stronger relationships with other countries of the world. However, those relationships have been with countries in the northern hemisphere, particularly North America and Western Europe. Becoming a multi-lingual and multi-cultural country affords Canada a doorway to non-English and non-French speaking countries. Africa, China, South and Southeast Asia, with about half the world's population, is a vast untapped source of human potential, natural resources and consumer market. Canada must be the dominant player in these markets by forging ahead with political policies and economic programs that will expand our influence and stature in these regions. Canada must insert itself into the psyche of the world's population by supporting and taking action to ensure law and order, safety and security, economic and political stability, democratically elected representation, technological advances, and the necessities of life are part of the lives of the world's peoples, particularly in Africa, South and Southeast Asia.

The continent of Africa will be the new frontiers of exploration and habitation in this millennium. People from the northern hemispheric region of the North Atlantic Ocean, particularly Canada, USA, and western Europe, are rapidly destroying the biosphere by polluting streams, rivers, lakes and seas; burying toxic chemicals on land; rapidly expanding cities, paving over valuable farmland and increased use of fossil fuels. Oppression, starvation and landlessness are major reasons for the increased migration from third world countries to developed countries. The increasing population in the developed countries causes an increasing demand for housing, transportation, energy and food in countries of the northern hemispheres. As the northern hemisphere becomes more polluted, its people in the first quarter of this millennium will begin a migration to Africa, looking for a simpler, cleaner and healthier life. Canada must begin preparation for its people to live in Africa by cultivating friendlier relations with all countries on the African continent. The continent once stigmatized as the "Dark Continent" by the colonialist will be the bright light of the world in the second half of this millennium. Canada must also help to foster the transformation of third world governments into democratically elected governments with judicial and security systems that respect human rights, freedom and the sanctity of human life. If we create better living conditions in the oppressed countries of the world, we will help their people to stay in their native countries, their first preference, if quality of life is good. We will then reduce the influx of immigrants to the developed nation and begin to reduce the depletion of resources in those nations.

International Intelligence Gathering

Intelligence gathering is an important part of building a great country. It is important that we know what is happening in our backyard, next door and around the world. It is incumbent on the Canadian government to engage in overt and covert intelligence gathering on other governments, corporations and groups in countries of the world, particularly in regions where government and national stability are identified problems. National security demands an awareness of developments in the entire world, twenty-four hours a day. Canada maintains diplomatic presence in almost every country in the world. Within every diplomatic mission, there must be a national security intelligence service whose role is to gather national and corporate intelligence within each country and deliver it to the security headquarters in Canada. Is it proper to gather intelligence on other governments and corporations around the world? Should we be gathering intelligence on our friends or only on the not so friendly governments? Should we be spying on the internal groups within foreign countries and within our own country? What would be the purpose of intelligence gathering and spying? When I was a young boy growing up in Jamaica, I heard a song on the radio that had one line of the lyrics that says, "It takes a friend to fuck a friend." One day, as the song played on the radio, I asked my Mother what it meant. She told me the more someone knows about you, the more harm they can do to you. It wasn't hard to understand what she was trying to tell me.

This is the reason Canada must engage in international intelligence gathering on the all governments and corporations of the world. Canada must also spy on groups around the world, and in our backyard, that may be engaging in activities that could be detrimental to the internal and national security of Canada and Canada's efforts at peacekeeping around the world. Those wishing to inflict military and economic harm on Canadians may very well be Canada's best friends and we must foresee, and be prepared to deal with these problems as they arrive on our doorsteps. Intelligence gathering prepares our government for quick, decisive actions against any government, corporation or group that threatens the welfare of Canadians. International and industrial espionage are well known to many around the world and in the "cloak and dagger" underworld. It is a profitable business to steal government and corporate secrets. Canada is a technologically advanced country and will continue to be in the centuries ahead. We must protect Canadian government and corporate secrets by actively seeking out those who may want to steal and trade these secrets for their own benefit or the benefit of a buyer.

Department of Internal Security

Each administrative region would have its own local police force to handle internal matters. The RCMP would handle national issues and all matters spanning other jurisdictions. "To protect and Serve," means we must be able depend on our police forces to do just that. Policing is a tough job and carries a risk of severe injuries and death. For the men and women who have chosen this profession, we must offer unwavering admiration and support, not adulation. Our political leaders must increase the number of uniformed officers patrolling our streets and protecting our people. Our community leaders must work in concert with police forces to diffuse tensions between mostly ethnic group and police officers. The management of our police forces must develop and implement ethno-cultural training for its officers in better understanding the dress, food, customs and other traits of ethnic communities. The judiciary must support police officers by ensuring the punishment fits the crime. A heavy workload and too many lenient sentences must certainly demoralize our police officers. Police officers are people like us, having stress, debt and family problems. Having the same weaknesses and are subjected to same influences as we do, too many police officers have yielded to temptation, getting involved in criminal activities and abuses of the very people they swore to protect. As with every profession, a few bad apples spoil the entire bushel. The actions of a few law-breaking police officers have tarnished the image of the many dedicated, caring and competent men and women of our police forces.

Many sectors of the communities have respect for, but no longer completely trust, the police. People are refusing to cooperate with the police, as they are themselves treated as suspects. Many immigrants are leery of police officers and with good reasons. Some police services have admitted their law enforcement personnel have been engaging in racial profiling in their enforcement practices. Enforcing the law based on racial profiling is abhorrent and requires punishment for those who practice it. Community organizations resent crime statistics compiled by race, colour, and place of origin and other marks of ethnicity, equating such actions to racial profiling. It most certainly is not racial profiling and is not different from collecting age-based statistics. Ask the young male drive how he feels after learning insurance companies classify males between 16 and 25 years as a high risk insured. There is a perception that persons of one racial group commit more crimes; gangs are more likely to be in another racial group; organized crime is the domain of another. That is racial profiling.

Crimes are the products of failures in sections of our society. The law enforcement community must be authorized to collect statistics on race, colour, place of origin, age, area of residence, for the sole purpose of identifying societal problems that might be the root causes of crimes. These statistics must never be used to portray any group as likely to commit crimes or in any other negative light. Crime statistics will allow governments and social agencies to identify society's failure points and develop programs to remedy these failures.

The difficulties in policing are a societal problem. The breakdowns of law are order in the home is telegraphed into businesses, the streets, our social groups and gangs. We must retrain our police officers to "protect and serve," to treat the people with respect and dignity, and to engage in more pro-active crime prevention measures. This would reduce the crime-solving budget and give officers more time to interact with the community, which would further reduce crime.

Guns and Gangs

> **"Violence is the last refuge of the incompetent."** *Isaac Asimov, (Born 1920 –Died 1992), author and biochemist.*

Guns, gun-related crimes and gangs are a part of life that urban residents must address. A gang, by definition, is nothing more than group of people, yet whenever we think of gangs, we think of biker gangs, street gangs, gangs of armed robbers and groups of people determined to wreck havoc on people and society in general. "Gang" is now synonymous with violence, guns, riots and mobs, all striking fear in our hearts. Gangs are the result of too many people with too much idle time on their hands. "Idle dog worry sheep" is a Jamaican proverb often repeated by the adults of my teenager years whenever their children had nothing to occupy their time. It is true now as in the days when I was a teenager. We must keep our youth occupied in meaningful endeavours to channel their energies into sports, community service and planning for a vocation in adult life.

After school and on weekends, many of our young have nothing to do, except hang around in a mall or on the streets with their friends. We glorify guns and gangs in movies, computer games and books. Gangs are glorified as a group of like-minded and free-spirited people bonding and caring for each other, without respect for property, life and authority. Gangs portray their members as fearless and invincible. For the teenager feeling rejected, gangs offer a sense of belonging, camaraderie, and strength though masochism. Friends hanging together to kill time, or walking the streets, are nothing more than idle hands. "Idle hands are tools of the devil." The powerful combination of fearlessness, invincibility, free-spiritedness and idle hands into a group of people, a gang, dedicated to destroying and asserting themselves, strikes fear into the hearts of law-abiding people.

The double-use of guns in providing protection and inflicting harm has appeal to gangs as tools of protection, control intimidation, and retribution. Combining gangs with guns creates a volatile mix in the impressionable minds of our young people. While gangs are not the exclusive domain of teenagers, adult gangs are populated with people who were once teenage gang members or exposed to gangs whilst a teenager. Where there are gangs, there are illegal guns, crimes and illicit drug use and trafficking.

The Federal Gun Registry is a necessity if we are to keep illegal guns out of our society. There are laws governing the possession of illegal guns.

How do we know a gun is illegal, if it does not have a registered owner? How do we know that a gun owner did not lend or sell his gun to someone who knowingly will commit a crime? Failing to register a gun will render that gun an illegal firearm warranting severe punishment.

The commission of a crime involving illegal guns will earn even more severe punishments. There are laws governing the commission of crimes and will be dealt with according to the laws governing each crime. Guns and Gangs are problems in society because of our lenient application of the laws, as are many other law and order problems plaguing our society. People using guns in the commission of crimes are bullies and cowards and require a special court of justice to inflict punishment. The government must construct a Gun Court that will address crimes involving guns. Punishment for gun crimes must be taken to the maximum limit of the law, without violating constitutional guarantees, even though the punishment may be considered cruel and unusual.

The powerful allure of guns and gangs attracts the teenager, feeling rejected at home or in school, looking for acceptance. The problems of gang activities are related to our children not having enough constructive activities in their spare time. We will help alleviate the creation of the gangs, formed mostly out of peer pressure and a sense of belonging, if we engage our children in more educational and productive tasks. We must challenge that sense of belonging, first through parenting and then schooling, in constructive groups that will offer development of the youth into adults. By extending the school day to nine hours and offering free education to students belonging to one of the cadet programs, we encourage our children to "belong," and keeping them engaged in local and international programs that will facilitate their development. We must, as parents and society, keep the "idle hands" occupied at all times.

Department of International Commerce

Canada is a country of traders and has been since the time of First Peoples vibrant society, when traded goods were skins, furs, birch bark, corn, beans, squash and tobacco. As Europeans moved into native territories, trading began with the Europeans desire to take fur back to Europe. World trade in motor vehicles, paper, timber, oil, natural gas, meat, electricity, telecommunications equipment and intellectual properties and many other goods and services, finances the Canadian standard of living. More than 85% of our trade is with the USA, with Japan and the European Union accounts for about 2.5% each, and the rest of the world the remaining 10%. Ninety percent of Canada's trade is with less than 20% of the world's population. There are markets of over four billion people waiting to be tapped!

International Commerce must promote Canadian products around the world; secure markets for Canada's goods and services; remove barriers to freer and fairer trade; monitor trade practices of other countries and develop Canada's responses and convince other governments and people around the world to "Buy Canadian." This department must explore the world as it seeks to diversify our trade portfolio into the markets of the more than 80% population where we earn a few dollars. Canadian businesses have been comfortable selling into a market that is much easier to understand than the other 80% of the world. Consequently, Canada is very susceptible to restrictive trade practices and the whim of the political climate in our largest trading partner. Government and the business community must work together, through this department, to develop a comprehensive plan to increase trade with Europe, Asia and Africa. Financial advisors tell their clients, "Diversify or you die" and not to "put all your eggs in one basket," lest you end up loosing everything. As a country, we have forgotten both and have relied on one trading partner to purchase more than 80% of our exports. In business, it is recognized that 80% of revenues will come from 20% of our clients. Canada receives 80% percent of its revenues from 20% its clients making Canada one very large business! It is a major responsibility of national government to sell western Canadian grains, Ontario and British Columbia apples, Saskatchewan Potash, New Brunswick and Nova Scotia paper, Quebec electricity, P.E.I potatoes and Newfoundland fisheries and attract tourists to the beauty of Nunavut, Yukon and Northwest Territories, to the world.

National governments, with their direct line of communications between each other, have influence in opening doors that may otherwise be closed in a business-to-business communication.

Department of Justice

Paying a debt to Society

We have often heard the phrase "the punishment must fit the crime" and the offender must "pay his debt to society." When a person is found guilty of committing a crime, what should the punishment be? How does society determine the severity of the punishment? Will the Supreme Court or even segments of society consider the penalty "cruel and unusual punishment"?

Criminal Record

A person convicted of a crime usually receives a punishment consisting of financial or jail time penalty or both. Associated with any punishment is a criminal record, for which the convicted person may apply for a pardon after a specified period has elapsed. A juvenile convicted for stealing a candy bar may receive a suspended sentence or a fine and tagged with a criminal record. This record may prevent him from becoming a peace office, seeking election to public office; even prevent him from holding a prestigious job. It certainly will prevent him from occupying a position of trust. While the offender paid his debt to society, society will never let him forget it and hold him hostage for the rest of his life. Even after being pardoned, and fifty years later, the offender must be extra careful in all his actions. For the next time he finds himself on the other side of the law, his criminal record file will be re-opened. That is a hell of a burden to carry from the teenage years until death. Even beyond death, the criminal record lives on. Convicted of committing a crime, accepting punishment and serving the imposed sentence more than fifty years ago, the juvenile offender did not pay his debt to society; he made a down payment on his debt. In effect, the offender paid a longer price than a convicted murder that spent 25 years in prison. It is cruel and unusual punishment to let a person carry that burden for the rest of his life. Once the sentence is served, the debt to society is paid in full and the criminal record must be destroyed after a fixed period.

Which one of us can say during our teenage years, we did not engage in activities that were dangerous to ourselves, broke the law, and as a prank, engaged in activities that could have seriously hurt our friends and ourselves, and even cause death? Have you ever been "dared" to walk out of a store with a candy or a magazine? These pranks are part of growing up to being responsible adults. While we had fun participating in these pranks, we probably knew we were breaking the law and putting others and ourselves in harms way, thinking nothing of the consequences because of peer pressure. Pranks and "dares" have resulted in criminal charges being laid against many teenagers. What is the appropriate form and duration of punishment for pranks? Was the act a prank? Was it a deliberate act to commit a crime? What is the right age for a person knowingly breaking the law? At what age do we consider a person accountable for their actions?

Child, Youth and Adult Offenders

The Child Offender

At age thirteen, the beginning of the teenage years, a person is aware of right and wrong although not experienced in understanding the consequences of their actions. Punishment should be meted out with some measure of leniency, with some responsibility transferred to the parents of the child. The police, parents, child and injured parties shall resolve the matter in an informal setting so as not to adversely affect the psychological well being of the child. Our efforts at this early age are to teach young offenders the values of right and wrong, law and order, crime and punishment. Responsibility to the parents should include appropriate restitution to the injured party and re-imbursement of costs for the resolution of the problem. These costs may include the services provided by the social services, justice and police departments. Parents and the young offender must be required to attend training classes specifically designed to address the issues of parental guidance and responsibility and identifying problems with the young offender and the methods of resolving these problems. Below the age of thirteen, criminal charges will not be laid. However, mandatory education will be required for parents and the offender.

The Youth Offender

As children grow older and gain life experiences, they are more aware of their actions and is therefore more accountable for said actions. Between the ages of thirteen and twenty, any person committing acts contrary to the rule of law will be punished more severely and the punishment made to fit the crime and the actual age of the offender. A lesser responsibility should be transferred to the parent of this child.

The police, parents, child and injured parties shall resolve the matter in an informal setting so as not to adversely affect the psychological well being of the child. These informal session should be presided over by a judge, and involve lawyers, parents, the child and an official from a juvenile prison or detention centre and social services department. Our efforts at this intermediate stage of adulthood are to remind the young adult of values of right and wrong, law and order, crime and punishment. These mediated meetings are a medium to teach the young adult about society's expectation of her behaviour in the pursuit of good citizenship and the punishment meted out for failing to live up to society's expectation and the rule of law. Punishment would be meted out and be properly supervised. If incarceration is the prescribed punishment, such time is served in an intuition that will help to rehabilitate the offender.

Responsibility to the parents should include appropriate restitution to the injured party and re-imbursement of costs for the resolution of the problem, even if the offender is incarcerated. These costs may include the services provide by lawyers, social services, the justice and police departments. Parents and the young offender must be required to attend training classes specifically designed to address the issues of parental guidance and responsibility and identifying problems with the young offender and the methods of resolving these problems. Between the ages of fifteen and eighteen, a criminal record will be attached to any person committing a crime. However, the criminal record would be sealed for five years from the date of conviction, except if the commission of the crime caused the death or maiming of another person or animal. All subsequent records of criminal convictions would be sealed for five years from the date of the first criminal conviction, meaning the period of sealing runs concurrently and not consecutively. After the end of the five-year period, all records of criminal convictions, except for crimes causing death and the maiming of persons or animals, shall be destroyed and so certified by the justice department to the offender and his parents.

For minor crimes committed by persons between the ages of thirteen and twenty years, criminal records would be destroyed after the fifth anniversary of conviction, and after successful application for a pardon. Regardless of the crime and punishment, at no time should an offender under age twenty years be tried in a court, or be incarcerated in an intuition, designed for adults.

The Adult Offender

Once a person has attained the age of twenty years they become an adult and are completely responsible for their actions. Parents will no longer be held responsible for the actions of their children, except if it is proven the parents aided and abetted in the commission of the crime, in which case it is a separate crime. The full force of the law, consisting of trial by judge or judge and jury with the offender represented by legal counsel, will be brought to bear on adults committing crimes. The offender must be present and take the stand to defend against all charges laid against him. Persons over twenty years convicted of a crime would have criminal record destroyed ten years after completing their sentence.

Persons committing crimes on the person, financial crimes or murder will have criminal record for twenty-five years after conviction.

Death Penalty

The finality of death makes it an action of last resort that is best carried out by God, our creator. It is easy to demand the death penalty when we are angry and seething with rage immediately after a murder, especially if the victim is a relative, friend, close associate or a well-known public figure. How can we forgive someone who killed a part of us, a mother, father, brother, cousin or very close friend. Is justice served by government-sanctioned execution? Is capital punishment a means of seeking revenge on the person committing murder? Is the death of a loved one any less important if it occurred at the hands of a drunk or careless driver, neglectful employer or because of teenage pranks? The premature death of a person, however caused, is a very serious matter punishable under law. The punishment meted out must fit the death, the cause of death, and the intent to cause the death.

When determining the punishment, a jurist must determine the cause of death, who caused it, who is responsible, was it neglect, pre-meditated, accidental or self-defense. If the death occurred, because of self-defense of one's life, no prison time for the accused. Causing someone's death due to willful neglect, a prank or an accident of any kind, then a minimum prison term of ten years shall apply. Pre-meditated murder would earn the guilty a "life time sentence without parole, for twenty-five years." It may seem harsh to sentence a person to ten years in prison for causing death by automobile accident, workplace accident or a teenage prank. One must respect life and be punished for denying someone the right to live until they die a natural death. Taking a life also denies family and friends the opportunity to enjoy the life of the victim. Not only murderers change the lives of their victim's friends and relatives; the person causing an accidental death robs victim, friends and relatives the chance of living a full life.

Financial Crimes

Amongst us are people who would rather make a living off the avails of criminal activity. Those I find most repulsive are responsible for fleecing money from others. Using lies, "get rich quick" schemes, and other deceptive practices these crooks destroy lives by taking the life savings of their victims. Punishment for these crooks must be severe and be similar to that of a murderer with the added penalty of refunding all the monies fleeced from their victims even if it take an entire life time to do it.

Position of Trust

Law enforcement officers, judges, politicians, corporate officers, senior government officials and other higher-ranking people in our society are all in positions of trust. Expected to behave in a manner commensurate with their position, many have breached the trust as they take care of themselves or their own. If the majority does not have confidence in the people in positions of trust, how then do we expect to build a Just Society? If the small group of people in positions of trust takes care of their relatives and friends, who will be taking care of the interest of the majority? Punishment for persons in beach of trust must be severe with incarceration, long term loss of freedom, financial restitution, loss of position and community status must be a mandatory part of any sanction.

Department of Labour

> "Labor is prior to, and independent of, capital. Capital is only the fruit of labor, and could never have existed if labor had not first existed. Labor is the superior of capital, and deserves much the higher consideration." *Sixteenth U. S President Abraham Lincoln, (Born 1861- Died 1865)*

Labour is the fuel for the economic machinery that drives Canada, yet the producers of labour are treated as the least important ingredient in the production of goods and services. Apart from the commodity it is, labour is people; it is the only marketable product of a human being. Labour is physical and intellectual and requires nurturing to produce. People market their physical strength and brainpower used to produce the goods and services we enjoy in our daily lives. Corporations treat people as expendable commodities and to some extent that is true. When one worker quits or is dismissed, there are many others waiting to fill the open position, sometimes at a lesser pay.

The quality of goods and services produced is directly related to the relationship existing between the employee and the corporation. When a worker feels exploited, he will find ways to extract more money from the company by reducing the output of his labour. Often it is by developing a "Who Cares?" attitude, with production and quality suffering. The company suffers by having products that are of lesser quality and more expensive to sell, beginning a downward spiral in company sales. Who will take the first step towards respectability and cooperation for the mutual betterment of the worker and company?

In the 1960's, Jamaica had a thriving banana export industry with an advertisement on the radio that said **"Look after the banana and the banana will look after you."** For the corporation and employees, one could easily see how "Look after the employees and the employees will look after the company," would benefit everyone. One could also see how "look after the company and the company will look after the employees" might benefit everyone. Unfortunately, looking after the company does not guarantee the company will look after the employees. Companies are now retiring their loyal and productive employees in order to eliminate higher wages and benefits to these employees. Replacing a single long-term, loyal, dedicated and productive employee with three or four lower paid part-time workers was the beginnings of employee disloyalty to the corporation. Corporate Executives must take the first step on the road to restoring employee loyalty by first treating employees as people with families, responsibilities and needs and as consumers. Employees will repay loyalty with loyalty. Were it not for the employee, the company would not exist.

Mandatory Retirement

Many years ago, men were the backbone of the labour force and most women stayed home to take of the family. In those days, the workday was about ten hours and the workweek was six days. People also started to work at a young age, as higher education was not affordable to all. Nutrition and health care were unavailable in most parts of the country and, where available, inadequate. With the poor working conditions that existed back then, and the poorer health of workers, retirement was a welcome relief after almost fifty years of working.

Healthcare is better, people are fitter and living longer, working conditions have been improved considerably, with people continuing to be productive many years past the current mandatory age of sixty-five years. Our Prime Minister, The Rt. Hon. Paul Martin, is beginning is first term at an age when most are forced to retire. Members of the Senate and Judges are allowed to work up to mandatory retirement age of seventy-five years. Forced retirement causes society to loose the valuable experiences and leadership of older Canadians, in favour of the younger, inexperienced workers. Older workers are viewed with resentment by younger workers instead of the respect they deserve for the wisdom of their years. Forced retirement sentences older Canadians to a life of mediocrity and near uselessness. Retired persons have options to volunteer and relax after a long working life, possibly living the rest of their lives feeling unfulfilled. Is this the best we have to offer retired persons after their contribution to building our country? Why must a healthy and experienced person be put out to pasture, like the unwanted bull and the aged race horse, when he is capable of contributing to society? At the beginning of the twenty-first century, many of our young corporate executives are in dire need of the wisdom and experiences of the retired executives they replaced.

Retirement is not an option for some as financial positions may dictate working a few more years. The desire to continue working past the official retirement age may be one of duty to continued contribution to society. The reason to retire or not must be the decision of the individual. In a Just Society, an official retirement age is necessary, with the earliest possible retirement age being set at fifty-five years. However, any person may continue their employment without any form of discrimination until an age of their choosing. There must be a national policy to determine the mental capacity and physical health of a person who has chosen to continue working into the later years for it is unreasonable to expect a person to work until death from old age. At some point, society must decide the age at which older persons will be better off in retirement. Seventy-five years is an age where people must retire, regardless of their mental and physical abilities to continue working. Judges on the Supreme Court of Canada must retire at age seventy-five; politicians need not retire at all, so why should working Canadians be forced to retire at sixty-five or face financial penalties if they choose to continue past sixty-five years?

In One Canada, every person will have a Guaranteed Annual Income of $20,000. Retirees dependent on Canada Pension Plan benefits will be in a better financial position than their present state. The financial reason for continuing to work past sixty years would have been removed, with many retiring as soon as allowed.

Department of National Defense

Some would say the only strong defense is peace. The power of peace over war is beyond debate. Peace creates; war destroys. It would be wrong to equate a strong defense with peace. Maintaining peace, in a free society, is one of the toughest jobs of any democratically elected government. Peace is the product of freedom, but freedom is not a product of peace. In many totalitarian governments of the twentieth century, people were at peace with each other and with other countries, yet freedoms were non-existent.

> **As long as there is one person willing to forcefully impose his will on another, we will have wars.**

Turf Wars, Gang Wars, Regional Wars, and international wars are all products of one person, one group, or one country wishing to conquer the other. Wars do not solve problems as we have seen in the many wars of the twentieth century, including two World Wars. More people ended up under oppressive governments after the end of World War II than prior to the start. The Vietnam War did not prevent the North from overrunning the South; the Korean War resulted in two Koreas separated by a demilitarized zone and occupied by a foreign army. World Wars I & II did not pan out to be the wars that ended all wars. Armed conflicts are ongoing in many parts of the world as groups and governments seek to exert control over others. A strong military will help to maintain the peace between countries by acting as a deterrent to invasion. At the apex of the cold war, the world was closest to complete peace, as it will ever get. The strong military might of the superpowers prevented one from attacking the other as mutual destruction was assured. With only one superpower, the world is closer to World War III than at any point since the end of World War II.

A Weakened Canadian Military

We sent about 650,000 to fight the First World War and fought fascism with an enlisted force of more than a million men and women. We sent almost 27,000 troops to Korea. Today, it is a struggle to keep a few hundred soldiers on the battlefield. Helicopters fall out of the sky, submarines leak; troops are ferried abroad by another nations transport. A once proud and respected military is broken and demoralized after decades of government neglect. Since the end of World War II, all our national governments have allowed our military capability to deteriorate; base closures, reduction in military personnel, deterioration of materiel, decline in troop morale and a woefully inadequate remuneration structure for the enlisted men and women. We have so destroyed our military that we now depend on a foreign power for our national defense. Transportation of our troops to foreign assignment is best served by foreign powers. On a force of 60,000 people, one-tenth the commitment of World War I, our government spent a paltry $11.8 billion, in 2003, rising to about $17 billion in 2008 under proposed financing. The deliberate destruction of our military renders it an impotent defense force, incapable of defending the territorial integrity of Canada, especially in the harsh terrain and frozen ocean of the North. The budget cuts of the past decade have forced military management to "make do" with very little to keep the military running. A culture of miserly spending has taken root in the military and a large cash infusion will not necessarily make a better military. An entire overhaul of the military is required, starting with a mission statement for our military role in the world for the next 100 years.

Strong Armed Forces

Canada has promoted global peace and the role of the United Nations as part of its foreign policy, supported mostly by words. When we speak of a nation's power, we are not only referring to its moral power; we are also referring to its military power. Despots and barbaric leaders around the world are not interested in moral power; only economic and military power will convince these despots and barbaric leaders to free their people from tyranny. We cannot promote global peace, NATO, NORAD and the United Nations with our weakened military. We must make a firm commitment in law to increase our military spending to at least 3.0% of Gross Domestic Product (GDP), in each of the next twenty-five years, which was $957billion in 2003. However, the increase in military spending should not be for supporting the weapons manufacturing industries of other countries. The increased military spending must be apportioned to research into newer and better military aircrafts, bigger and more effective battleships, more effective and less costly weapons, and a better remuneration package for our soldiers.

Canadians and Canadian companies must be in the forefront of any research and development of these military products. A strong military will only protect our sovereignty if the military equipment is developed and built in Canada, with the labour of Canadian workers. Canceling the Avro Arrow was the biggest blow to asserting Canadian sovereignty over the waters, airspace and land it claims. We now rely on a foreign nation to provide us with fighter planes and military transport. Purchasing used, mothballed, and problem plagued, submarines did not help in enhancing our military credibility nor did it increase our military capability. The world's only military superpower is forcing Canada to increase military spending, ostensibly to sell more of their weapons and to ensure they have control over the Canadian military. Canada needs a strong and agile military to protect its air, sea and land sovereignty and to help secure and protect peace and freedom around the world. As the second largest country in the world and with one of the smallest population of the industrialized world, protection of our sovereignty is vital to becoming the Greatest Country on Earth. A strong country and a strong nation need a strong and efficient military force. The territorial integrity of Canada's 9.9 million square kilometers and two hundred and forty three thousand kilometers of coastline, coupled with varied and harsh weather, demands a strong military presence. With three oceans and the world's longest undefended border, we need a military machinery capable of patrolling the air, on land and beneath our lakes and oceans. No part of Canada should be greater than five minutes access by fighter planes. A strong military will allow us to exert our sovereignty over all our territory, internationally recognized or as we claim. The USA does not recognize portions of our Arctic and have several times trespassed under our Arctic waters. At other times, they have "notified" us of their intention to use the passageway, rather that ask our permission to traverse these waterways. Other nations have also refused to recognize Canada's claims over certain parts in the Arctic

Military might does not equal right. Military might brings caution from both sides, which helps prevent wars.

More Soldiers, More Equipment

Our military personnel should number seven and one half percent (7. 5%) of the population with two and one half percent (2. 5%) in reserve forces. The National government should embark on a program to modernize the military hardware with new destroyers, new and more submarines, new aircraft carriers, new battleships, new and more fighter and bomber aircrafts all developed and built in Canada. Increasing personnel and increasing remuneration will reduce the workload and increase the moral of our uniformed personnel. Do we want our national interest defended by a tired and demoralized military? Do we want our territorial integrity defended by men and women eking out a living on near-poverty remuneration from our national government? That is our expectation today as successive governments have deliberately treated the military with contempt by reducing funding, personnel, and too many foreign commitments, supported by inferior and outdated equipment. Many Canadians holding positions of prominence have compared our military spending to that of the United States of America, suggesting our spending should be in line with America's military spending. We cannot afford to keep military spending in line with the Americans. Canadians, and the rest of the world, pays for a substantial portion of America's military spending through the profits American companies taken out of Canada and the rest of the world. We must spend to meet out military needs for a country of our size, which is not the case today. Now is the time to modernize and enlarge the military. Let us not wait for war to break out. Let us save lives by having a rapid deployment force.

United Nations Rapid Deployment Force

Canada should support and contribute to a United Nations Rapid Deployment Force (UNRDF) of one million troops and materiel for peacemaking and peacekeeping duties. Deployed to protect peoples of the world from oppression, rape, pillage and murder by despotic government, the UNRDF will work to install democratic governments, offering people liberty and safety. We must turn our efforts to protecting human life. Too many lives have been lost in many countries as the rest of the world collectively takes a "hands off" approach and "sovereign nation" mentality to these despotic leaders. Many of these murderous regimes are in far away places and do not have oil or other precious natural resources, rendering them of less import to many western countries. Since World War II, millions have died in civil wars and fights for freedom, in areas such as Rwanda, Vietnam, North Korea, South Africa, Namibia, Rhodesia, Uganda, Cambodia, Russia, Czechoslovakia, Hungary, Haiti, Nicaragua, Argentina, and Chile. The world watched and supplied weapons and military intelligence in these conflicts and genocides, in the name of playing one ideology against another. The re-arming of our military is not only for the protection of Canadian territorial integrity but for the benefit of our Allies and for those nations around the world that seek freedom from despots. A larger military will also benefit Canadians in times of emergency. The military helped in the Manitoba and Quebec flooding, the Quebec and Ontario ice storm and the Toronto blizzard. These peacetime missions help our people cope with disasters, lessening stress and offering support when we are most vulnerable. Help from our military personnel gave Canadians an insight into the operations and caring nature of the military. The military personnel gained the respect and trust of the people, learning to respect the people and freedoms they defend.

Our peacekeeping role is world-renowned and respected. Our peacemaking role is emerging and will be well respected in due course. Whenever we send our troops into harms way, we must support them with advanced military machinery so they may protect the oppressed and protect themselves from the oppressors. We must be vigilant in preventing other genocides in the world. We must never again allow holocausts and genocides in any part of the world.

Department of Natural Resources

Natural resources are precious gifts from the Earth, created and grown over thousand, millions and even billions of years. They belong to all Canadians and not to whomsoever owns or leases the land under which these resources lie. Rivers, lakes, oceans, oil, gas, forests, minerals and animals are but a few of the major natural resources in Canada. Once depleted or made extinct, natural resources are gone forever and generations will be denied the benefits they once offered. It is our responsibility to use the natural resources to meet present needs but also to aggressively conserve for future generation while we wait for the Earth to create more in its own good time. We must also plant more trees, cleanup our waters and protect our animals, if we the human race, wish to survive. Corporate greed, supported by governments, has continuously trumped conservation on the road to ever increasing corporate profits.

Department of Prisons and Corrections

Mistakes are an unpleasant fact of everyday life and a characteristic of our imperfection as human beings. This imperfection is not an excuse to continuously make mistakes and not atone for these mistakes. A free society will be plagued by crimes from misdemeanor to the most heinous. It is difficult not to feel rage when a loved one, an innocent person, or a public figure is maimed, harmed or murdered. We want revenge, death to a murderer, or lifetime incarceration for a convicted felon. Incarceration must be a part of any penal system. Rehabilitation must also be an even bigger part. Crimes are a product of our social deficit; a failure of society to identify and resolve problems that are the root causes of crime. Whether it is stealing a chocolate bar from a variety store, stealing software or embezzling funds from investors, there are root causes for all crimes. Some who break the law do so out of contempt for, and daring of, the law.

We must rehabilitate convicts by re-educating them, after identifying the cause of their criminal behaviour. If lack of moral values is the root cause for criminal activity, them we must re-educate the felon with the right moral values. Every convict must be given hope of being rehabilitated and returned to a free society to lead a productive and crime-free life. Reintegrating convicts into society will be of financial benefit to society in the form of reduced costs to the Prisons and Corrections department. Sophisticated monitoring and positioning technology exists to allow convicts to serve their sentence is a community institution, in the home of family or living on their own, while being tracked by law enforcement personnel. Society will be better off if monies saved from incarcerating convicts are redeployed to hiring more police offices, judges and people trained in human rehabilitation.

Department of Public Information

In every democracy, the dissemination of public information is crucial to freedom and security. The peoples' ignorance of government, political parties, politicians, our laws, policies and programs are directly related to poor dissemination of public information on these matters. People require information to ensure their quality of life is enhanced by taking advantage of public services offered by the government. Government is dynamic, with laws changing to meet the political needs of the day. A better-informed person will be a better Canadian. Knowing where to turn for government assistance will improve government service.

Keeping informed and knowledgeable of politics and the political processes, will help to build a stronger democracy. I have campaigned on behalf of several candidates' at all three levels of government. I am appalled at the apathy demonstrated by the population. The distrust of politicians and the feeling of helplessness against behemoth governments seem to be a common feeling amongst the population. Many Canadians feel powerless to effect changes for their benefit. In federal and provincial general elections, the percentage of eligible voters casting a vote seems to be decreasing in subsequent elections. Public education is lacking in our democracy. Often times Canadians do not know where to turn for help whenever they need it. The list of government services available must be better communicated to the population through the media. How many Canadians know that approximately two million card-carrying members of Canada's political parties decided who will be the members of our parliaments after every general election? I bet you thought that the general population made that decision. Using their respective nomination process, political party members chose a slate of candidates, offering them up to the voting population as their respective party's standard-bearer in the next general election. We, the voters, then choose the ones that shares our vision of Canada. Do we realize the lives of Canadians are controlled by the political party forming Government of Canada and selected by about one quarter of the eligible voters? We are destined to have mediocrity in governance if only ten percent of adult Canadians belong to a political party and less than one quarter of eligible voters chooses our government.

Public information is about people, culture, party politics, governance, and government; what they do, how they do it and how the people may get help from their government and better use government services.

Department of Public Safety and Emergency Management

As we go about our daily lives, safety must be paramount in our thoughts and deeds. Without safety and security, society will deteriorate into lawlessness and fearfulness. Public Safety is ensuring the food we eat, the car we drive and all the goods we purchase are safe and free of defects. Natural and man-made emergencies are unpleasant facts of life. Lives have been lost, communities devastated, and families destroyed as catastrophic events befall communities. Whether it is an individual rushed to a hospital after a serious accident, flooding, forest fires, an ice storm or an electricity blackout, we must always be prepared for a rapid and effective response to ensure safety of everyone and minimize loss of life. I lived through the Mississauga train derailment and subsequent evacuation where almost a quarter of a million people were orderly evacuated after a train carrying chemicals derailed in the middle of the city. I lived through the electricity black out that hit more than fifty million people in Ontario and parts of eastern USA. I have lived through one hurricane, on the island of Jamaica, and it is the scariest event I have ever witnessed. There is no greater feeling of emptiness as when one looses a loved one or all their possessions. The feeling of being alone and helpless as one watches a basement flooding, a roof torn of a house or another person drowning, is the greatest pain one could ever feel. Emergency preparedness and management must be a crucial part of any government plan to protect its citizens from natural and man-made events and to ensure timely and meaningful help will be available for the people.

Department of Revenue

Someone must collect the billions of dollars that will be flowing in to the government treasury after the implementation of the Government Services Fee. The Department of Revenue will be the collector of all government monies.

Department of Science

In our world, science plays a major role in our daily lives, and will continue to play an ever-increasing role as the decades go by. Science offers a wide range of possibilities, with huge benefits and pitfalls. Genetically modified plants and genetically modified foods are causes for serious concern in the population of many western countries. These concerns stem from the relatively little known facts about the genetically engineered plant and food and their long-term effects on human cells. Scientific research will produce new medicines from the many plants in pristine forests of the world. As we move to reside in space stations, and colonies on the Moon and other planets, experiments will produce differing results than when conducted under the influence of Earth's atmosphere and gravity. Purer chemicals may be produced in environments without gravity. Canadians produced some great discoveries that have benefited all humanity. We must be among the world leaders in funding all forms of scientific research. We must also continue to be at the forefront of scientific research and discoveries as we create the greatest country on Earth.

Department of the Solicitor General

The Justice Department will create laws to be enforced by the Internal Security Department and the Solicitor General will ensure the application of our laws to those choosing to break them. Our present judicial system is plagued with long delays and cases being dropped for many reasons. These delays are not the sole fault of the government; organizations and individuals in the legal and enforcement fields also contribute to the delays. Resolving these delays must be a priority for any government. We cannot maintain an orderly society if we cannot timely enforce and apply our laws. Offenders must speedily have their day in court, justice quickly served and sentencing applied immediately. Everyone needs to get on with life after a crime is committed and the full weight of the law is brought to bear in a conviction or the accused feels the ecstasy of exoneration.

Department of Sports and Recreation

From birth, kids love to have fun. Lying in a crib and unable to freely move around, a healthy baby smiles, plays with the crib rails, listen and laugh as he moves the "rattle" and other toys we provide them. In all this excitement for the baby, he is accomplishing one of the most important human traits. He is learning new things, soaking up everything much like a sponge soaks up water. Unlike a sponge, the human brain does not get saturated; it continues to absorb new information for as long as we are alive. As the baby grows, it learns more and require a better and more sophisticated method of teaching him new things. At the same time, the young child's curiosity causes him to be pleasantly mischievous; to have a very short attention span; to want to play instead of learn; to want to be on the move instead of sitting around; to want to be free instead of being constrained. Oh, to be a child again! All these traits makes it difficult to teach children the basics of life in a structured classroom setting. A teacher cannot take a child in a classroom setting and concentrate solely on teaching manners, respect, camaraderie, cooperativeness, and all the other lessons in human relations. Teaching these attributes by themselves is boring to the student and creates discipline problems for teachers. Removing the teachings of these attributes of human relations create the many problems we are witnessing in our society.

Physical education is an extremely important part of the human experience on Earth. We are designed to be active and creative. Our physical and intellectual beings are created to improve and grow. Living a long, prosperous and productive life requires regular exercise of our physical and mental beings. At the same time, humans prefer to take the path of least resistance and least pain to an end. We will perform at the minimum if allowed; we will avoid pain and challenges at all cost. The majority of us have resisted the challenge of exercise, reading and physical work because we consider them difficult and boring. Our senses have become numb by the "programming" images on man-made devices that have retrained us to be sedentary. After about grade 10, most children begin to reduce their physical activity, giving up soccer, hockey, football, track and field and many other sports in favour of hanging with their friends, hanging around in a mall, playing hours of computer and video games, watching television and browsing the internet. The reduction or elimination of physical education in school curriculum and the emphasis on fast food in our daily lives have contributed to obesity in young children. By the mid-teen years, schoolwork increases, youths begin to have part-time jobs, leaving little time for physical activities. The free spirit of children starts to disappear as they become aware of the demands of life, the need to survive and as responsibilities arrive at their doorstep.

We must educate our children in the art of diplomacy; the need to be disciplined in all aspects of life; the requirement to have respect for people and property; the vitally important traits of competition, camaraderie, cooperation, deportment and togetherness. Sporting activities are the most effective ways to educate our children in a manner that is pleasurable for them. This means developing programs that includes sports and recreational activities combined with the arts and science curriculum. We must devise means to help our children to love school. Constantly we heard our children say "**School is boring, teachers are boring, and subjects are boring.**" How, then do we make school and learning more fun for our children?

Recreational, Amateur and Professional Sports

Amateur Sports

Tens of thousands of our youth dream of being one of the greatest athletes in the world. Dreams of playing on professional sports teams, playing for a pay cheque or winning gold at world sporting events drive many of our young athletes to strive for excellence. Even with broken-down equipment, shortages of facilities, chronic under funding and shortages of qualified coaches, our school athletes pour their hearts into many sports, hoping to get a scholarship or make it big in professional sports. At major world events, our amateur athletes have made Canada proud, bringing heart thumping pride to our people as the Maple Leaf is raised and O Canada is played for all to hear. Earning national pride in the sporting arena must never be forgotten as being the sacrifices of many amateur athletes, their parents, friends and a few loyal sponsors. Missing from support groups are our governments and, to a lesser extent, national sporting associations who are continually struggling to fund athletes and their sports. Politicians, who cannot see an immediate vote in our athletes while they are training, clamour to heap praise on the champion athlete, basking in the glow of publicity earned by the athlete. People who have long forgotten the meaning of sportsmanship operate Nation Sports Associations, their policies and procedures carved in stone. Our governments have almost eliminated funding for sports at all levels of education and in community sporting groups. In 1976, Montreal hosted the Summer Olympics and Canada became the only country not to win a gold medal when hosting the summer games. In 1988, Calgary hosted the Winter Olympics and once again, Canada became the only host country not to win a gold medal. For 50 years, Canada did not win an Olympic gold medal in ice hockey, a game we taught the world and have dominated for decades. In 2002 Winter Olympics, a team of excellent players defeated a spirited Team USA to win the gold medal. As significant as it is, our amateur ice hockey players did not achieve the win; rather a contingent of mostly multi-millionaire professional players made us proud. They are Canadians and we are very proud of them.

Our amateur athletes, many trained and funded in foreign countries, are beginning to compete and win at major world events. Canadian based and trained amateur athletes are beginning to have success. Greater success is possible if larger and more secure funding were available from our governments and corporations. Soccer is the largest sport in Canada, by registered players, surpassing hockey. Despite the numbers, we do not have a strong national soccer league of the caliber found in Europe and South America. Our National Soccer team reached the FIFA World Cup once, in Mexico, in 1986. Since that time, we have not fared well, with the exception of winning the 2000 Gold Cup. Like the athletes in all other sports, some good young talent is on the way, training locally and internationally. Sadly, due to lack of competition of the highest level, our athletes migrate to other countries to ply their professional trade, coming home long enough to play on a Canadian national team. Athletes in many other sports are toiling away in anonymity and in near-poverty lifestyles to achieve the fame and success a gold medal or championship will bring. We must be their morale and financial booster every step of the way.

Recreational Sports

At the school and community level, the mediocrity of sports development and management is shocking. Professional management must be a part of the operations of all our community sports clubs, supervised by a volunteer Board of Directors directly elected by the members. We must develop tiered competitive and recreational sports program that will encourage participants from four years and above. The health and financial benefits of keeping millions of children, youth and adults active and fit will help build a stronger, smarter and healthier society. As both a recreational and competitive coach, I have witnessed both desires to win and just to have fun. Our world is competitive in everything we do. We must encourage our children to be competitive, to win, but not at all costs. We must be dignified in winning and graceful in accepting defeat. That is what sportsmanship is all about!

Professional Sports

Professional sports are a major part of Canadian culture. Regardless of the sport, hockey, football, soccer, baseball or basketball, professional athletes enjoy a reverence not seen in any other sector of society. The more prominent ones also enjoy a whopping pay cheque. When our revered professional athletes fall off the podium, our image is shattered and we become disappointed, wondering how is it possible they misbehaved so badly. Arguably, professional athletes are overpaid and are spoiled brats with a body of evidence existing to support these points. They are entertainers, just like highly paid movie stars in Hollywood. Professional sports teams are businesses, created to generate profits for their owners and a job for the professional athletes. While the main product is a contest between two teams, or two athletes, revenues stream in from gate receipts, broadcast rights and branded merchandise. Professional sports team draw out discretionary expenditures from the surrounding population, which provides an added stimulus to the local economy. We have lost professional teams in major cities, mainly to similar sized cities of the USA. Our governments must find ways to help professional team strive in our small markets, without resorting to subsidies, giveaways, tax reduction or any other programs not available to every other business in Canada. Government and the people must not allow themselves to be held hostage by professional sports organizations threatening to move operations elsewhere unless the government ponies up bags full of money.

International Sporting Events

The world's most prestigious sporting event is the International Olympic Committee's (IOC) Summer Olympic Games. The most watched is Federation International de Football Associations' (FIFA) World Cup of Football (soccer). Canada hosted the Summer Olympics in 1976 and made unsuccessful attempts to host it again. Some in our community believe hosting major international sporting events, such as the Olympics and World Cup, is a waste of money, arguing money for financing these events be redirected to the homeless and the poor. Admirable as these causes are and warranting everyday attention, Toronto did not solve its homeless and poverty problems after loosing in its bid to host the 1996 and 2000 Summer Olympics. Many planned projects were put on hold after each loss. There were grandiose plans to revitalize Toronto's waterfront. I haven't seem much revitalization since Toronto lost the 1996 bid in the 1990 IOC announcement awarding the 1996 Summer Olympics to the city of Atlanta, Georgia, USA. Canada should definitely be bidding to host the FIFA World Cup, an event Canada had never hosted. Even though we do not have any world-class soccer facility, a successful bid would most certainly result in the building of many world-class stadiums, which are badly needed for the national soccer development program and national teams. These stadiums will fill the need of other sports such as track and field and football. People are worried about large deficits after the major world sporting events are over, fearing a repeat of the Montreal Olympics of 1976. Montreal Mayor Jean Drapeau, after Montreal won the right to host the 1976 Olympics, was quoted as saying, **"The Olympics can no more lose money than a man can have a baby."** Following the 1976 Olympics, the city of Montreal was left with a debt of $1 billion which is continues to payoff, almost thirty years, and seven Olympics later. The Los Angeles Games of 1984, the first privately financed games, generated over US$200million in profits. With these two contrasts in mind, hosting a major world-sporting event is not only about the event and about money. It is the construction legacy and the multi-year worldwide advertising campaign to promote the host country, seeking to increase short- and long-term tourism, increasing the inflow of cash into the host country. The cost of hosting the event is amortized over the many years between hosting the same event. Hosting a major worldwide sporting event is also about increasing the local profile of each sport and local competitors. Studies have shown an increase in local and national interest in sports in the years immediately following the event.

Department of Supply and Services

This department will be responsible for the procurement of all goods and services supplied to government departments and parliament. From time to time, we have hard horror stories of governments paying too much for goods and services, not getting the quality it paid for, and other mind-numbing waste. Just like the individual family and the corporation, government must be frugal with its money.

Department of Technology

In the latter part of the twentieth century, the mechanized Industrial Revolution became fully developed and a shift towards Knowledge Revolution began. Industry requires more physical and intellectual capacity from it employees. The shipper-receiver now requires computer skills to complete his job. Customer service representatives use databases to store information on clients and products. Consumers are accessing their banks and shopping via the internet with the "bricks and mortar" merchants feeling the effects of reduced store visitors. Technology offers us instant communication, biometric recognition, community link in a computer network, and medical devices that peek into our insides without a scalpel, among many other marvelous advances. Technological developments of the past gave us national standards. We may by a television set or AM/FM radio receiver without considering the content we might be watching or listening to, or ownership of the TV or Radio station. We need not worry about the manufacturer, as we know that all TV sets and radio receivers will work on the Canadian broadcasting system. Radio and television broadcasts were developed into a "standard." National Television System Committee (NTSC) is the standard in Canada, the US and the Caribbean. Amplitude Modulation (AM) and Frequency Modulation (FM) broadcasts are the standards for commercial radio stations. There are many more standards for various technologies. History will show that many of these standards were agreed to before the 1980's the beginning of decade of greed. Fast forward to the 1980's and the advent of the cellular telephone and satellite television broadcasts. A cell phone from one provider is not compatible with the system of the other provider and likewise for the satellite television receiver. While there are technical standards, interoperability is not possible because we do not have a standard system. If a customer is fed up with his cell phone or satellite provider, he is stuck between a rock and a hard place, for he must lay out additional monies to purchase the equipment to switch to the competitor. Not so with the Plain Old Telephone System (POTS), the wired telephone service provider. Whether we purchase wired telephone service from the large companies or one of the resellers, the services are interoperable because there is a standard. No additional money is required to switch service. Nowhere is the absence of standards having a more profound impact than in the computer hardware and software industries. The set of specifications, agreed to at the lowest common denominator, ensures people and corporations struggle for interoperability in these two very significant industries. Industrial standards ensure that consumers spend less money and have choices while the lack of standards ensures the consumer becomes captive to individual corporations, costing the consumer more money and eliminating choice.

There will be many technological breakthroughs in the decades and centuries ahead. Canada must be at the forefront in technology research and implementation. Canada must ensure national standards are in place and every Canadian government must work with industry to ensure the benefits of technological advances are reaped by the consumer and the developer of the technologies.

Even though writers have been around for millennia, I could not imagine writing this book without my computer, a word processing application software and the power of the internet. The internet, almost completely unavailable to the public in 1990, is a lynchpin of today's communications and an important part of business practices. E-mail messaging have become so pervasive in our society individuals are lost without it and corporations begin to loose profit whenever an e-mail service is not working. As an illustration, one of my company's current clients did not have a computer network, e-mail or internet connection when I was called to revamp their computer system. The technology solutions proposed envisioned a computer network with a dedicated server, workstations, internet connection, e-mail and web site. The network infrastructure so transformed the organization to a dependence on internet access, e-mail, and file and printer sharing that a recent problem with the Internet Service Provider prompted a threat of legal action for a service interruption that lasted days instead of a few hours. This transition to such dependence on technology happened in less than eighteen months for this nine-person organization.

Department of Travel and Tourism

Promoting and Traveling Canada

One could spend a lifetime traveling Canada and not see all the villages, hamlets, towns and cities, and even the vast wildernesses. The vastness of the land, the majesty of its rivers, lakes and mountains are exhilarating. I have visited many places in most provinces and thoroughly enjoyed every one of them. One of my goals is to visit every country of the world at least once, spending at least one day in each. Notwithstanding my lofty goals, I am committed to giving at least one week every year, for the rest of my life, to vacationing in Canada. There is a hotel, cottage, cabin and campground to suit every need. The sunshine and warmth of southern destinations are great for our bodies and the beautiful tan we desire. Our memories of Canadian destinations will last forever, even as were are saving for a yearly southern vacation to reapply tanning.

Promoting Canada to Canadians

Early in our time in Canada, my wife and I met an older person, and at our workplace. As the friendship developed, we met her husband and children, who were about our age. I was surprised to discover this couple knew many areas of the USA, particularly Florida, but did not know where Mississauga was, even though she lived in the west-end of Toronto, adjoining Mississauga. Later, as we met more people in our travels throughout southern Ontario, we came across many who knew more places outside Canada than they did of places inside Canada. Usually, people would tell us they wanted sunshine, so they took vacations to the south. Others would cite the high cost of vacationing in Canada compared to other parts of the world. It still seems more Canadians take prepackaged vacations to the sunnier southern climes than across Canada. Lately, I have encountered Canadian vacationing to sunny places during Canadian summers. While Canadian summers are short, we are not wanting for heat right across Canada.

Canada has many celebrities in the entertainment and sports world. We have prominent corporate executives and national leaders. The Department of Travel and Tourism should sponsor competitions to select groups of people who would receive all-expense paid vacations for a week with prominent Canadian political, sports and business people, at Canadian locations. Imagine a corporate executive and a group of Canadians hiking the Rockies, or whitewater rafting down one of Canada's magnificent rivers, taped and broadcasted on a television network. Imagine the Prime Minister and Canadians from all lifestyles camping in Cape Breton National Park, or going to see the midnight sun in the high Arctic. Imagine a famous Canadian movie star or popular singer touring the Quebec Winter Carnival or Toronto's Caribana Parade with adults and youths from all over Canada. Imagine the premiers spending a week vacationing with a group of people from their respective provinces, promoting provincial attractions to the rest of Canada. The tourism boost to the locale would be enormous. Canada offers so much to see and do, it would take a lifetime to see its major attractions, pristine wilderness, beautiful wildlife, and participate in the many festivals of all seasons. Every Canadian should commit themselves to spending one week of their vacation every year, for the rest of their lives, in a Canadian location. Fall is beautiful; winter is exciting and spring prepares us for the awesome sunshine and heat of summer. Canada is beautiful. Canada is wonderful. Spend some time to travel throughout Canada, meet its people, see its places and enjoy our country. The memories will last forever.

Promoting Canada to the World

Canada is a magnificent country; its expanse, varied weather and people offer visitors an enjoyment of nature, friendship and many things to see and do. The four seasons offers visitors activities such as skiing, snowboarding and tobogganing in the winter; camping, hiking, and whitewater rafting in the summer; observing the foliage in the fall. We have cultural activities throughout the year that attracts visitors to Canada. Promoting Canada to the world through cultural exchanges, foreign aid, world-renowned sporting events, government-to-government cooperation, and people-to-people interaction will improve our quality of life by bringing more money in to Canada. Tourism will flourish in Canada if Canadians travel within Canada and visitors continue to consider Canada as a safe and attractive place to visit, despite our creeping political alignment with a regime that oppress poor and less fortunate countries around the world. We must fiercely maintain an independent foreign policy that promotes peace, cooperation, freedom and democracy. This will encourage many more foreigners to visit Canada.

Paradise in the Sun – The Caribbean Islands

Canadians love the sunshine; summer is great in Canada. Picnics, boating, fishing, camping, and cottaging are major activities that relieve the pressures and stresses of the winter months. Winter forces many Canadians to hibernate, dreaming of the southern sunshine destinations of the Caribbean islands, Mexico, and the many warm vacation places in American states, particularly Florida and Hawaii. Billions of dollars are drained out of Canada each year. Would it not be nice for Canada to have a Paradise in the Sun? It is quite possible for Canada to have a province in the sun; much like the U.S.A have Hawaii and Puerto Rico and the island colonies Britain have in the Caribbean. Various Canadian Prime Ministers have had their favourite places in the sun. Prime

Ministers Pierre Trudeau and John Turner loved and often visited Jamaica. Prime Minister Brian Mulroney preferred the Florida sun. Even our premiers have there favourite sunshine destinations. Every Canadian has their favourite sunshine spot. Many love the Caribbean islands for their "laid back" life, sunshine, beaches, rum and friendliness of the Caribbean peoples. In the Caribbean islands, Canada and Canadians are well respected and loved. Our own Canadian province in the sun would be a perfect addition to Canada and its people. The Canadian government should approach one or two islands to become provinces of Canada. They would benefit from Canadian technology, Canadian jurisprudence, and share in Canadian wealth by uplifting their own standards of living and quality of life. Peoples from these islands would reap the benefits of Canadian citizenship we enjoy everyday.

The two islands best suited to be provinces of Canada are Barbados and Jamaica. Both have strong British heritage, vibrant tourism, friendly and educated people, and an industrious and competent workforce. Canadian-educated political and business leaders in Barbados and Jamaica have very strong ties to Canada. Barbados and Jamaica have large expatriate population in Canada with Jamaica having the larger population. Barbados is a five-hour flight from Toronto while Jamaica is a just over three hours away, closer than a Vancouver-Toronto flight. The national Canadian government would propose to the governments and people of Barbados and Jamaica to join Canada as provinces. All three countries would hold national referenda to determine the wishes of its people, I believe all three peoples would vote in favour of forming a union, much the same way as Newfoundlanders joined Canada in 1949.

A sunshine province would keep billions of tourist dollars in Canada; offer Canadian businesses an economically attractive manufacturing base, keeping more money in Canada. Barbados and Jamaica would offer Canadians the opportunity to own sunshine property for retirement, keeping the retirees money in Canada. Canadian retirees would spend Canadian money, without the hefty conversion to the US dollar at their US retirement communities. Retiree's health care costs would be lower as they are part of Canada and would not require extra health insurance. The boost to the Canadian economy would offset any costs associated with bringing the standard of living of Barbados and Jamaica to Canadian level.

Paradise in the Sun - Jamaica

Jamaica is a member of the Commonwealth, with the British Monarch as Head of State. It is located in the western Caribbean, approximately 150km south of Cuba and one-hour flight from Miami. About the size of Lake Ontario, with a population just over two and one half million, Jamaica is a constitutional parliamentary democracy with a legal system based on English common law, much like English Canada. Jamaicans rely on European, American and Canadian tourism for a large part of its foreign earnings. Exports of bauxite, alumina, rum, and bananas, also contribute to its foreign earnings. The United Kingdom accounts for 10% of Jamaica's exports; Canada, 12%; and the USA, 28%. Many of the modern conveniences found in Canada are available in Jamaica. There are Canadian, British, and American Banks, North American telephone, television and cellular telephone system; world-class hotels and some of the best beaches in the world. Jamaica's educational system is predominately British, but influences from Canada and the USA are prevalent. Many Canadian and American companies operate in Jamaica, shipping their products to North America. Canada's Seasonal Agricultural Workers Program affords 5000 Jamaicans temporary seasonal employment on farms in Ontario and Quebec.

Paradise in the Sun - Barbados

Barbados is a small island located in the Atlantic Ocean, near the boundary with the Eastern portion of Caribbean Sea. With the British Monarch as Head of State, and a member of the Commonwealth, Barbados' parliamentary democracy follows the British system. Tourism is an important trade as is sugar, molasses, and rum. Predominantly Christian, Barbados has 97% literacy. Barbadians, "Bajans" for short, enjoy the many modern conveniences of Canadians; North American telephone, television and cellular telephone system; Canadian, British and American banks; and world-class hotels and hospitality services. Barbados's largest trading partner is the USA at 41% and U.K at 7%. Barbados is part of the Canada's Seasonal Agricultural Workers Program, which allows Caribbean farm workers the opportunity for temporarily working on Canadian farms, primarily during the harvesting of fruit and vegetable crops. Canada has a close and longstanding relationship with Barbados covering major areas such as banking, migration, development cooperation, financial services. Canadian banks have long held a dominant position on the island. Barbados is a favourite vacation destination for many Canadians. Canada is a preferred tourist destination for Barbadians, many of whom have strong family connections in Canada. Among the current generation of Barbadian leaders, many have family connections, or received part of their education, in Canada. The Canadian Women's Club is the oldest service organization in Barbados.

The similarities and commonalties of Barbados and Jamaica to, and with, Canada makes for an excellent fit with Canadians' desire to have "Paradise in the Sun" at Canadian dollar value. As it becomes more difficult and unfriendly to travel to sunny locations on our continent, it is more imperative for Canada to have its own territories in the sun, with the freedom to travel as every Canadian deserve. Having our own territories in the sun will help keep tourist dollars in Canada; helping to maintaining our standard of living. I believe Paradise in the Sun could be all the islands of the Caribbean Sea, affording Canadians the opportunity to be citizens and homeowners in the sun.

Department of Transportation

In any society, the need to move people and goods from place to place is vital to the survival of that society. Whether the movement is by rail, road, water or air, it must be cost effective and efficient. Transportation systems must be developed to its fullest without sacrificing the environment. In urban areas, local governments must be encouraged to construct efficient people movers in the form of public mass transits, such as underground and aboveground trains, buses and ferries. In our present form of government, urban and intercity public transit systems receive inadequate attention. Cities are expanded with little regard for efficient public transit systems. Municipal government and landowners are more interested in cramming more houses and industrial buildings on a given piece of land. The municipality's goal is to generate increased property taxes while the landowner is to generate more profit. Long after these goals are met, public transit begins to receive attention with the rudimentary designs makes getting from point A to B, a scenic journey where a fifteen-minute automobile trip would take about an hour by bus. Buses travel a scenic route along streets, avenues, roads, lanes crescent, courts and places as they pick up and drop of passengers in residential areas. For the most part, urban planning prefers the personal automobile, with efficient public mass transit an afterthought. With the vast distances from sea to shining sea, an integrated system of roadways and railways are essential to the movement of people and goods. Canada has a vast network of rail, road, air, and water transportation systems serving mostly urban areas, where profit is greater. While service is better in urban areas, a Canadian may travel to almost any part of Canada by either private or public transportation, if time is not of the essence. The sheer size of Canada, and the meager public transportation system, dictates that the private automobile will always be king of the road. We must create a fast and efficient public transportation system to service distances greater than 200 km at the same time as we are improving existing, or building new, urban public transit systems. The number of passengers using air, rail, and bus transportation systems has been declining over the years, mainly because of poor quality of service and lack of investment in these infrastructures. The private automobile is the "king" of people movers and will continue its dominance for years to come, despite its pollutants killing the environment and adversely affecting the health of many Canadians, adding billions of dollars to our health care costs.

Everyday the number of drivers and motor vehicles increases as is the number of accidents and injuries. Motor vehicle insurance and driver competencies are major sore points among all Canadian drivers. Whether our insurance is from a private company or government agency, we all agree motor vehicle insurance is more expensive than it ought to be. While private insurance companies are in the business to make a profit, there is some merit to the perception of greed on the part of these private companies. Why is it mandatory to have motor vehicle insurance and it is not mandatory for companies to offer insurance coverage to everyone? With less than stellar public transit, it is unimaginable that a Canadian could go through life with the use of an automobile. Automobile insurance companies may deny insurance coverage at their pleasure, an act that could devastate the life of one person or an entire family. Government must ensure that an automobile insurance company cannot deny coverage to any person, regardless of driving record. Reducing the number of accidents and injuries require better driving skills. We must institute a national driver-training program by highly certified driving instructors with experiences and certification in controlling motor vehicles in all driving conditions. Driver education must include extensive classroom training, including driving simulator, akin to an aircraft flight simulator. Driver training and testing must include urban and highway driving. A license to operate a motor vehicle must relate to the weight class of the vehicle used in the driver road test and the issued driver license endorsed accordingly. Every driver must be retested in five-year intervals, with the severity of the test increasing in each five-year increment.

Roads and Highways construction

A great country needs a great transportation system. With a 50-year plan, a series of east-west and north-south highways built, or reserved, at convenient distances apart would allow easy access to every city, town and village, improving movement of goods and people. Governments must build a public network of major multi-lane highways in grid pattern to improve the flow of vehicular traffic and reduce pollution from idling cars stuck in gridlock. Any network of roads and highways must be integrated with other forms of transportation systems to ensure a seamless transfer of people from one mode to the other. Why it is possible to drive from Toronto to Miami and Key West in Florida, or Montreal to New York City, exclusively on multilane highways, yet it is not possible to drive from Toronto to Regina and Vancouver exclusively on multilane highways. It is simply because our governments have concentrated in building road links in the north-south direction and neglecting the east-west direction.

Railway construction

Integrated with major highway construction would be high speed and regular speed commuter trains for intercity transportation. In major urban centres, subways, buses and above ground rail service would provide fast, efficient intra-city transportation. Inter-city travelers would also benefit from more bus and train transportation services, instead of depending on our gird-locked highways of the mostly single passenger automobile and massive transport trucks. The National government must provide leadership in transportation areas where the private sector has no interest. For decades, there has been talk of building a high-speed railway system in the Quebec City, QC and Windsor, ON transportation corridor. For years, all talk and no action from government have resulted in a slow and inefficient passenger rail system in this corridor that is only now getting better. The GO transit system, in the Greater Toronto Area, works very well in peak hours and strand commuters in the off peak hours. Passenger rail system needs a major expansion in the frequency of trips and communities served. Over the decades, our rail system was rationalized to serve on profitable routes and fewer communities. The closing of rail lines and stations, when combined with discontinued air routes, denied affordable public transportation to many Canadians. When the last spike was driven to complete the trans-continental rail service in the east-west direction, the vision was that rail service would serve all Canadians and provide another means of transportation and a vital link between all regions of Canada. Even with recent cash infusion into the federal government-owned VIA Rail, it is inadequately funded, cannot develop into a viable and efficient national passenger rail service.

Public Transit

"The car is king" is probably the mantra of the automobile manufacturing and oil producing sectors of our economy. For nearly a century, we have bought into it, creating parking nightmares, and polluting the environment. The private automobile has significantly contributed to the deteriorating health and breathing problems of our people. The heavy reliance on the automobile has contributed to urban sprawl and a significant reduction in farmland. In the major metropolitan areas, gridlock exists and is getting worse day by day. Commuting time via the private automobile continues to increase, resulting in a twelve-hour workday for most commuters on an eight-hour shift. The private automobile, with its single driver/passenger, will kill the economy in the years to come. Productivity will decrease as time lost, stress and accidents keep people away from the workplace. The increased distress and injuries from accidents will drive our health care costs to the moon in the next twenty five to fifty years. Governments must place greater emphasis on, and implement, public mass transportation technologies. The start of such a mass, public transportation infrastructure must be at the municipal planning level. Today, municipal planning benefits the landowner and house builders, universally and misguidedly referred to as "developers." The house construction sector is more concerned with the number of houses built on a given parcel of land, with a view of maximizing profits. Municipal governments, starved of funds by their provincial masters, encourage developers to squeeze more houses on to a given plot of land as a means of exacting more lot levies and a continued property tax base to fund local services. In 2003, a group of us were investigating the possibility of building a major sports facility in one of the cities around Toronto. After identifying a 200-acre parcel of land, we approached the city planning and economic departments to discuss rezoning and possible land uses for the identified property. The head honcho of the economic department advised me he had no interest in building a sports facility on the parcel of land when houses would generate ten times more property taxes than the proposed facility, and that recreational uses for land is no of any big concern to him. He certainly represented his Economic Development department very well. The Recreational and Parks department were excited to hear about our proposal, which is still in the developmental stages. As city finances are property tax driven, we will continue to see urban planning and construction focused on increasing the construction density on any given parcel of land. One need only look at a geographical map of the city to see the maze created in order to build more houses. After these land barons gather their profits and run, government is left with the responsibility of maintaining a maze of urban roads and sidewalks. In planning new residential and business districts, government must give public transit the highest priority, while assuring a measure of peace and quiet in residential neighbourhoods.

Department of Veterans Affairs

We send our men and women to war in far off places to defend our values and protect our freedoms. Upon their return the government and people they served barely remember the sacrifice they made for the entire country. Our federal government has a pathetic record of helping our veterans. Many suffer physical and psychological trauma, and are unable to take care of themselves, live in poverty and an otherwise miserable life. We must properly provide for the men and women whom fought for our freedom. They are not asking to live as Kings, Queens and Royalty, just live a meaningful life like most Canadians.

Building One Canada

Canada must be remodeled if it is to become the Greatest Country on Earth. The bickering between all levels must cease. Our ethnicity and culture are of infinite value to Canada and must be supplanted by Canadiana. We must be Canadians first. Nationalism must replace parochialism. We must take back government from the political parties, corporations and wealthy Canadians.

Taking Back Government

> "Throughout history, it has been the inaction of those who could have acted; the indifference of those who should have known better; the silence of the voice of justice when it mattered most; that has made it possible for evil to triumph." *His Excellency, Haile Selassie, (born 1893 - Died 1974) Emperor of Ethiopia.*

Government belongs to all the people of Canada and not corporate Canada, wealthiest of Canadians or the political parties, their members and supporters. The three partners to building a Great Canada are the people, its government, and businesses. We cannot build a country at the expense of anyone of the three partners. Government creates the legislative and social infrastructure; business provides capital and ideas and Canadians provide physical and intellectual labour to produce marketable goods and services. Each party to the building of Canada is a consumer of goods and services produced by the others. This is a fact ignored by all three parties, to the peril of Canada.

As a people and society, we believe, and expect, our government to lead our country and its people into a better life. We work very hard knowing we will better our own standard of living, improve the Quality of Life for all Canadians, and enhance our stature in our world. Government must equally serve all Canadians, regardless of their political beliefs and financial power. Most of our governments throughout the last century have forgotten its role. We have had governments supporting businesses at the expense of people; we have had governments supporting people at the expense of businesses and we have had governments that have tried to balance the needs of the people against the wants of businesses. Unfortunately, governments that implemented policies and programs intended to balance the wants and needs of the people with the wants and needs of businesses have been short lived. Corporate Canada is an integral part of building Canada into a Greatest Country on Earth, in partnership with government and Canadians. Corporate executives would have us believe their companies are here to create jobs for Canadians. Nothing could be further from the truth; they are here to make profits and increase there wealth. Jobs are created as the need to produce more goods and services arise. Once the business environment changes for the worse, corporations and their capital will flee to a more favourable environment.

Over many centuries, government did lead its people to greater conquests. At every step of the way were rich and powerful men, as either government leaders or advisors to government officials. These rich and powerful men controlled everything; they were large landowners with peasants, or slaves in an earlier time, farming the land; they were industrialists building railroads; they were oilfield owners and oil producers. During the twentieth century, government became the pawn of rich men and large companies. Powerful men, largely the leaders of powerful corporations, exerted influence on aspiring political office seekers and political office holders. Often these powerful men and their corporations purchased influence with large financial contributions to political parties; working on a political campaign or just giving a public endorsement of the future politician. Influence peddling is now a big business in itself with large corporations employing lobbyists or purchasing the services of business whose sole purpose is influence peddling. Often, senior political party campaign workers and strategist become lobbyist after "their man" find himself with a seat in one of our legislative chambers. Defeated politicians become "government consultants" selling access to their former peers.

Those giving large sums of money and countless hours of time to politicians eventually want a return on their investment. They want it all back, and much more. Those "gifts" must be returned a hundred or a thousand fold, no question about it. Politicians now become beholden to the contributor and as the old saying goes "he who pays the piper, calls the tune." The return on investment for these gifts will manifest itself in the form of an appointment to a government board or agency, employment in a constituency office, government contracts to friends and relatives and many more, too numerous to mention here.

"One of the penalties for refusing to participate in politics is that you end up being governed by your inferiors." *Plato, (born 427 BC – Died 347BC)*

Taking back government starts with us gaining political knowledge and becoming a member of a party. Many people are reluctant to join a political party, fearing they do not know enough about politics. Like the "chicken and egg" situation, you must decide which comes first. In politics, joining the party comes first and all the knowledge you will need to effect change will come rushing in. Politics is the reason political parties exist and governments are the creation of political parties. If we are ever to take back government, every Canadian must understand two political processes. The first is the political party process, which is private and internal to every political party, requiring membership in the party. The second political process is the public process during an election campaign, culminating on Election Day. Our Constitution and our Canadian citizenship guarantee our right to participate in general elections, after we have met eligibility requirements. As infrequently as we have exercised it that "right" is the most powerful right any Canadian will ever hold. That right gives us the power to change our lives by changing our governance. Taking back government requires an understanding of both political processes and political parties.

The first step in understanding the political processes is recognizing the sole reason for the existence of a political party is to control the government for the benefit of its supporters. Political parties create grandiose platforms and seek out high profile candidates to convince the voters that a particular political entity is best able to govern Canada. In understanding the political processes, we must recognize the role of the governing political party is to increase its chances of re-election by implementing programs that finds favour with the population. During an election campaign, political parties promise everything and nothing. Political parties are not accountable to the population, are generally accountable for the promises made during the course of meeting its objective, which getting enough of its candidates elected to the form a majority government, but would be happy with a minority government. The Election campaign period is crucial to every political party. Many voters decide their preference of parties based on family voting history, party membership, candidate's stature in the local community, and friendship to the candidates. Very few voters base their voting preference on party platforms unless there is a "pie in the sky" promise such as reducing taxes, reducing crime, mortgage-interest tax deductibility, reducing the size government or some other hot button issue. Our everyday understanding of life and our political education and enlightenment will enable us to filter out political garbage spit out by the electioneering machinery of every political party. Political education begins with common sense! In our personal lives, if our pay cheque decreases, will we not have less money to spend between pay periods? The government has a payday and it does get a regular pay cheque. At specified intervals, corporations remit to the government all monies collected on behalf of the government. If government reduced taxes, will it not provide less, or poorer quality of, services? A politician promising to reduce taxes is also promising to reduce services to us!

Many of us refuse the see this reality. A government promising to increase spending on health care or any other areas of vital interest to the people is also promising to increase taxes. One more many of us refuse to acknowledge this. We, the people cannot have it both ways. We must either support paying higher taxes for the higher quality of government services we desire, or lower taxes, and consequently lower levels of services, paying for any additional services we may require. Either way, we will either pay now or pay later!

Taking back government is joining a political party, getting the right to participate in the internal political party process. The most important party process is the nomination of a candidate for the forthcoming general election. Every candidate seeking the nomination embarks on a campaign to signup as many party members to gain a numerical advantage over his opponents. By joining the party, you help to determine who carries the party banner into the election. This is where the self-serving politicians-to-be are weeded out. The more members joining, the more worried the party brass becomes. The more members, the more the party hierarchy looses their iron grip on the internal party political machinations and the more rooted democracy becomes within the party. By joining a political party, you get a political voice and you exercised one part of your vote to elect a member to our legislative chambers.

Taking back government requires our constant vigilance, between elections, on the actions of the government. Knowing that the next election campaign begins the morning after the last Election Day will help in understanding everything government does is geared towards its re-election. Government is nothing without the people and their money to pay for government services.

Taking back government means never surrendering our voice to another and never letting someone lead us down a path of their choosing. That is exactly what most of us do as we go about our daily lives, without a care about government and its actions. The majority of us, calling ourselves the "Silent Majority," are lost in the political wilderness, unable to filter out political deception from reality and grabbing on to straws of political promises of salvation. A minority of us, labeled 'Special Interest Groups" by the silent majority are vociferous on the subjects that matters to us, working very hard to get our way with the politicians. The special interest group engages the political process and the silent majority is afraid of the political process. In Taking Back Government, the silent majority, having long surrendered it voice, must become the vociferous special interest group, with the special interest being "Canada."

If you do not belong to a political party, you will not gain an understanding of the party political process, which is crucial to get good governments. No one wants to show an outsider the machinations of the political process. Not having a clear understanding of the political process and governance makes us feel alone, powerless and lost, surrendering our rights to people and politicians who purport to know what is best for us. No one can take away our rights, we must fight to keep our rights and never surrender to "backroom boys," political party "bagmen," and "spin-doctors." Montreal-born Singer/Songwriter Cory Hart says it best in his song "Never Surrender"

> "...And nobody wants to show you how
>
> So if you're lost and on your own
> you can never surrender
> And if your path won't lead you home
> you can never surrender
> And when the night is cold and dark
> you can see, you can see light

**No one can take away your right
to fight and to never surrender…"**

Taking back government means that we must "get up, stand up for our rights," the rights guaranteed in our Constitution and Charter of Rights and Freedoms.

Taking back government means staying in constant contact with our elected representatives. Once elected, politicians normally vote the party line, forgetting the opinions of the constituents they were elected to serve. Our telephone calls, e-mails, letters, and opinions on every major government action, will serve as a constant reminder to the politician of his duty to serve the people first. A politician's worst nightmare are letters, e-mails, faxes and telephone calls from his constituents, especially if expressed opinions are negative. I have seen it, they shake in their boots!

Taking back government means holding the entire elected assemblies, not just the government and the governing party, accountable between elections and at election time.

Taking back government may increase our trust in politicians, enhance the reputation of the governments; we may even get to like and appreciate politicians and politics.

Canada is our property; the government belongs to us and it is our servant. Are we ready to take back our property, reconstruct it, and once again have prosperity and cooperation? Only you can answer that question.

The strength of democracy depends on the collective efforts of every person living in Canada, whether citizen or resident. Democracy is not just voting at election time; it is staying in constant contact with elected representative and government departments; expressing our opinions so others may hear them and standing up for our beliefs are parts of democracy. Democracy is not surrendering you voice to anyone. Democracy is not being a proxy by depending on others to be the agent of changes you want to see implemented. Democracy does not necessarily equate to freedom. Democracy is the power of individual choice to be who we want to be; how we want to live.

If we do not fight for democracy, we will become someone's puppet or pawn.

The time to Take Back Government is NOW.

Who will build One Canada?

"Never be afraid to try something new. Remember, amateurs built Noah's Ark, professionals built the Titanic."
Unknown

Who will build one Canada will depend on the will of the people. The present crop of federal and provincial politicians certainly will not build it. We have national and provincial political parties representing governments at both levels. National political parties are a federation of provincial parties even though they may be acting as separate entities and purporting to represent specific interests within their jurisdictions. They are cousins to each other and will eventually act in supporting each other with a view to getting the other elected in their respective jurisdictions. They will act against each other whenever protecting their self-interest of getting elected or re-elected. In 2003, there was speculation that the Federal government did not join the Americans' war on Iraq because the pending Quebec election would be influenced by sending Canadians, and particularly Quebecers, to die in a war. One might remember that Quebecers opposed conscription during World War II. A federal Liberal government sending Canadians to war in Iraq would certainly have had a negative effect on the Liberal party in Quebec, a cousin of the Liberal Party of Canada. Like all Federal political parties, assisting the election of provincial cousins is the primary goal close to a provincial election. There were also speculation that the hard line taken by the by the federal government over Ontario's Conservative government's demand for $1 billion in compensation for costs related to SARS and the electricity blackout were not heeded because of an impending provincial election where it was hoped the Ontario Liberals would win the election. Fuel was added to the fire when the newly elected Liberal government immediately accepted a smaller amount of compensation from the federal Liberal government. Here we see two cases where it is speculated that cousins are taking care of each other. Sometimes in politics, it is difficult to identify the real reasons for government action, blurring the line between serving the people and serving their political cousins. After all, politics is getting and staying elected.

The present Federal political parties are incapable of building one Canada, as their primary goal is to be elected, cater to their own regional needs and the needs of their provincial cousins. This makes it impossible to put Canada first and impossible to build Canada into the Greatest Country on Earth. Regionalism will definitely be an obstacle to building one strong Canada, one Great Country, as a model for the world to emulate. A new nationalist political movement is required to build one strong country. This new nationalist political movement must not have any affiliation to any provincial political party because it would prevent the objective of creating one country with two levels of government by eliminating the provincial bureaucracy.

Are will willing to put regionalism aside for stronger Canada, creating the Greatest Country on Earth?

Are we willing temper our parochial nature to build one great country?

Do we support Canadian nationalism or Canadian provincialisms?

Are we ready for stronger local governments supported by a strong national government?

Are we willing to pay for government services used?

Are we ready to adopt a new governance model, preparing Canada for maturity?

Will we put Canada first?

We must positively answer these questions if Canada is to become the Greatest Country on Earth.

One Canada must be built by its people!

Building One Canada, with a two-tier governance system, will take time and inevitably cause some confusion and consternation during the implementation stages. Convincing Canadians that this new paradigm governance will best meet their needs will be a very difficult and an almost insurmountable task. We are so accustomed to government bureaucracy, inefficiencies, inaction, and a heavy tax burden, we will be bewildered by any suggestion there is a better governance model that will bring better government and put more money in our pockets without reducing the level of service required to improve our quality of life.

The many people and corporations that benefit from the inefficient bureaucracies will fight "tooth and nail" to prevent the implementation of a system of governance that is efficient and serve its customers, the citizens and residents of Canada. There will be strong opposition from federal and provincial politicians, federal and provincial governments, businesses and some of the wealthier members in our population. Members of the general population will oppose creating One Canada out of fear mongering by one or all of the afore mentioned groups. Collectively, politicians will object as it reduces their numbers and holds them accountable to the people. In one Canada, it will be difficult for politicians to make grandiose promises and then break them. If a politician could not promise more jobs, reduce taxes, add more police officers, teachers and nurses, and more money for "hot button" issues, what would he promise you? How about good government"? With fixed election dates, politicians would no longer be able to "time" a general election to coincide with expected good economic indicators. The people would know that increase spending near an approaching election date is all about vote buying, all about politicking.

Spending limits during an election and immediately after a candidate is nominated will ensure there is a fair and equitable process for all to participate. Bringing a political party's internal election process under the rules of Election Canada will eliminate the manipulation, deception, and shenanigans characteristics of internal party election processes.

One Canada would compel all politicians to work for the good of Canada and its people, setting aside political ambitions until an election is underway. With the possibility of Department ministers having years of experience in their appointed area, we may actually have a minister who understands his portfolio. With a starred General as Defense Minister, a Farmer as Agriculture Minister, a Lawyer as Justice Minister, Attorney General and Solicitor General it would no longer take years to educate a minister about his portfolio.

Provincial governments will bemoan their loss of a kingdom, as their parochial nature prevents them from seeing the greatness that awaits One Canada. Provincial governments are well aware they have outlived their purpose and are demanding more powers and money from the Federal government to prolong the perception of their usefulness. The infighting between federal and provincial governments is juvenile, irresponsible and counterproductive, with billions of dollars wasted in the process as people suffer in joblessness, poverty and poor health.

For the first one hundred years of confederation, provincial governments served us well as Canada grew from infancy into adolescence. In 1967, Canada began its growth into adulthood and like any adolescent person, no longer needs to be nurtured into adult nation by parochial (provincial) governments. Since its centennial, and after a little more growing up in 1982, the nation that is Canada been discovering and understanding our adolescence, letting the world know we are learning and getting ready to play on its stage. In the latter half of the last millennium, we had moments of brilliance and gained the respect of other peoples and nations, reflective of an adolescent growing into adulthood. Our brilliance was demonstrated in battles and victories in World Wars I & II, peacekeeping, technological advances, social and cultural diversity and our voice of reason around the world.

Provincial governments and parochial politicians must now let the adult nation of Canada grow into maturity by voting themselves out of existence and embracing one Canada. Former Prime Minister The Rt. Hon. Lester B. Pearson placed Canada's future in perspective when he said, in 1966,

"As we enter our centennial year we are still a young nation, very much in the formative stages. Our national condition is still flexible enough that we can make almost anything we wish of our nation. No other country is in a better position than Canada to go ahead with the evolution of a national purpose devoted to all that is good and noble in the human spirit."

Since that speech, Canada became more mature, displayed more confidence and earned the respect of many countries in the world stage, while bickering between levels of government continued at home.

Corporations and wealthier Canadians will oppose one Canada because they will be required to pay of the full cost of government services used. A few larger companies and wealthier Canadians always bombarded governments with requests for financial grants, subsidies, tax reduction, deferrals and credits and other handouts to build professional sports arenas, expansion of auto plants, and investments in oil, gas and mineral exploration and many more mega projects. Treating governments and the people as bottomless pits of money, these individuals and companies have no compunction in making their financial demands, even threatening to move their investments, professional teams, manufacturing, and assembly plants to another country. Where does the hard working Canadian man or woman move to if they encounter financial difficulty? Nowhere, they must tough it out until better times come along, however long that might take.

Some of our fellow Canadians will object to creating one Canada out of fear of the unknown, a common human trait. Certainly, we must question whether one Canada will be better than today's feudal Canada. The new paradigm in financing government will be portrayed as increasing "taxes" when, in reality it is all of us paying the full cost government services consumed. The parasites in our present system of taxation will oppose creating One Canada for fear of loosing their "free ride" on the backs of those who pay taxpayers. One Canada will unleash the pride and entrepreneurial spirit in every one of us. One Canada will give us the choice to be whomsoever we want to be; to maintain the Quality of Life befitting our own desires.

One Canada – The First Phase

Section 91 of the Constitution Act, 1867, (formerly the British North America, 1867) authorizes the federal government to **"make Laws for the Peace, Order, and good Government of Canada,"** in relation to matters not exclusive to the Legislatures of the Provinces. One such power is **"the raising of money by any mode or system of taxation."** Section 92 of said constitution act grants the provinces powers over **"direct taxation within the Province in order to the raising of revenue for provincial purposes."** Nowhere in the constitution does it obligate the federal government to collect all taxes and then redistribute to the provinces. The federal government now collects personal and corporate income taxes, retail sales taxes, and many other levies then redistribute a portion to the provinces, based on an agreed formula, to fund areas of exclusive provincial jurisdiction. Quebecers file a provincial and a federal tax return while all other Canadian files a single return, customized for their province of residence. Most provinces impose a retail sales tax on a majority of purchases, payable at the cash register. The federal government imposes a national sales tax, its Goods and Services Tax (GST) in some provinces and the Harmonized Sales Tax (HST) in others. In Quebec, the GST is provincially administered under an agreement with the federal government.

Creating One Canada begins with the will of the federal government in the National Parliament. The first step in creating one Canada is the abolition of federal income tax, goods and services tax and all other forms of duties, levies and taxes currently imposed by the national government and replacing these taxes and levies with the a twenty percent (20%) Government Services Fee.. All the monies collected will remain with the federal government, as allowed in Section 91 of the Constitution Act, 1867. Provinces will then be solely responsible for direct taxation for provincial purposes, as allowed under Section 92 of the Constitution Act, 1867. We are all familiar with provincial governments complaining the federal government collects taxes from, and not sending an equal amount to, the provinces. The federal government has become the scapegoat for the financial ailments of the provinces, perceived as mismanagement by many citizens and corporations. The federal government's implementation of Phase 1 of building One Canada will return direct taxation and accountability to the provinces. No longer will provincial governments hide under the skirt tail of the federal government. The buck will finally stop at the provincial governments, making them completely accountable to their respective populations

Step II of creating One Canada is the collection of fees on fossil fuels and water and electric utilities and the disbursements of said fees detailed in the "Financing Government" section of this book.

Step III of creating One Canada is the provincial implementation of the proposals put forth in this book under "Financial Municipal Governments."

One Canada – The Second Phase

The transformation of Canada from a multilevel government system into two-tier national and local governance model proposed in this book requires constitutional amendments, a much more daunting task given the history of attempts at constitutional amendments. Section 38(1) of the Part V of the Constitution Act, 1982, "Procedure for Amending Constitution of Canada," generally provides for an amending formula that requires two-thirds of the provincial legislatures, consisting of at least fifty-percent of population of all the provinces of Canada. With Quebec and Ontario having 62% of Canada's population, any amendments to the Constitution must be approved in the legislatures of one of these provinces plus at least six other provinces. The proposed Constitution Act 1987, better known as the Meech Lake Accord, proved the difficulty of constitutional amendment.

All levels of government and their respective peoples must want and understand the benefits of a new system of governance that will bring prosperity to Canadians, influence around the world and be a beacon of democracy and governance for countries of the world.

Priorities in One Canada

In attempting to manage the affairs of the population, government must meet the needs of many differing constituencies. Each differing constituency believe their objectives are the highest priority, whether it's education, housing, defense, health, homosexuality, social services, farming or one of the many other responsibilities of the government.

Government's highest priority must be in the areas where its actions will produce the greatest results. In our present governance model, government priorities shift to match opinion polls. At all times, and regardless of political ideology, the highest priority must be Education as it encompasses every facet of society. Why must Education be the highest priority? Education produces knowledge and the use of knowledge is power. Many of society's ills will be solved through better education in many fields. By educating our people, we give then the knowledge to make decisions for themselves. Health and finances are always major concerns for many Canadians. Will we retire healthy and with enough money to live in retirement until death? If we educate people about the environment and conservation, we will have people that are willing conserve nature's resources as we use these resources to meet our everyday needs. Educating our children to respect people and property will definitely reduce violence, theft, and gang related activities. The silent killers of people today, heart disease, obesity, hypertension, high stress levels, and high cholesterol are a direct result on failing to give proper and early health education to our young children and adults. Even adults could benefit from education on controlling these silent killers. Early sexual health education will bring hope of reduced teenage pregnancies and sexually transmitted diseases. Our society is educating our people but has failed to show them the use of that knowledge. The other priorities should be the environment, health, justice, security and in the order that, firstly, to protect life then goods and profits. Without life, there will be no goods and no profits.

One Canada is Simplicity

The goals of creating one Canada are simplicity in governance and giving Canadians greater control over their own lives. Restructuring the governance model into two levels will reduce the bureaucracy required to serve the people. Government services will be more efficiently delivered to the people at lower cost, and will actually meet the needs of the people. The entire funding for government services will be simplified by reducing the number of collection points, and the number and types of fees collected. This simplicity will ensure efficient management of the collection of government services fee. Government services, rather than taxes, duties, and other levies, will ensure everyone pays the entire cost of government services used. The yearly cumulative cost of purchasing government service will be much less that it is today as the many corporations and wealthier Canadians who do not now pay the entire cost of government services used will be required to do so in this new paradigm of governance. Having one national representative Senate, with every Senator belonging to a government committee will better utilize the intellect of all the members of the Senate. Creating more government departments to reflect the needs of the people will simplify the development and delivery of services. Giving more autonomy to the municipalities will ensure they are continually capable of meeting the needs of their residents. Regular consultation between the Governing Council, the Senate and the Mayors Executive Board will facilitate the development of national programs that meet the needs of all Canadians. With three hundred and fifty administrative regions, each having one senator, one mayor and twenty-four councilors, and with one prime minister, one deputy prime minister, the people's elected representation will number less than nine thousands, far less than the present number. One Canada is about simplifying governance, simplifying the way we do business and simplifying the lives of Canadians so that they may enjoy their lives and their country to the fullest. One Canada is about simplifying the legal infrastructure and business operations so we may create and enjoy prosperity.

It is not enough...

It is not enough that we love our country; we must promote and defend it from all threats, perceived and real.

It is not enough we educate our people; we must teach them to use the knowledge they received.

It is not enough that we tolerate the differences in other cultures; we must learn to understand and accept the difference in our many peoples.

It is not enough that we compete in science and technology; we must be leaders in every field.

It is not enough that we compete in sports; we must always be on the podium, raising the flag at every major world event.

It is not enough we sell farm and agricultural products; we must be the leading and preferred supplier.

It is not enough we complain about what is wrong with Canada; we must work to fix all the problems.

It is not enough we think the grass is greener on the other side of the fence; we make cultivate our own greener grass.

It is not enough to blame politicians for all our ills; we must take them to task and hold them accountable everyday and every step of the way;.

It is not for us to dominate the world but to cooperate, live in, and make it a better place for all to enjoy.

It is not for us to dominate people, but to free their spirit to pursue happiness.

If you believe

If you believe....

... Canada is one country and indivisible,

> **.... Every Canadian -**
>
> ... is equal one to another;
>
> ... has a right to his personal belief system;
>
> ... has a right to live a life free from all forms of discrimination
>
> ... has a right to live in a safe and secure environment;
>
> ... has a right to be free to pursue their hearts desire;
>
> ... has a right to receive an education;
>
> ... has a right to a just legal infrastructure;
>
> ... has a right to live anywhere in Canada they desire;
>
> ... has a right to own property anywhere in Canada;
>
> ... must be treated with dignity and respect;
>
> ...If you believe everything costs someone something.

…... Then you believe in One Canada!

The future is not to be forecast, but created.

Sir Arthur C. Clarke, Author of 2001: A Space Odyssey

Canada Facts and Figures

Canada facts and Figures provides a summary of Canada's geographic facts, climatic conditions, economic output, military state and readiness and human potential as of the year 2000. Our internal political representation, international status, contribution to the world and membership in world organizations will enlighten the reader on the importance of Canada to the world community.

Map of Canada

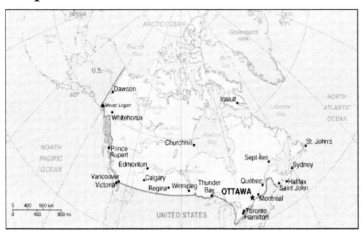

Geography

At 9,976,140 sq km, Canada is the second-largest country in world (after Russia), strategically located between Russia and USA, via north polar route. Approximately 85% of the population lies with within 300 km of the US/Canada border. Canada is located in the Northern portion of the continent of North America, bordering the North Atlantic, and North Pacific, and Arctic Oceans. Canada's only land border is with the USA and at over 8000kms, is the longest undefended border in the world.

Maritime claims -
contiguous zone: 24 nm
continental shelf: 200 nm or to the edge of the continental margin
exclusive economic zone: 200 nm
territorial sea: 12 nm

Climate: varies from temperate in south to sub arctic and arctic in north

Terrain: mostly plains with mountains in west and lowlands in southeast

Elevation extremes - Canada's lowest point is the Atlantic Ocean at 0

meters and its highest point is Mount Logan, rising to a height of 5,959 m

Natural resources: iron ore, nickel, zinc, copper, gold, lead, molybdenum, potash, silver, fish, timber, wildlife, coal, petroleum, natural gas, hydropower

Land use: About 5% of Canada's land area is Arable land, supporting 3% permanent pastures; 54% forests and woodland, with the remaining 38% in other forms of vegetation, (1993 est.)

Environment: air pollution from metal smelting, coal-burning utilities, and vehicle emissions resulting acid rain killing lakes and forests and impacting on agricultural; ocean waters becoming contaminated due to agricultural, industrial, mining, and forestry activities

Environment - international agreements: *Canada is a party to several international anti-pollution agreements, most notably:* Air Pollution, Antarctic Treaty, Biodiversity, Climate Change, Desertification, Endangered Species, Environmental Modification, Hazardous Wastes, Marine Dumping, Nuclear Test Ban, Ozone Layer Protection, Ship Pollution, Tropical Timber, Wetlands, and Whaling. Canada has ratified the Climate Change-Kyoto Protocol and has begun programs to ensure it meets the targets set out in the protocol.

People

Population: 31,902, 268 (July 2003 est.)

18. 7% of the population is less than *14 years;* 68.4% is between *15-64 years and the remaining* 12. 9% *is over 65 years.*

Canada's population is increasing at about one percent (1%) per year. The contributing factors are the increased life expectancy of 76 years for males, and 83 years for females; a birth rate of about eleven (11) births per 1,000 population, a death rate of about seven (7) deaths per 1,000 population and a migration rate of about six persons in every one thousand.

Canada's gender ratio remains almost constant from birth until age sixty-five, at about one male for every female. The longer life expectancy contributed to the over sixty-five year ratio of two (2) males for every three (3) females. However, the average over the entire population is still one to one.

Infant mortality rate: 4.95 deaths/1,000 live births (2002 est.)

Total fertility rate: 1. 6 children born/woman (2002 est.)

The multicultural composition of Canada is a result of its diverse ethnic groups from the British (28%), French 23%, other Europeans (15%), Amerindians (2%), other, mostly Asian, African, Arab (6%), mixed background (26%). With multiculturalism comes a multi-faith society. Canada is made up of Roman Catholics (46%), Protestant (36%), and others (Muslims, Sikhs, and Jews etc) (18%). Canada's two official languages are English (59. 3%) and French (23. 2%). The language of immigrants and First Peoples are spoken by about 17. 5% of the population.

Literacy

Ninety-seven percent of all persons age fifteen and over can read and write.

Government

Country name: On the international stage the abbreviated name for Canada is CA

Government type: confederation with parliamentary democracy

Capital: Ottawa

Administrative divisions: 10 provinces and 3 territories

Independence: 1 July 1867 (from UK).

National holiday: Canada Day, 1 July (1867).

Constitution: 17 April 1982 (Constitution Act); originally, the machinery of the government was set up in the British North America Act of 1867; charter of rights and unwritten customs.

Legal system: based on English common law, except in Quebec, where civil law system based on French law prevails; accepts compulsory International Court of Justice (ICJ) jurisdiction, with reservations

Suffrage: 18 years of age; universal

Executive branch

Head of State: Constitutional Monarchy, represented by Governor General of Canada and Lieutenant Governor in the Provinces, all appointed by the Monarch on the advise of the Prime Minister.

Head of government: Prime Minister, Leader of the Majority Party.

Cabinet: Federal Ministry chosen by the prime minister from amongst the members of his own party sitting in Parliament;

Elections: The monarch is hereditary and lives in a foreign country; the monarch, on the advice of the prime minister, appoints his representative, the governor general' for a five-year term. Following legislative elections, the leader of the majority party in the House of Commons is automatically designated by the governor general to become prime minister.

Legislative branch: A bicameral Parliament consisting of the Senate and the House of Commons

The Governor General, on the advice of the prime minister, appoints Senators, who serves until reaching age of 75 years. The Senate normal limit is one hundred and four (104) senators. Members of The House of Commons are elected by popular vote. At the 2000 elections there were three hundred and one (301) seats in the House.

Elections

House of Commons: normally held every five years, though a general election may be precipitated by the defeat of a minority government.

Senate: The Senate is a body of appointed representative, with appointments made by the governing party. Considered a "chamber of sober second thoughts," Senators are mainly stalwarts, rewarded with a public position.

Judicial branch: Supreme Court, judges are appointed by the prime minister through the governor general

Political Parties: Political parties vie for control of government and presently the Liberal Party of Canada, Conservative Party of Canada, New Democratic Party of Canada, and the Bloc Quebecois are represented in the Parliament of Canada. Other smaller parties have contested general election, garnering less than 2% of the popular vote.

International organization participation

Canada participates in many International and United Nations organizations. The following are the most renowned:

Agence de Cooperation Cultrelle et Technique (La Francophonie) (ACCT); Asia-Pacific Economic Council (APEC); Commonwealth of Nations, (C); European Space Agency (ESA, cooperating state); Group of Seven Nations (G- 7); Inter-American Development Bank (IADB); International Atomic Energy Agency (IAEA); International Civil Aviation Organization (ICAO); International Chamber of Commerce (ICC); International Confederation of Free Trade Unions (ICFTU);International Energy Agency (IEA); International Federation of the Red Cross and Red Crescent Societies (IFRCS); International Health Organization (IHO); International Labour Organization (ILO); International Monetary Fund (IMF); International Maritime Organization (IMO); International Mobile Satellite Organization (INMARSAT); International Telecommunications Satellite Organization (INTELSAT); International Criminal Police Organization (INTERPOL); International Olympic Committee (IOC); International Organization for Migration (IOM); International Standards Organization (ISO);International Telecommunications Union (ITU); North Atlantic Treaty Organization (NATO); The Nuclear Energy Agency (NEA); Organization of American States (OAS); Organization for Economic Cooperation and Development (OECD); Organization for Security and Cooperation in Europe (OSCE);United Nations (UN); United Nations Educational, Scientific and Cultural Organization (UNESCO); United Nations High Commissioner for Refugees (UNHCR); World Health Organization (WHO); World Intellectual Property Organization (WIPO); World

Meteorological Organization (WMO); World Trade Organization (WTO);

Diplomatic representation around the World

The Canadian government maintains diplomatic and consular offices in most countries of the world. Canada's worldwide diplomatic missions are headed by Ambassadors, High Commissioners and Consulate Generals.

Flag description: Adopted in 1965, The Canadian Flag has three vertical bands of red (hoist side), white (double width, square), and red with a red maple leaf centered in the white band.

Economy

Economy - overview: As an affluent, high-tech industrial society, Canada closely resembles the USA in its market-oriented economic system, pattern of production, and high living standards. After World War II, impressive growth in manufacturing, mining, and service sectors transformed Canada from a largely rural economy into one primarily industrial and urban. Over the last generation Canada's growth rates fluctuated with the rest of the industrialized countries. However, growth rates averaging nearly 3. 0% was common in the last decade of the twentieth century. Public debt continues to plague governments even after having budget surpluses were partially devoted to reducing the large public sector debt. The Canada-USA Free Trade Agreement (FTA) and the Canada-USA-Mexico North American Free Trade Agreement (NAFTA) touched off a dramatic increase in trade and economic integration with the US. With its great natural resources, skilled labour force, and modern capital plant, Canada enjoys solid economic prospects. Canada's economy is closely tied to that of the USA, where 90% of its exports are sold. The constitutional impasse between English- and French-speaking areas has caused uncertainty in the political stability of Canada. This political instability cause economic uncertainty that, from time to time affected economic growth. Canadians have long had serious concern about the brain drain of professional persons to the USA, lured by higher pay, lower taxes, and the immense high-tech infrastructure and the perception of a better Quality of Life in the USA. .

GDP: purchasing power parity - $923.3 billion (2002 est.)

GDP - real growth rate: 3.4% (2002 est.)

GDP - per capita: purchasing power parity - $29,400 (2002 est.)

GDP - composition by sector (2001 est.)
Agriculture: 2%; *Industry:* 27%; Services: 71%

Population below poverty line: Depends on one's point of view. There is significant poverty in Canada.

Household income or consumption by percentage share
lowest 10%: 3% (1994)
highest 10%: 24% (1994)

Inflation rate (consumer prices): 2. 2% (2002 est.)

Labour force: 16.4 million (2001 est.)

Labour force - by occupation: services 74%, manufacturing 15%, construction 5%, agriculture 3%, other 3% (2000 est.)

Unemployment rate: 7.6% (2002 est.

Budget: *revenues:* $178.6B *expenditures:* $161.4B (FY 2000/2001)

Industries: processed and unprocessed minerals, food products, wood and paper products, transportation equipment, chemicals, fish products, petroleum and natural gas

Industrial production growth rate: 2.2% (2002 est.)

Electricity: Canada produces almost 550 billion kilowatt hours (kWh) of electricity, each year, from fossil fuels (25%), hydro plants (61%) and nuclear generation (12%). About 500 Billion kWh is consumed in Canada and 50 billion kWh exported to the USA. We import about 13 billion kWh from the USA as our peak demands exceed production, mainly due to our own plants shutdown for maintenance and refurbishing.

Agriculture - products: wheat, barley, oilseed, tobacco, fruits, vegetables; dairy products; forest products; fish

Exports

Exports: $260.5 billion (2002, est.)

Exports - commodities: motor vehicles and parts, newsprint, wood pulp, timber, crude petroleum, machinery, natural gas, aluminum, telecommunications equipment, electricity

Exports - partners: US 85%, Japan 2. 2%, UK 1. 6%, EU 2. 2%, others 9%, (2000 est.)

Imports: $229 billion (2002 est.)

Imports - commodities: machinery and equipment, crude oil, chemicals, motor vehicles and parts, durable consumer goods, electricity

Imports - partners: US 72. 7%, U. K 3. 4%, Japan 3%, EU 3. 2%, others 17. 7%, (2001)

Debt - external: $1. 9 billion (2000)

Economic aid - donor: ODA, $1. 3 billion (1999)

Currency: Canadian dollar (Can$) = 100 cents

Communications

Telephones - main lines in use: 20. 8 million (1999)

Telephones - mobile cellular: 8. 7 million (1997)

Telephone system: excellent service provided by modern technology *domestic:* domestic satellite system with about 300 earth stations *international:* Five coaxial submarine cables; satellite earth stations - 5 Intelsat (4 Atlantic Ocean and 1 Pacific Ocean) and 2 Intersputnik (Atlantic Ocean region)

Radio broadcast stations: AM 535, FM 53, short wave 6 (1998)

Radios: 32. 3 million (1997)

Television broadcast stations: 80 (plus many repeaters) (1997)

Televisions: 21. 5 million (1997)

Internet Country Code: CA

Internet Service Providers (ISPs): 760 and declining (2000 est.)

Internet Users: 16.84 million and growing (2002 est.)

Transportation

Railways: There is over 36,114 km or standard gauge rail tracks across Canada used mostly by two major transcontinental freight railway systems, Canadian National and Canadian Pacific Railways and the government-owned VIA Rail passenger service.

Highways: The vast distances of Canada is served by almost one million kilometers of highways of which 40% is paved and 60% unpaved. Less than 5% of the paved roads are multi-lane expressways.

Waterways: 3,000 km, including Saint Lawrence Seaway

Pipelines: crude and refined oil 23,564 km; natural gas 74,980 km

Ports and Harbours: Becancour (Quebec), Churchill, Halifax, Hamilton, Montreal, New Westminster, Prince Rupert, Quebec, Saint John (New Brunswick), St. John's (Newfoundland), Sept Isles, Sydney, Trois-Riviere, Thunder Bay, Toronto, Vancouver, and Windsor.

Merchant Marine: Canada has 122 ships in it merchant marine, not including ships used exclusively in the Great Lakes.

Airports: There are almost 1500 airports serving Canada; 33% having paved runways and the remainder having unpaved runways. Canada is also served by twelve heliports.

Military

Military branches: Canadian Forces (includes Land Forces Command, Maritime Command, Air Command, Communications Command, Training Command, and Royal Canadian Mounted Police (RCMP)

Military Manpower

A person of 17 years is considered military aged. Approximately 8.36 million males age 15-49 are available for military service. However, "fit for military service" is 7.14 million

Military expenditures: For the fiscal year 2002/2003, Canada will spend $11.0 Billion, or about 1.1% of GDP on its military.

Trans-national Issues

Disputes – international -Maritime boundary disputes with the United States of America at the **Dixon Entrance, Strait of Juan de Fuca in the Beaufort Sea and Machias Seal Island.** The **Dixon Entrance** is a narrow passage (80 km wide) of the eastern North Pacific, stretching 80 km east from the open ocean to Canada's Hecate Strait. The **Strait of Juan de Fuca** is a 160 km long and from 24 to 32 km wide waterway linking the Pacific Ocean and the Strait of Georgia and Puget Sound. Part of the U. S. A. - Canada border lies in mid-channel. The **Machias Seal Island** is part of New Brunswick, off the coast of Maine, USA. The USA claims this island, as does Canada.

Saint Pierre and Miquelon is a French territory located in the north Atlantic and South of the Newfoundland coat. This two-island territory is a focus of maritime boundary dispute between Canada and France; in 1992, an arbitration panel awarded the islands an exclusive economic zone area of 12,348 sq km to settle the dispute.

Bibliography

Year of personal experiences and many hours of research made this book possible.

Government of Canada and all its departments	www.gc.ca
Alberta	www.gov.ab.ca
British Columbia	www.gov.bc.ca
Newfoundland and Labrador	www.gov.nf.ca
Manitoba	www.gov.mb.ca
New Brunswick	www.gnb.ca
Northwest Territories	www.gov.nt.ca
Nova Scotia	www.gov.gns.ca
Nunavut	www.gov.nu.ca
Ontario	www.gov.on.ca
Prince Edward Island	www.gov.pe.ca
Quebec	www.gouv.qc.ca
Saskatchewan	www.gov.sk.ca
Yukon	www.gov.yk.ca
Constitution Acts, 1867 to 1982	
The Toronto Star	www.thestar.com
The Globe & Mail	www.globeandmail.com
MacLean's Magazine	www.macleans.ca
Microsoft Encarta 2004	http://encarta.msn.com/
How Canadian Govern Themselves	Senator Eugene A. Forsey
CIA World Fact Book 2003	www.cia.gov

About the Author

Cecil Young was born at Rose Hall, 20km east of Montego Bay, on the Caribbean island of Jamaica. In 1968, while attending Mount Zion Primary School Cecil earned a scholarship to attend the prestigious all-boys high school, Cornwall College, in Montego Bay. An avid follower of the political process, he became active in local and national Jamaican politics at the tender age of fifteen, campaigning for a family friend in the 1972 General Elections.

Cecil was delighted in moving to Canada in 1972, where he attended Glendale Secondary School in Hamilton, Ontario, completing Grade Eleven, before returning to Jamaica a year later. After a three-year employment in the communications sector, Cecil returned to Canada in 1976. In 1983, he graduated from Sheridan College with a Diploma in Electronics Engineering Technology. After graduation, Cecil gained work experiences in the government, manufacturing and communications and technology sectors. Today, Cecil is a principal in a computer consulting business.

For more than thirty years, Cecil has been active in the community, serving on at least one Board of Directors in each of those years. Today he is active in federal and provincial political parties, is a Coach in Erin Mills Soccer Club and strong supporter of soccer the Mississauga. Living and raising a family in Canada for more than a quarter of a century, Cecil believes greatness awaits Canada if only the political bickering and buck-passing would stop. Cecil believes in two levels of government, a strong national and effective local government that involve the people in all aspects of governance.

ISBN 141202235-5